To Ken,

Thank you for your help,
and for coming,

Michael

The Convent of La Santa Trinità at La Cava visited by Marianne Talbot and party in September 1831 and by Sir Walter Scott in February 1832.

LIFE

IN THE

SOUTH

THE NAPLES JOURNAL OF MARIANNE TALBOT 1829-32.

edited with notes by

Michael Heafford.

POSTILLION BOOKS, CAMBRIDGE
2012

Published by Postillion Books, Cambridge, 2012.

ISBN 978-0-9558712-1-4

Printed and bound in Great Britain by Joshua Horgan,
246 Marston Road, Oxford OX3 0EL.

Contents

Illustrations:
Cover illustration: adapted from the title-page of [Lewis Engelbach], *Naples and the Campagna Felice*, London, 1815.

Frontispiece: View of Convent of La Santa Trinità, from Thomas Roscoe, *The Tourist in Italy*, London 1833. The illustration was drawn by J.D. Harding, published by Jennings & Chaplin, and dated 28 Oct. 1832.

Picture pages:
Page 1. Reproduction of one page of the manuscript.

Page 2. a. View of 'The Hermitage on the Road leading to the Cone of Vesuvius' from John Auldjo, *Sketches of Vesuvius*, London, 1833.
b. View of the Camaldoli della Torre del Greco from an early 19th century coloured gouache (private collection).

Page 3. a. Title page of *Pompeiana: the Topography, Edifices and Ornaments of Pompeii*, by Sir William Gell and John P. Gandy, London, 1817-19.
b. Portrait of Sir William Gell from the frontispiece of Volume 1 of *Pompeiana: the Topography, Edifices and Ornaments of Pompeii, the Result of Excavations since 1819*, by Sir William Gell, London, 1837.
c. Portrait of James Justinian Morier from the frontispiece of *The Adventures of Hajji Baba of Ispahan*, ed. C.J.Wells, London, 1897.
d. Title page of Volume 1 of *The Adventures of Hajji Baba, of Ispahan, in England*, London, 1828.

Page 4. a. Portrait of Sir Henry Lushington from a painting reproduced with the kind permission of Woolley and Wallis, Fine Art Auctioneers of Salisbury.
b. Portrait of Stratford Canning from Volume 1 of: Stanley Lane-Poole, *The Life of the Right Honourable Stratford Canning*, London, 1888.
c. Portrait of Francis Seymour Conway, third Marquis of Hertford, from Volume 4 of: William Jerdan, *National Portrait Gallery*, London 1833.
d. Portrait of Sir Walter Scott from Volume 12 of: Edmund Lodge, *Portraits of Illustrious Personages of Great Britain*, London, 1834.

Introduction

The setting

During the summer of 1817 or 1818, two gentlemen were discussing English poetry just south of Naples. The location of the discussion imprinted itself on the mind of one of them:

> It was that lovely village-dotted plain, between the mountains and the sea, *Il piano di Sorrento*, in that quiet shady nook, embosomed in groves of orange and citron trees, called 'La Cocumella.'...... We sat for an hour or two on a rustic seat at the edge of an orange-grove which overhung the sea and commanded a full view of the bay, Mount Vesuvius, the whole of the city of Naples, with the castles and monasteries, behind it and above it, the enchanting promontory of Posilipo, the Cape of Misenum, the coast of Baiae, the low, bright, glittering island of Procida, and the lofty, volcanic island of Ischia - a view which I shall always maintain, and religiously believe, to be the finest in the beautiful globe which God has allotted to us for a habitation.[1]

At the centre of this quasi-paradisiacal landscape, described in similar effusive terms by many visitors at the time, lay the city of Naples itself, considered by Stendhal as 'beyond all comparison the finest city in Europe',[2] by Charles Greville, 'the most beautiful and the gayest town in the world'.[3] Although the French Revolution and the Napoleonic wars had imposed so many fundamental changes on Europe, all making an impact on Naples, none had turned this city, surrounded by such magnificent scenery, into a backwater, a place to live 'careless of mankind'. Indeed, a number of factors ensured it remained one of Europe's mainstream cities. Important amongst these was its position on the traffic route between Northern Europe and the countries of the Mediterranean and beyond, and its provision of harbour facilities facilitating movement of people and trade. For the British, many of its foreign policy concerns focused interest on the area - fear over the expansion of Russia, the desire to create an independent Greece without over-diminishing the power of the Ottoman Empire, consolidating its new Crown colony of Malta, establishing its protectorate of the Ionian

---

[1] Charles Macfarlane, *Reminiscences*, p.84. N.B. Bibliographical information is abbreviated throughout for titles in the Bibliography.

[2] Stendhal, *Rome, Naples and Florence in 1817*, London, 1818, p.118

[3] Charles Greville, *The Greville Memoirs*, Vol.1, p.432-3.

Islands, and guarding its shipping from the pirates operating off the North African coast. As a result of these concerns, the Royal Navy maintained a strong presence in the Mediterranean and made regular use of the port of Naples.

While the city, through its port, was open to traffic from the Mediterranean and the Orient, it retained its attraction to those engaged in what had, in the eighteenth century, been designated as a 'Grand Tour', but which travellers in the new century rather more modestly called their 'Continental Tour'. At the key sites of Pompeii and Herculaneum, new discoveries were regularly being revealed, and for those willing to travel only slightly further, the three magnificent Greek temples of Paestum were easily accessible. Even if, for the British, the time available for their tour diminished over the years, for many of them it remained a leisurely affair. On a typical tour, they crossed the Channel during the early summer heading first for Paris or for a trip up the Rhine. In August and September, they lingered in Switzerland, but with the onset of autumn and the possibility of early snow closing alpine passes, they headed south, first to Florence, and then on to Rome in time for Christmas. Their stay in Rome reached its climax with the celebrations of Carnival in which they actively participated. The beginning of Lent provided an opportune moment to leave Rome for Naples and a quiet period visiting the Classical excavations and remains, climbing Vesuvius, exploring the coastline townships of Sorrento and Amalfi, and crossing to the unspoilt island of Capri. After five weeks, Rome summoned the visitors back to witness the Easter celebrations. These concluded, the visitors headed for home often varying their itinerary in order, on their return journey, to enjoy different places and experiences.

Naples, destination for travellers, was, most importantly, the capital city of the Kingdom of the Two Sicilies, with all the social and cultural activities which such a status implied. The ruling Bourbon family, deposed by the French revolution but restored in 1815, had particularly close ties with both the French and Spanish royal families. In 1829, during the course of the journal, King Francesco I accompanied his daughter Marie Christine to Spain where she was to marry the widowed King Ferdinand VII. The party from Naples included, amongst others, the King's oldest daughter, Marie Caroline, widow of the Duc de Berry who had been assassinated in 1820 and the mother of the Duc de Bordeaux, the prospective heir to the French throne. The party had scarcely returned to Naples from Paris in July 1830 when

Louis Philippe seized power. He too had close family connections to the royal family of Naples for his wife, Marie Amelie, was a younger sister of Francesco I. The Bourbons of Naples were naturally sensitive to the fortunes of their close family. At the same time they could not afford to forget events of the recent past which had, little more than twenty years before, deposed them. The Carbonari insurrection of 1820 served as a constant reminder that any sign of weakness or lack of judgment could either lead to a renewed occupation by the Austrian army or topple them completely from power. It follows that the death of Francesco I in November 1830 and the accession of his son, the young Ferdinando II, heralded a particularly critical period, a period Marianne Talbot experienced and described.

Before the journal: the Talbots in England
In spite of the far from stable political situation, it was here in Naples in the autumn of 1826 that Sir George Talbot and his two daughters came to set up their main residence for a period of over five years. Marianne Talbot, the author of this journal, was thirty eight, her sister Georgina five years younger. Their lives before their stay in Naples are not well documented, but a brief sketch of them can be built up. George Talbot had been born in 1767, the younger son of Sir Charles Henry Talbot, a descendant, though not a direct one, of the first Earl of Shrewsbury. In 1787, he had married Anne Preston, the daughter of an Irish clergyman, in Bath. The couple had had three children - in addition to the two girls born in 1788 and 1793 respectively, a son, Charles William born in 1796. In the earliest years, with their father serving as an officer in the Scots Guards, the family seem to have lived mainly in Bath with their mother and their widowed grandmother, Mary Preston. During the course of August 1810, Mrs Talbot died, but there is uncertainty as to the place or precise date of her death. On the subsequent death, two years later of George's elder brother, Sir Charles Talbot, George assumed the baronetcy, and inherited the family estates in Kent and in London. In 1816, with peace firmly established after the Napoleonic conflicts, and with his son, Charles William, a student at Christ Church, Oxford, Sir George accompanied by his daughters took up residence on the Continent. Apart from a few periods back at home, they were not to return to England until 1832, some sixteen years later. It is with their final journey home that this journal concludes.

This brief history of the early years of Marianne Talbot's life can be only sparsely supplemented from other sources. In the journal itself Marianne describes her childhood as an unhappy one, but does not explain why. She recognised the debt she owed to her grandmother, Mrs Mary Preston, especially in passing on to her a love of books. Lady Louisa Stuart, portrays Grandmother Preston as a warm person with an independent mind, a neat turn of phrase, and a wide circle of acquaintance.[4] In her journal, Marianne also points to happy moments spent with the Drummonds of Charing Cross, the family of London bankers. She does not make mention in the journal of the death of her mother in 1810, of that of her grandmother, Mary Preston, in April 1817, or of that of her brother a few months later.

Her father, Sir George Talbot, moved in socially exalted circles. He much enjoyed entertaining at his house in New Burlington Street, and his parties were regularly reported in the press throughout the London season. For instance, the *Morning Post* reported a party given by Sir George in February 1815 which had been attended by: the Foreign Ministers, the Dowager Duchess of Rutland and Lady Manners, the Marchioness of Salisbury and the Ladies Cecil, Viscount and Viscountess Melbourne, the Earl and Countess of Uxbridge, the Ladies Paget and the Hon. Berkeley Paget, the Dowager Duchess of Leeds, and Lady Francis Osborne, Lady Henley and Miss Eden, the Earl of Tyrconnell, Lord Alvanley and Mr Raikes, Sir John and Lady Shelley, Mr and Mrs Pigon, Mr Lambe, Mr and Mrs Freemantle and Miss Harvey, Mr and Mrs Drummond, Mr Champneys, Mr Brummell, and Mr Brand. A few months later in June, when the Battle of Waterloo was fought, Sir George was giving a ball on the 18th at which news of the victory was received. One guest, the Austrian chargé d'affaires, recalled how 'the joy it excited was lessened by the losses which it brought to many English families.'[5] In view of his regular and lavish hospitality, it is not surprising that Sir George was in turn invited to many of the fashionable world's most select events, to the Marchioness of Salisbury's concerts, and to the Countess of Sefton's parties. To most of these, he would have been accompanied by his daughters, as he would on his visits to operas performed at the King's Theatre.

It will have been noted that Sir George's party guests included three of the most famous men-about-town: George Brummell, Lord Alvanley and Thomas Raikes. All three were, along with Sir George, members of the ultra-exclusive White's Club. The Betting Book of the Club

---

[4] See letters of Lady Louisa Stuart to Miss Louisa Clinton, ed. Hon. James Home, Edinburgh, 1901.

[5] Neumann, *Diary*, II, p.169.

shows that Sir George was ever ready to take out a wager, not only on horse races, but on such matters as the date when Napoleon would be deposed, the date when Louis XVIII would be in Paris, and whether Lady X would marry before Lady Y. So prolific was his betting that it was recorded on one page of the Betting Book that his name was appearing for the 150th time.[6] In spite of the frequency with which he laid a wager, there is no evidence that, like some of his illustrious fellow members, he overstretched his finances. His bets were, for the most part, for relatively modest sums, and appear to have been won as often as lost. It seems unlikely, therefore, that financial difficulty played any part in his decision to set off for the Continent in April 1816. This conclusion is further supported by Sir George's readiness to return to England for occasional quite extended periods over the following sixteen years. When he did so, he returned to his betting at White's and continued to be invited to the parties of London's elite society. He also returned to his own lavish entertaining. This included, in March 1824, a concert presided over by Gioachino Rossini and attended by, amongst others, Prince Leopold and Prince Polignac, the Duke of Wellington, the Marquis of Hertford, Earl Talbot, the Countess of Harrowby, and Countess Sefton. Through these social events, both before and during their Continental residence, Sir George's daughters became part of an extensive social network, and knew, or knew of, most of the leading figures in London society.

Before the journal: the Talbots on the Continent
Only the most scant information about the Talbot residence on the Continent has emerged. They left England in April 1816 reaching Switzerland at the end of June. In mid-July they took up residence for a few weeks in Lausanne, presumably then heading south into Italy. Certainly early in 1817, they were staying on the Chiaia, the most fashionable street in Naples, where Sir George was giving a ball every Friday. They arrived back in London at the end of August, but there seems to be no record of when they left again for the Continent or where they stayed. Their next sojourn in England began in March 1819, and Sir George managed to give a few dinners in May and June before he and his daughters returned to the Continent. We only catch up with them again in 1820 when Marianne's journal informs us that they visited Sorrento and were in Naples to witness the entrance of the revolutionary Carbonari on 9 July. Later that year Sir George funded an excavation in Rome. Mary Berry visited it on 22 December and re-

---

[6] *The Betting Book of White's*, [London, 1892], Vol.II, Part I, p.122.

corded that there was 'little to see as yet'.[7] They returned to Switzerland during the summer and autumn of 1821 and again in the summer of 1822 when they spent four weeks in Geneva, leaving for Paris on 6 August, and continuing to London for the briefest of stays - by mid-September, they were on their way back to Paris.

The Talbots returned to London in April 1823 and stayed long enough for them to give and receive hospitality. They attended Prince Esterhazy's Grand Ball and Supper on 1st May and the Duke of Devonshire's Fête on the 23rd. In September, the family attended the grand sale of items at the doomed Fonthill Abbey before the new owner took it over from William Beckford. It is not clear whether after this, they returned to the Continent or not. Certainly, from January to July 1824, they were firmly based in London, with Sir George giving regular dinners. In August, the family left for Paris, and in September, they found themselves in Spa, the famous watering place in Belgium. By March 1825, they were in Rome, where Sir George, according to Sir William Gell, was giving 'great and good dinners'.[8] In the autumn of 1826 they were back in the Naples region, where they rented a villa at Castellamare, the favourite summer resort of wealthy Neapolitans. They probably moved into Naples during that winter; certainly in March 1827, Sir George was entertaining there. It seems likely that, apart from a couple of months in London during the summer, they remained in Naples for the remainder of 1827 and the whole of 1828. Finally, after over a decade of occasional sightings and long periods of uncertain whereabouts, the Talbot family move firmly into the spotlight with the first entry of Marianne's journal on 1st March 1829.

The journal
Marianne Talbot did not pick up her pen on 1 March 1829 to embark on writing a journal for the first time: as the manuscript volume is designated as Volume 10, it must be assumed that she had begun confiding her thoughts and activities to paper many years earlier. Whether any of the preceding journal volumes still exist is uncertain - in this journal she mentions burning some earlier ones - but as a run they would surely have provided a fascinating record of the early decades of the nineteenth century. As it is, we must, for the time being at least, be content with a glimpse of what might have been through this single volume. It was clearly not written with any intention of wider publica-

---

[7] M. Berry, *Extracts of the Journals*, Vol.III, p.272.

[8] See Madden, Vol.2, p.40.

tion in mind, though it was singled out by its writer as containing more of general interest than other volumes. Its main function seems to have been as a personal reminder of times past and as a means of personal reflection on life. As a result, it does not emerge as continuous, self-explanatory narrative, but as a succession of vignettes recording people, places and events. Sometimes these are fragmentary, sometimes they contain unexplained allusions; however, what we occasionally lose in full comprehension is more than made up for by the way in which the entries, however brief, come together to create a vivid impression not only of the writer, not only of leading members of the British community in Naples, but also of important events and key concerns in Britain and in Europe at the time. The latter are not introduced or discussed in any formal way, but emerge from the responses of the writer to the people she meets, the events she witnesses, and the information she receives.

A multitude of individuals appear on the pages of the journal. What makes the journal so readable is the writer's ability to describe them briefly, yet vividly, and to draw our attention to stories linked to them. Her focus is concentrated on those with whom she has regular, if not daily, contact. Alongside more or less permanent residents, these included both those seeking improved health and cheaper living, who often settled in Naples for a considerable time, and those with more circumscribed aims, e.g. visiting the Classical sites, climbing Vesuvius, attending carnival. Diplomatic staff, especially the British, Austrian, French, Russian and Spanish ministers, made regular invitations which were reciprocated by the Talbots. These manifold contacts, whether on-going or one-offs, ensured that Marianne was well informed and well entertained.

The British community in Naples
Presiding over the British in Naples was its Minister, William Noel Hill. In the early years of the century, an aspirant for the hand of Lady Hester Stanhope, he may have received preferment through her help, but was spurned by her as a prospective spouse. Appointed Minister to Sardinia in 1807, he entertained Lady Bessborough in Turin in 1821 and created a positive impression on his guest:

> Mr Hill is very attentive to us, and makes us almost live with him, and is very amusing in his odd way. .... You know his lisp-

ing, mumbling manner of speaking, which often gives more appearance of humour to what he says than it deserves.[9]

However, Hill could also prove extremely unpleasant, as Mary Berry
was to discover. Harriet, Countess Granville, reported the incident:

> She [Miss Berry] has had a violent quarrel with William Hill.
> She complained of his rudeness, and, upon it being reported to
> him, he said, 'Lord bless the woman, what would she have? I am
> sure I'm very ready to have her to dinner!' Upon hearing this she
> stormed. 'Mr William Hill have me to dinner, ready to have me!'
> The Genoese States rung with her larum.[10]

In Naples too, he proved capable of rubbing people up the wrong way.
Harold Acton quotes a letter sent to Hill by a resident aggrieved that
he was excluded from a 'public assembly' hosted by Hill, while on
other occasions being called his 'old friend' and 'oldest
acquaintance'.[11] Marianne Talbot's journal gives many further in-
stances of his moodiness, whimsicality, lack of consistency in relationships, and downright rudeness. At the same time he could be an
extremely entertaining and amusing raconteur.

As a bachelor, there were limitations to the degree to which Hill could
be seen as the leader of the British community, especially as far as female residents were concerned. For them, the leading lady seems to
have been Lady Drummond, the widow of Sir William, who had been
Minister in Naples at the beginning of the century, and had returned to
Italy later in life to devote himself to writing on archaeological topics.
He had died in Rome in 1828. Although Lady Drummond entertained
regularly, she does not figure large in Marianne's journal. Marianne
often refers to her by her nickname of 'Lady Dry' and one one point
designates her a 'fierce old idiot'. Not surprisingly, on meeting the
young Lady Canning, she declared her 'a nice gentle person whom I
would willingly have to reign over us.'

To support them in their everyday concerns, British residents were
fortunate to be able to call on the British Consul General, Sir Henry

---

[9] Acton, *The Last Bourbons*, p.6.

[10] H.F. Leveson Gower (ed.), *Letters of Harriet, Countess Granville*, London, 1894,
Vol.I, p.124.

[11] Acton, *Last Bourbons*, pp.7-8.

Lushington. It was he who supported the British merchant community in their petition to establish a Protestant Chapel in the city. When this was rejected by the King, he appropriated a large hall at the entrance of his house where Protestant services could be performed.[12] In 1799, Sir Henry had married Fanny Lewis, sister of Matthew, just three years after the latter had published his tour-de-force, *The Monk*.

Amongst the most firmly entrenched of British residents was an unofficial medical practitioner to the British community, John Roskilly. He arrived in Naples in 1814-15 and, having married a Sicilian lady, settled there until his death in 1864. Whenever illness or accident struck a British traveller, he was regularly called in. However, he does not appear to have been a regular social guest at the formal dinners and entertainments attended by the Talbots.

The British family longest established in Naples was that of the Actons. Sir John Acton, born into a Catholic family in 1736, had been called on to reform the Neapolitan navy, and had so impressed the King, Ferdinand IV, that he ended up as Prime Minister. In 1800, at the age of sixty three, he received Papal dispensation to marry his thirteen year old niece, Mary Ann. When he died in 1811, he left three children. After the disruptions of the Napoleonic period had settled, Lady Acton kept an open house in Naples and was fond of putting on amateur dramatic performances and creating *tableaux*. By the end of the 1820s, her younger son had entered the priesthood, while her older one, Sir Richard, was keeping an eye out for a potential bride.

Amongst the long-term residents who feature frequently in the journal were two friends, Keppel Craven and Sir William Gell, who had both served as vice-chamberlains to Princess Caroline, the ill-fated wife of the Prince Regent, the future George IV. They had accompanied the Princess on her travels on the Continent until the point when she decided to turn northwards again. Craven decided to stay in Naples with his mother, formerly the adventurous Lady Craven and now the widowed Margravine of Anspach. Although, according to Marianne, a rather stolid bachelor, he had somehow acquired an illegitimate son. Matchmakers proposed that Keppel and Marianne might make a successful pair - but she would have none of it.

---

[12] In 1831, some 200-300 British subjects attended. See *British and Foreign State Papers, 1834-1835*, London, 1852, p.883.

In contrast with the stiff Craven, Sir William Gell, in spite of chronic gout which meant that he walked with sticks and had to be lifted in and out of carriages, played a central role in the social life of the British community. He not only related easily to people, but also, having published two works popularising the discoveries at Pompeii, was regularly called upon to act as *cicerone* to wealthy British visitors. Residing mainly in Naples, returning frequently to a *pied-à-terre* in Rome, and with a large circle of acquaintance, Sir William was a rich source of information about people and events. That he was also a lively raconteur with a gentle sense of humour, which he turned on himself as well as others, made him a popular dinner guest. With little money, especially after the pension accorded to him by Princess Caroline had been cut off after her death, he welcomed the hospitality and the benevolence of his better-off acquaintances. He was a regular and welcome guest of the Talbot household.

The strategic position of Naples as a Mediterranean port had encouraged the development of a sizable British merchant community within the city. Yet of the dozen members of this community who signed the petitions in favour of founding a dedicated British church in Naples,[13] not a single one is named in Marianne's journal. This absence would point to as sharp an acceptance of class divisions as would have been expected at home. If exceptions are to be found, they are in the persons of Mme Dupont and Mme Falconnet. Harriet Dupont was the daughter of Captain Sir Andrew Snape Douglas and had married the rich French merchant Maurice Dupont in Naples in 1827. Isabella Pulteney married the Swiss banker, François de Palézieux Falconnet, in 1829. Both the offspring of prosperous gentry stock and married to wealthy spouses, they were able to become participants in the elite British social set in Naples.

On the fringes of this set were Thomas Uwins, Thomas James Mathias, and Anna Baptista White. For five years between 1825 and 1830, the painter Thomas Uwins resided for much of the time in Naples. He received hospitality and commissions from Sir Richard Acton, but was also able to send paintings back to London to be sold there. The Talbot sisters certainly encouraged him in his work and probably bought from him.[14]

---

[13] See *British and Foreign State Papers 1834-1835*, London 1852, pp.878 & 882-3.

[14] See Uwins, II, p. 41.

Thomas Mathias was a man of letters whose main claim to fame lay in a work entitled *The Pursuits of Literature*, a satirical poem in four dialogues published in the 1790s and which reached its fourteenth edition in 1808. According to Gronow, the work had created 'an extraordinary sensation not only in the fashionable, but in the political world.' It had been pronounced by some 'the most classical and spirited production that had ever issued from the press,' by others 'one of the most spiteful and ill-natured satires that had ever disgraced the literary world.'[15] Mathias had been a fellow of Trinity College, Cambridge, and subsequently librarian at Buckingham House. He seems to have moved to the Continent around 1815, possibly for financial reasons - he had encountered difficulties as a result of an over-ambitious publishing project. His long-standing interest in Italian language and literature would explain his decision to move to Italy. Established in the Pizzafalcone district of Naples, he dedicated himself to writing and to translating works into and from Italian.

Most intriguing is the person of Miss Anna White (also spelt Whyte) who seems to have moved to Southern Italy at the same time as Mathias. However, she took up residence at La Cava, a small hill town closer to Salerno and the Amalfi coast than to Naples. As her residence lay on the route to the ancient Greek temples at Paestum and in close proximity to the famous Benedictine convent above La Cava itself, it was mainly on their excursions that she encountered members of the British community. When she did, she proved kind and hospitable. Her attempt to support Thomas Welch Hunt and his young wife Caroline after the attack on them by *banditti* in 1824 was long remembered. It was not her character but questions about her past and her motivations for living in such an isolated spot which were found puzzling. 'What an odd existence is this Miss Whyte's whom no one knows the hist'y of but who knows everyone,' was Marianne's reflection when staying at La Cava in 1830. Later in the same year, Sir William Gell took man-about-town Henry de Ros to visit her and reflected:

> It was quite wonderful to find an old Lady in the mountains capable of conversing with & entertaining a young man of fashion fresh from London just as if She had lived there last year. How the devil did she contrive to know all the people not only by name but

[15] Gronow, I, pp.143-4.

what they did & who they lived with - I could not make it out but so it was.[16]

A couple of years later, it was Sir Walter Scott whom Sir William Gell took to stay at La Cava where he

> expressed himself at all times much delighted with our amiable hostess Miss Whyte, remarking very justly that she had nothing cold about her but her house, which being in the mountains is in fact by no means eligible at that season of the year.[17]

Anna White seems to have readily provided hospitality to those who called on her at La Cava, but she never appears, in Marianne's journal at least, to have received it from the Naples residents. No doubt the distance, along with her own intention of leading a retired life, prevented it. Her generosity is further manifested in the provisions she made in her will, not only for her long-serving chamber-maid, but also for the latter's illegitimate daughter.

The visitors to Naples
A constant stream of visitors arriving by sea and by land prevented the British community remaining long unaware of events back at home. Some of those passing through were engaged in diplomatic missions, the most pressing of which related to the negotiations over the creation of an independent Greece. Thus, in 1829, Stratford Canning, after his attendance at the Conference of Poros, found himself in Naples; he was joined by his wife travelling from England. The couple struck up an enduring friendship with Marianne. After falling out with the British Government over policy relating to Greek independence, Stratford Canning tendered his resignation. Before he and his wife had left Naples, his replacement, Sir Robert Gordon, arrived with a group of aides including Lord Yarmouth, Lord Douro, and Robert Grosvenor.

Most British travellers touring the Continent in the early decades of the nineteenth century were men travelling singly or in small groups. To penetrate into the social set in Naples, it was not sufficient to be seeing the sights; the right connections were also essential. For Charles Greville the diarist and for man-about-town Henry de Ros, mem-

---

[16] Letter of 19 Nov. 1830 from Sir William Gell to Georgiana Gell, Derbs. County Record Office, D258/50/140.

[17] Gell, *Reminiscences*, p.20.

bership of White's must have been recommendation enough. Henry Edward Fox, the future Lord Holland, had lived for long periods at Rome and had a wide circle of acquaintance, and thus was able to introduce his friend Edward Cheney. His cousin Henry Stephen Fox had served as attaché and chargé d'affaires in various Italian postings including one at Naples. The latter had terminated in 1828 when he was appointed to a post in Brazil. However a couple of years passed before he was able to take up his appointment and during this time he appears to have lingered in Italy.

The number of women travelling seems to have increased sharply in the new century. Very few of these travelled alone, but many in the company of their husbands and often with their children. A consideration of four couples who feature quite prominently in the journal gives an indication of the range of their backgrounds and possible motivations for travelling. Peter and Elizabeth Langford Brooke, prosperous proprietors of Mere Hall in Cheshire, had been married some ten years before they set off on their prolonged Italian tour. They arrived in Naples towards the end of November 1828 and based themselves in the city for almost three years. As well as participating fully in the social life of the community, they seem to have expended much time and money in acquiring works of art both in Naples and Rome. The contents of Mere Hall when they came to be sold in 1994 indicated the range of the Brooke purchases: Etruscan style etchings by Tischbein, a painting of the Penitent Magdalene after Guido Reni, Italian landscape scenes in oil and watercolour, classical alabaster figures, and two white marble busts of the couple themselves commissioned in Rome from the sculptor Richard James Wyatt.[18] Even factoring in expenditure on works of art, they were able, over their three year residence in Italy, to achieve a saving of over £2000 on what they might have spent in England over the same period.[19]

Joseph and Lady Isabella St John had married at the end of August 1829 and had set off immediately for the Continent. They travelled under something of a cloud. Lady Isabella, daughter of the Duke of Grafton, had married against the wishes of her parents, and although the latter had become reconciled to the *fait accompli*, it was felt that a honeymoon tour abroad would allow the dust to settle. Marianne on her return from Paris met Isabella in Florence in October 1829 and

---

[18] See Christie's Mere Hall catalogue of the sale, 23 May 1994.

[19] Ibid., p.131.

again in November after the Talbots were back in Naples. The St Johns spent the winter in the city only leaving in May 1830 in order to spend the summer in Florence. They returned to Naples briefly later in the year.

The poor state of health of his wife had induced James Justinian Morier to travel to the Continent in 1829. As a young man, he had been involved in two prolonged diplomatic missions to Persia, and had received widespread acclaim for the published descriptions of his travels. Subsequently two fictionalised accounts of Persian life, *The Adventures of Hajji Baba of Ispahan* (1824) and *The Adventures of Hajji Baba in England* (1828) made him one of the most popular and successful authors of his day. The Moriers arrived in Naples in April 1830 and remained there through the summer and autumn, only heading to Rome towards the end of the year.

The journal also introduces one of the most famous, indeed notorious, couples of the age, the Marquis of Hertford and his companion Lady Strachan. The former was fabulously wealthy, not only through inheritance, but also from his marriage in 1798 to Maria Fagnani, the illegitimate daughter of the Marquis of Queensberry. Although depicted in Thackeray's *Vanity Fair* as the profligate Lord Steyne and in Disraeli's *Coningsby* as Lord Monmouth, both portrayals undoubtedly distort the reality of this complex individual.[20] Marianne Talbot certainly finds good qualities in him. His companion Lady Strachan proved an object of disapproval for many of her contemporaries. Mrs Arbuthnot described her as:

> one of the most vulgar women I have ever met with, having all the pretension of a fine lady. The terms she is on with Lord Hertford are most extraordinary; one cannot look at him, crippled with the gout & looking like an octogenarian, & imagine there can be any real impropriety & yet she is the depository of all his secrets .... & she seems complete mistress of the house.[21]

While also designating her as 'vulgar', Marianne developed an amused liking for her, stating that she preferred meeting her to 'any excellent good precise woman'. It would seem probable that Lady Strachan confided the extraordinary details of her birth, her upbring-

---

[20] See, for instance, Bernard Falk, *"Old Q's" Daughter,* p.116.

[21] Mrs Arbuthnot, *Journal*, Vol.I, p. 431.

ing and her marriage to Sir Richard, to others apart from Marianne Talbot, but while perhaps known at the time, they seem to have been forgotten since. If, as she indicates, Sir Richard was an unwilling bridegroom, his acquiescence in his wife's behaviour might be explained, along with his agreement that his three daughters be placed under the guardianship of Lord Hertford, a man with whom he had long been on friendly terms. After the death of Sir Richard in 1828, the Marquis along with Lady Strachan and her three daughters regularly visited the Continent and particularly favoured Naples.

Many other individuals and family groups are mentioned in the journal, for instance the Townley Parkers from Cheshire, the Ridleys from Newcastle, and, confusingly, another family of Talbots. There are occasional incursions from members of the British set in Rome, including the remarkably eccentric Lady Westmorland as well as Lady Mary Deerhurst with her daughter. As the Talbot residence in Naples approached its end, Britain's most famous living writer, Sir Walter Scott, arrived from Malta with his daughter Anne and older son, Walter. Having anchored in the bay on 17 December, they were only released from quarantine a week later when Sir Walter's younger son, Charles, working as an attaché under William Hill, was able to join them. On arrival at the hotel Gran Bretagna, Anne immediately wrote an invitation to Marianne Talbot. This resulted in the first of a number of meetings with Sir Walter and his family over the following three months.

British social life in Naples.
Various forms of social event brought individuals and groups together. Day excursions to Pompeii, Herculaneum or to the summit of Vesuvius were well suited to small groups of acquaintances. These could be extended over a number of days to take in the temples at Paestum, the monastery at La Cava, or the coast as it ran from Castellamare to Sorrento and round to Amalfi. House concerts, amateur dramatics and the creation of *tableaux* were also popular, along with visits to San Carlo, the opera house. However, the most important event was the dinner party. In a letter to his family in Derbyshire, Sir William Gell describes how central it was in his own life in Naples:

> One goes out a dining as usual, & a weeks dinners will give You a better idea of the people than any other description. Dec. 8 Wednesday dine at Mr Cravens .... having dined on tuesday at the Spanish Ministers. Thursday dine with Mr & Mrs Langford Brooke. Friday at Lady Drummonds with a rout. Saturday dine

with Ld Harrowby. Sunday with Mr Hill. Monday at Sir George Talbots that is tomorrow & on tuesday a dinner to the Harrowbys in state at Mr Cravens. By this You will see how the world wags here.[22]

It had come to be expected that British representatives on the Continent would extend dinner invitations to all those who arrived with a letter of recommendation:

> [British] travellers .... think that envoys are merely sent abroad to facilitate their touring fancies, and to invite them to dinner. This pleasing hallucination seems to preoccupy the minds of nine out of ten English who wander abroad.[23]

Perhaps for financial reasons, the eccentric William Hill seems to have resisted the pressure to some extent, while nevertheless offering frequent but select hospitality. In contrast, Sir George Talbot clearly loved entertaining and good food, and thus seems to have outdone the British minister in the quantity and quality of his dinners.[24]

As Sir William Gell's weekly engagements suggest, William Hill and Sir George Talbot were far from being the only hosts. Owen Blayney Cole was invited to a soirée by the rich Garniers:

> In the saloon of the Palazzo Garnier were more than a hundred guests of various nationalities, style, and rank - counts, marchesas, and be-diamonded dowagers, many of them with musical Italian names. On a raised platform at the other end of the room were Lady Strahan and her lovely daughters .... In an ante-chamber was the Marquis of Hertford, seated at whist, his well-developed leg graced with the garter and gallant motto, on his breast the star.[25]

The British regularly received and offered hospitality outside their own national set. Some foreign ministers, particularly the Russian Count Stackelberg, were frequent hosts, as were some of the Italian aristocracy. Important social events might well have involved an invi-

---

[22] Letter to Georgiana Gell, 12 Dec. 1830, Derbs. Record Office D258/50/141.

[23] Charles White, *Three years in Constantinople*, London, 1845, I, p.144.

[24] See journal entry for 24 April 1830, p.68.

[25] Owen Blayney Cole, *A last memory*, p.258.

tation from or to the Neapolitan royal family, but there appears to have been little of that intimacy between the royal household and the British upper class set which had existed fifty years before in the days of Sir William Hamilton.

The journal - stories, revelations and mysteries.

Through the spontaneity and conciseness of her writing, Marianne Talbot conveys an impression of her world - her interests and preoccupations. Books were important to her and she informs us directly about some of her current reading and, through her quotations and references, about what she has read in the past. Information about current events is gleaned from newspapers and journals, through letters she receives from friends, principally Lady Belhaven and the unidentified Charlotte, and, of course, from the British travellers arriving in Naples. Political debates about Catholic emancipation and parliamentary reform are followed with interest. As a member of a social elite, she had contact with many of those engaged in the international politics of the time, particularly in diplomacy - Sir Stratford Canning, Sir Robert Gordon, Sir Charles Stuart, Sir Brooke Taylor, the Duc Dalberg, Graf von Lebzeltern amongst others. Sometimes events came directly to Naples - in 1830, the occupation of Algiers by the French was followed by the arrival in the city of the deposed Dey and his suite. The following year, a volcanic island emerged out of the Mediterranean. The hoisting of a union jack on the island by the British Navy might have led to a serious political incident between Britain and the Kingdom of the Two Sicilies. In fact, the British made no stand over the matter and the island itself sank back into the sea. News of a much more serious nature, the political turmoil in France, quickly reached Naples because of the relationship between the two royal families and through the change of diplomatic personnel; in particular the Comte de Ferronays, former French minister and, at the time, French ambassador to the Vatican, found himself, along with his family, marooned at Naples. More feared even than political unrest, because unpredictable in its movement and seemingly indiscriminate in its choice of victims, was the cholera epidemic as it gradually moved north and west. First mentioned by Marianne in 1830, by the time of the Talbot return to England in 1832, its presence played a major role in determining the timing and route of their itinerary.

Alongside events taking place in the wider public arena, Marianne reported on those occurring in a more private sphere; here there is much to intrigue with some semi-revelations and mysteries. Of Marianne's relationships with men, we learn little. She had had one great, but doomed, love affair when she was young. A close relationship with Henry Stephen Fox seems to have been on the cards at one point in the past, but circumstances intervened - an intervention which she came to see as a lucky escape. The arrival of Sir Robert Gordon on his way to Constantinople apparently led to a sentimental flutter. By way of contrast, she has no hesitation in rejecting the proposal of Foley Wilmot, and does not countenance for a moment the attempts to tie her to Keppel Craven - she values her independence much too highly.

Marianne's interest in marital matters extends to the relationship between the couples who cross her threshold. She considers how well matched they are, who dominates, whether the woman has made financial concessions to her husband; the Langford Brooks, the St Johns, the Moriers, the Falconnets and the Duponts are all put under scrutiny. She also introduces hearsay stories on the marriage theme, for instance that of the British lieutenant who captured his bride from a Spanish convent. She noted at the same time that Admiral Fleming had also married a nun. She touches on the remarkable story of Mr Swift and Miss Kelly, which preoccupied William Hill and Sir Henry Lushington at the time. The couple were allegedly married in Rome against the wishes of Miss Kelly's mother. According to Charles Greville, who took up the mother's cause, even the daughter had not realised that a meeting she had attended with William Swift, had, in fact, been a marriage ceremony.[26] The mother challenged the legality of the marriage and effectively prevented the bridegroom from gaining access to his bride. If Marianne dismissed Miss Kelly as 'an illbehaved young lady', she reserved much greater disapproval for Lady Mary Hill who married her courier and left him a substantial legacy on her death. Lady Mary was the daughter of the 2nd Marquess of Downshire, and during the 1820s, had travelled extensively on the Continent with her widowed mother. The scandal seems to have erupted after her death in 1830.

Over these stories, Marianne could not be accused of being reticent, but she was not in a position to give full details. However, as well as her affairs of the heart, there is much relating to her own life during the period of the journal about which she reveals little, if anything. There are clear hints that there were tensions in her relationship with both her father and her sister. When returning to Naples from Paris in

---

[26] Charles Greville, *The Greville Memoirs*, Vol.1, p.479.

October 1829, she records, when in Parma, a major incident in her life: 'I have another misery, one that makes me wretched, but on this family misery, I will never write.' Precisely a year later, she seems to return to the same source of misery, quoting the last verse of Thomas Gray's *Ode on a distant prospect of Eton College*, and in April 1832 she is still tormented by the episode of 1829. It would seem that her sister was the source of the problem but there is no indication of its nature. Equally mysterious are the plans for the return to England. Initially, it had been decided that the family, after some sixteen years on the Continent, would return permanently to England in 1831, but when, where, by whom, and above all why the decision was made, is not indicated. It becomes no clearer when suddenly the date of departure is postponed by a full year.

Other topics, touched upon or omitted, reflect the interests and preoccupations of the writer. Curiously, for one whose father was for ever entertaining and who, herself, often took up several dinner invitations in a week, Marianne expresses little interest in food - not once does she describe the dishes served up at a dinner; her pleasure derived from the people she met and the quality of their conversation. Prior to the return to England, the family plate was sent home, the silver sold to Rothschild, but in general, we learn next to nothing about the domestic arrangements, the daily routine, the lay-out or furnishing of rooms, or the employment or duties of the servants. In contrast, fashion is something which clearly was of importance to her. She noticed what the ladies were wearing, their dresses, their hats and their jewelry, and she herself spent large sums on these items herself. To make such purchases she was not dependent on hand-outs from her father - she clearly had control of her own money and enjoyed investing it - the financial advice of the Marquis of Hertford was welcomed.

Naples after the Talbots.
The departure of the Talbots from Naples in 1832 was followed by a more general break-up of the British set with the departure of two of its leading personalities. On a visit to Naples in the autumn of 1832, Lord Berwick, the older brother of William Hill, died, and so the British Minister in Naples since 1825 resigned and returned to Shropshire to take up the title to his family's estate. He died, unmarried, in 1842. Even more involved in the day-to-day affairs of the British community had been Sir Henry Lushington. He had been appointed British consul-general at Naples in 1815, but in 1832 this appointment was

terminated, apparently in a cost-cutting exercise: his replacement was a plain 'consul' with a much reduced salary.

Death caught up with the older members of the group: Anna White died in 1833, James Mathias in 1835 and Sir William Gell in 1836. Keppel Craven lived on until 1856 and his illegitimate son Augustus married Pauline Ferronays, daughter of the French politician and diplomat stranded in Naples when Louis Philippe ousted Charles X. Lady Strachan loosened her ties with the Marquis of Hertford, married an Italian, acquired the title of Marchesa di Salza, and settled in Naples where she died in 1867. Using Joseph St John as go-between, Sir Richard Acton finally succeeded in persuading the Duc and Duchesse Dalberg to allow him to marry their daughter. After Sir Richard's death in 1837, his son, Sir John, played an influential role in British politics, and was subsequently appointed to a Regius Professorship at Cambridge. His widow married Granville Leveson-Gower in 1840.

The Talbots after Naples.
With the termination of the journal in August 1832, the account of the Talbots' life again becomes fragmentary. They re-established themselves in Burlington Street, and, in 1833, Sir George reintroduced his regular dinner parties during the season. Later in the year, he purchased a property in Hanover Square and, having made the move, he let out his Burlington Street house. In 1841, he concluded his final property purchase in London when he leased 21 Grosvenor Square. It was here that he died, aged 89, on 15 June 1850. During the last years of his life, he had continued to give and attend dinner parties. He was also a regular theatre-goer, for instance attending, in 1847, three different operatic productions starring the operatic mega-star of the period, Jenny Lind. Apart from a stay in Paris in the summer of 1839, the Talbots do not seem to have crossed the Channel. However, they did settle into a routine of visiting some of the increasingly popular health resorts. Initially, they favoured Brighton, but subsequently they sojourned at Leamington, Malvern, Ryde in the Isle of Wight, and Bournemouth.

During the final years of their father's life, little information has emerged about the individual activities of Sir George's two daughters. Marianne maintained the interest in writing which she mentioned in the journal. At least two publications emerged from this activity. In 1835 there appeared a collection of pieces in a work entitled *The Sketchbook of the South*. Here are to be found some of the essays the preparation of which she mentions in the journal: 'The Cardinal Lover', 'The Monastery of Monte Vergine' and 'The Santa Trinità of La Cava'. She also began working on a novel which was ultimately published anonymously in 1850 under the title of *Past, Present and Future*. Of Georgina, nothing seems to be known until, after her father's death, she set about establishing a village for the working poor just outside Bournemouth. Marianne's involvement in the project is uncertain, but, after Georgina's death in 1870, she gave it her support. During the remaining years of her own life, Marianne seems to have resided mainly in the family house in Grosvenor Square, but when she died in 1885, aged 96, her body was buried alongside that of her sister, in the churchyard of St Mark's Church, in Talbot Village, the village they had created - not in the Protestant churchyard in Rome as she had at one time wished, but also not in the family vault in Dorking which she had so much dreaded!

Editing the journal.
The most pressing editorial problems arose from the nature of this particular type of journal: one written, not systematically or on a regular basis, but as the fancy took the writer, and essentially for herself, not for others. Details of events and people and the personal responses to them were often thrown onto the page without any need being felt to clarify the context or to identify individuals with precision. As a result, the text is dense and the script hard to read. The combination of uncrossed 't's and undotted 'i's with a sequence of 'n's and 'u's meant that without context to help, many individual words, often elided together, would have been unreadable. The unexpected introduction of French words added a further difficulty, as did casual and intermittent punctuation, along with Marianne's occasional failure to write what she clearly intended to write.

Faced with such a text, I decided to excise nothing - all editing out is liable to distort the impact of the writing and the reader's perception of the writer. It also presupposes that the editor's judgment in distinguishing what is important from what is less so will coincide with that of future readers. I did, however, intervene by inserting and adjusting punctuation in order to increase readability. I also corrected spelling, but only in those few cases where idiosyncrasies might have puzzled or misled the reader. Otherwise, I have endeavoured to maintain the original text and decided not to insert *sic* on those occasions when spelling or usage deviated from current practice. Within square brackets, I have sometimes added one or more missing letters, again with the aim of enabling a smoother read. Completely unreadable words are replaced by a spaced [?] ; words which I may not have read correctly are directly followed by[?]. Apostrophes were used casually and intermittently. Here too I have tried to let the manuscript version stand. To standardise appearance in notes and following Marianne's practice in the text, I have used capitals in foreign titles, e.g. Comte, Duc.

The journal is thronged with names - people who Marianne met or referred to. Where possible and where it seemed useful, I have endeavoured to identify these. Similarly events are described or alluded to, and here too I have sought to add background details. Where information would seem warranted but is lacking, it should be assumed I tried, but failed, to find it! To those who find the footnotes excessive in length and number, I apologise. For me the by-ways into which the journal led were one of its fascinations - but following them may reduce the impact of the rapidly moving account.

The task of editing of the journal benefited enormously from the advent of the computer and internet age. By means of digital photographs, the transcription of the text was completed much more rapidly and accurately than would have been possible in the past. It was much easier to consult colleagues over difficult words and phrases in the text. Internet searches led to chance discovery of Marianne's involvement in the two books already mentioned - they had been published anonymously. Through versions helpfully scanned and made available on internet sites, the texts could be read on screen. Sites containing genealogical material, historical newspapers, biographies, and literary works were invaluable in identifying individuals and quotations, and in clarifying allusions to people and events.

Any editor turning to publication will have regrets about unfinished business. As well as the usual frustrations at words or names I unsuccessfully struggled to decipher, I failed to uncover the identities of the rich Mr and Mrs Garnier who appear on a number of occasions, or of the other Talbot family living in Naples with numerous children. Although there is a painting of Marianne in her old age, I found no illustration of her in her youth or middle age which would have been an appropriate addition to this publication. Of the hundreds of letters which Marianne must have written, the only one I know of is that written to Sir Walter Scott during his stay at Naples.[27] Similarly, I found no trace of the 'beautiful drawings' which were to be Marianne's 'last recollection of Naples'.[28] Finally, there were those intriguing puzzles and stories a fuller investigation of which would have required much more research time than could reasonably be allocated. These included the extraordinary life of Lady Strachan, including the identity of her father, the identity of Augustus Craven's mother, the post-elopement life of Captain Stuart and the nun, the remarkable marriage in Rome of William Swift and Elizabeth Kelly, their forced separation for some seven years until their second marriage in Folkestone, and then their subsequent life together, the marriage of Lady Mary Hill to her courier and its circumstances, the causes of her death, and the sequence of events leading to his suicide.

Acknowledgments.
I am grateful to all those institutions, public and private, in both the UK and Italy, which allowed me access to their archives, and whose staff provided friendly assistance (see Bibliography). I am particularly grateful to my home library at the University of Cambridge. Those libraries and archives which permitted digital photography deserve special thanks, because its use enabled study and transcription to be completed more rapidly, more efficiently, and more cheaply. The Bibliothèque de Genève gave useful information about the Coindet collection. Woolley and Wallis, Fine Art Auctioneers of Salisbury, kindly gave permission to reproduce the image of Sir Henry Lushington. Christie's gave me a copy of their Mere Hall catalogue from 1994.

My correspondence with Carol Medlicott, longtime researcher into the history of Talbot Village, proved stimulating and useful. The Earl of Elgin provided confirmatory information about the relationship of his family to the young Louise Dillon (subsequently Lady Strachan). Simon Ditchfield and Carlo Knight gave helpful answers to particular questions. As well as to these, I am grateful to all my friends who provided support and advice - especially those called on to suggest interpretations of Marianne's difficult handwriting. Finally, my thanks are due to Pat Story for a careful reading of the draft and to Clare Yerbury for realising practically my ideas for the cover and for the insertion of illustrations.

---

[27] National Library of Scotland, MS 3517, ff.243-4. It was probably written on 1 March 1832.

[28] See p.170.

Prologue to the Journal (written by the editor).

In March 1829 when this volume of the Marianne Talbot's journal opens, she, along with her sister, Georgina, and father, Sir George, were firmly established in Naples and renting a suite of rooms in the Palazzo Serracapriola on the Chiaia, the elegant sea-front street over-looking the Bay of Naples. Harboured in the Bay was the British Mediterranean fleet under its commander, Sir Pulteney Malcolm. He, along with his officers, had recently attended a ball laid on for them by the British community for which the residents were now being called on to pay their contribution.

At the residence of the Russian Minister, Count Stackelberg, an amateur dramatic performance involving the acting out of a proverb and apparently including a character called The Humorist had led to a spat between British attaché Foley Wilmot and his Russian host. The performance also involved Count Beugnot, a French diplomat, and Madame Apraxin, a Russian resident.

In the city itself, in the run-up to Ash Wednesday on 9 March, Carnival was approaching its height. Its exuberant and carefree activities, including the throwing of bouquets, sweets, and sometimes bags of flour, were hardly ones in which Britain's ultra-serious Stratford Canning would naturally participate. He had arrived a few weeks before, after representing Britain at the Conference at Poros where Greek independence from Turkey had been discussed. He was now engaged in correspondence with London over the future of his mission. He had recently been joined from London by his young wife.

The text of the Journal of Marianne Talbot 1829-1832.

****

"This journal is a relief - when I am tired - as I generally am - out comes this, & down goes every thing. But I can't read it over - & God knows what contradictions it may contain. If I am sincere with myself (but I fear one lies more to oneself than to anyone else) every page should confute/refute, & utterly abjure its predecessor."[1]   Lord Byron.

****

1 March [1829].   The paper came round to ask for the 56 ducats for the ball & with it 'Sir P. Malcolm[2] & the Capt. & Officers of his Squadron present their comp'ts to the gentlemen at Naples who honoured them with the ball last E'g & they cannot take their leave without expressing to those Gentlemen their sense of such a flattering mark of attention towards them.'
His Majesty's sloop *Asia*, Naples bay, 20th Feb'y 1829.

Mr Wilmot[3] continues in a Fury with old Stack[4] - he has written a song beginning "Hush, Hush here's old Mother Apraxin."[5] There is not much in it except bitterness; but the following Verses he has shown about addressed to Beugnoit,[6] the French attaché who acts:

> 'Pour bien jouer l'humoriste,
> Si tu veux montrer ton zèle,
> N'invente rien, sois copiste,
> Et prends ton hôte pour modèle.'

thus translated:

---

[1] See Thomas Moore, *Letters and Journals of Lord Byron*, 2 vols., London, 1830, Vol.I, p.463. The date of publication indicates that M.T. must have inserted the quotation into the journal after reading Moore's work in 1830 (see entry for 1 July 1830).

[2] Sir Pulteney Malcolm, commander-in-chief in the Mediterranean 1828-31.

[3] Foley Wilmot (1796-1852) had been appointed a British attaché in Naples in 1828.

[4] Count Gustav Ernst von Stackelberg (1766-1850), Russian minister in Naples.

[5] A Russian resident of Naples.

[6] Gustave Adolphe Beugnot (1799-1861) had been Secretary at the French embassy in Constantinople and was to serve in an equivalent position in Rome from 1829-1835.

'Beugnoit! you know that l'humoriste
Depicts a strange ill-tempered beast
So, if you'd beat our Garrick hollow
That thunders of applause may follow
Take - tho' he now begins to twaddle,
Your host the Calmuck as your model.'

Mr Canning[7] has the very maddest eyes I ever saw. I am not sure whether a man who is said to be as aware of his temper can be said to have a bad one, but for all my admiration for genius & abilities, I don't know that I sd like to be Mrs Canning. The other Morn'g, they were at the balcony of the Accademia looking at the Masks & Mrs C. was much pelted from the higher window[8] - it is a proof of love & attention that does try one's English temper; however he fell into a fury & exposed himself to the Italians who were charmed. Luckily Mr Wilmot, Papa & Sir Ed. [Stopford][9] had all come away as it wd have been a distressing scene. Mr Wilmot was telling me of his conduct with the French Ambassador somewhere some years ago whom he sent to, to ask him, why he did not challenge him. They had quarelled about the words *franchise* & *politesse*; people say that he can't take a joke. Prince Leopold's[10] Ball was thin & cold. The King of Bavaria[11] was there looking like a tamed Hyena & Mrs Barrington[12] was there much admired; she is young & beautifully made & has a fine complection. Mr Bisse[13] asked Mr Canning to dance, more a subject for fury than sugar plums to my mind. Prince Rics[?] was there & Mrs Barrington told me that she met him one day at North'd House where

---

[7] Stratford Canning (1786-1880) had attended the Poros Conference on Greek independence in the autumn of 1828 and had arrived in Naples in January 1829 where he was joined by his wife.

[8] It was customary during Carnival to pelt people with sugar-plums (small sweets). It appears Canning was slow to enter into the spirit of the occasion.

[9] Sir Edward Stopford (1766-1837).

[10] Prince Leopold of Saxe-Cobourg (1790-1865), former husband of Princess Charlotte (d.1817), daughter of George IV. After turning down the crown of Greece, he became King of the Belgians in 1830. He had spent the winter of 1828-9 in Naples.

[11] Ludwig I (1786-1868), King of Bavaria between 1825 and 1848.

[12] Presumably Jane Elizabeth (1804-1883), the wife of William Keppel Barrington, who became Viscount Barrington of Ardglass on the death of his father on 4 March 1829.

[13] Thomas Bisse (1788-1872) had moved to Naples with his wife after the Napoleonic war. They returned to England during the course of 1829.

she had taken the old Bishop of Durham[14] to see the house & there she met P'ce Rics, who said "Apparement c'etoit un mariage de convenance!"

Nothing is talked of but Saturdays Post. The Duke of Wellington is in for ever & ever. It is said that the King said to the Duke of Wellington "For this business you'll go to Hell & I to Heaven."[15]

I have had a wonderful Letter from one of whom I cannot give the name she assumes of P'cess of Radzivill. Now our correspondence must cease for her conduct is too bad. It is evident that Pozzo di Borgo[16] don't acknowledge her & that she sees but Men. That Spa friendship of mine[17] is quite out of the common, as the Scotch say; & I had often misgivings as to the ultimate end of this wild cleverness. She sends me Autographs of her literary society at Paris: Notes of Tissot, Azaïs, B.Constant, C'te de Segur, Fonig & Gerard. Mr Mellish[18] has given me Notes of the writing of Mr Canning, Capo d'Istria, Guilleminot & M. de Ribeaupierre. Mme Delmar[19] sends me a Note of the Duke of Raguze's; & M. de Varenne[20] has given me one of P'ce Mav-

---

[14] Shute Barrington, Bishop of Durham from 1791 until his death in 1826, was the great uncle of William Keppel Barrington.

[15] Presumably on the topic of Catholic emancipation which George IV had opposed.

[16] Count Pozzo di Borgo (1764-1842), a Corsican who had been fiercely inimical to his fellow-Corsican Napoleon, had, in 1814, been appointed Russian ambassador in Paris.

[17] People encountered in a watering place like Spa may not live up to first appearances.

[18] Richard Charles Mellish (1801-1865), attaché at the embassy in Constantinople between 1828 and 1830.

[19] Emily Rumbold (1790-1861) had married the rich Prussian baron Ferdinand de Delmar in April 1827. In her twenties, she was regarded as one of the belles of society. She was present at the Duchess of Richmond's famous Ball in Brussels on the eve of Waterloo, and when she danced the last dance with Captain Horace Seymour of the Life Guards, William Pitt Lennox, the Duchess's son, considered 'a handsomer couple were never seen. They would have formed as fine a subject for Millais' splendid picture, as did the "Young Brunswicker".' (See William Pitt Lennox, Celebrities I have Known, 2nd series, London, 1877, Vol.I, p.333). In *tableaux vivants* of Olympus and its gods presented at the Congress of Vienna, she was chosen to portray Diana. After her marriage and subsequent residence in Paris with her husband, she became a fashionable salon hostess. (See Sir Horace Rumbold, *Recollections of a Diplomatist*, Vol.1, London,1902, pp.42-53).

[20] Jacques Edouard Burignot de Varenne (1795-1873), French diplomat involved in the negotiations over Greece

rocordato, & Sommery[21] a Letter of Châteaubriands but with his usual distraction he sends me the note of the person who sends it to him which is too curious not to keep too.

We said goodbye to Sir E. Stopford, a good natured man to live with in a house. I hope he will come back. We begin to see Mrs Brooke,[22] Figit Brooke, as Sir W. Gell calls her. Today a dinner of tiresome Italians. Our Minister[23] is the very oddest person alive - sometimes so very fond of us, & at others asking Papa to dinner when he knows he is engaged, which he calls doing a civility. We went to Ly Ridley's ball.[24] The Ridleys are a rich, prosperous family all very unhappy. Ly Ridley dresses herself after Ninon[?], is gentily vulgar, spends hundreds & thousands upon patent lace, indian muslin & trinkets, looks like a fool, has half a dozen daughters all dressed to match, but who will not match, I sd think. How many english ressemble them!

6th March [1829]. We meant to have (literally) a goose & gander feast today, but the leading goose & gander were sick & the flock dispersed, & we mixed in some specimens of intellect. Mr Ch[ristopher] Talbot[25] who is clever & takes a book after dinner & sits reading like a bird on a perch. I sat next my gretna green friend[26] at dinner who is a jabberer of the first class but having seen many people & countries has much to tell worth hearing. Such a letter as Sir Wm. Gell & Mr Wilmot penned to Ly Belhaven!![27] giving an acc't of Sir William Gells elder brother having fallen into the sea from the road between Nice & Genoa!

---

[21] Augustin Mesniel de Sommery (1800-95) had been a secretary at the French embassy in Naples since 1825.

[22] Elizabeth Langford Brooke and her husband Peter, of Mere Hall, Cheshire, had arrived in Naples at the end of November 1828.

[23] William Noel Hill, British Minister in Naples 1825-1832.

[24] In 1803, Laura Hawkins had married Sir Matthew White Ridley (1778-1836) who was M.P. for Newcastle between 1812 and his death. According to Sir William Gell, the Ridleys gave 'balls great & expensive like 200£ each & dinners without end'. (See letter of 10 March 1829 to Mrs Georgiana Gell, Derbs. County Archives, D258/50/131).

[25] Christoper Rice Mansel Talbot (1803-90).

[26] Presumably, Foley Wilmot who is about to propose formally for M.T.'s hand - see below.

[27] Lady Belhaven (c.1790-1873), née Hamilton Campbell, had married Sir Robert Montgomery Hamilton, 8th Lord Belhaven (1793-1868) in 1815. The Belhavens had recently been in Naples, having attended a ball given by Prince Leopold. (See *The Morning Post*, 25 March 1829).

I have had such a kind letter from Ly Belhaven as melted my heart. She is the woman I love the best in the world. A letter arrived from Charlotte of 8 sides of kindness & amusement & one from Mme Delmar of Paris gossip - she had been of the *Tableaux* at the D'esse de Gontauts where the D'esse de Berri personated Marie Stuard in the marriage of François deux with the Duc de Chartres.[28]

12 March [1829]. For a long time past Mr W[ilmot] has found his way into this house twice a day. I can't help it. I wish he wd not come. He gives me a great deal of trouble in going out to prevent it. I am a Bear to him & cut him in public to show it cannot be, but it seems that the saying comes true, "Use your lover as you would your dog & he will be as faithful as a Dog." The Bisse screeches[?] & Mme Dupont[29] will talk[?] of him, & also of Mr Hill marrying Ly Dry.[30]

14th March [1829]. There was a *triste* party at the Stacks. The Grand Duchess[31] has chosen l'Humoriste to be the Proverbe, a piece of Malice to her host & Mme Apraxin is scandalized at *la liberte grande* of everything. Hating Royal presentations & it being Sunday Night we would not go. M. de Varenne is one of the few french Men I can bear. He was giving me yes'y an acc't of Ly Hester Stanhope. George 4th has paid her debts. He says that she is his *philosophe* in her religious opinions.

15th March 1829. Papa told me that Mr W[ilmot] has proposed for me. He made the usual answer that he always does on every disagreeable occasion. "My daughters always do as they like, I have nothing to say to it." I never dreamt of accepting Mr W. yet he is certainly attached to me & is very clever. I have seen him twice a day since Oct. & incessant has been his attendance, "For this hands, lips, & eyes

---

[28] i.e. played by the Duc de Chartres. The event was described in some detail by the Duchesse de Maillé in her *Souvenirs* (pp.267-9). She noted that it was a 'singulier rapprochement' in which the Duchesse de Berry (mother of the Duc de Bordeaux, the heir to the French throne) made king the Duc de Chartres (the eldest son of Louis-Philippe).

[29] Harriet Dupont (1786-1860) was the daughter of Captain Sir Andrew Snape Douglas (1761-1797). She had married the prosperous French merchant Maurice Dupont in Naples in April 1827. Her brother Andrew had been Secretary of the British legation in the Kingdom of the Two Sicilies 1813-24.

[30] Lady Drummond, née Harriet Anne Boone, widow of Sir William Drummond (c.1770-1828). 'Dry' was Sir William Gell's nickname for Sir William.

[31] Helena Paulowna, daughter of Prince Paul of Würtemberg had married Grand Duke Michael in 1824. He was the brother of Czars Alexander I and Nicholas I.

were put to school".[32] As an agreeable companion, he is unrivalled. I shall miss him terribly & yet - I don't like him. We yes'y dined at Mr Stratford Cannings. I think both he & she represent well, tho' she is young & shy; he is stiff & like Sir Ch. Grandison, but he loves the society of learned persons but wh. Sir Chas. did not.[33] Mr Wilmot says that Mrs Canning is as pleasant as milk & water can be. I sat between him & Sir W. Gell. One was grave, very grave, & the other funny, notwithstanding Gout & illness. Near[?] us was Abelard or now called Babilard Steward.[34] We have hardly spoken since the Affair of 1825, but yes'y he was very coming, said that *if* there was any religion in the world it was the Catholic, & said a number of very silly things, to which Sir Wm. Gell said "Miss Talbot likes a rakish air & manner like yours."

17 March. I am totally unfit for a gay select dinner today, being much too tender hearted, & Georgina is worse than I am. I did not suppose that I sd mind saying Goodbye to one I had often wished gone - he was in a terrible state of agitation & nerves. He is gone to Rome & to Russia to Ld Heytesbury[35] as Attaché. The sight of strong feeling is painful, life is such a scene of strong dislikes & likes, such wear & tear of temper & feeling. Women go thro' much when it is not supposed they do.

18th [March 1829]. The ides of March are so always to rue. The woman who has to refuse a Man she knows really well is quite as unhappy as he is. We had yes'y a little dinner; the scene in the Morn'g had agitated me, appearances were against me, & Mrs L[angford] B[rooke] & the Men must have thought I really liked Mr Wilmot! I got a Note from Sir Wm who loves a marriage beginning "Dear Mlle Herod".

---

[32] See George Lyttelton's poem of 1733, *Advice to a Lady*. The lines are quoted by Maria Edgeworth in the first chapter of her novel *Belinda*. M.T. may well have been aware of both sources.

[33] Sir Charles Grandison, hero of Henry Fielding's epistolary novel of the same name, which was first published in six volumes 1753-4.

[34] *babillard* - a gossip. Thomas Stewart (1802-1845), a nephew of Lady Drummond, was to join the Benedictine order in Sicily. In 1845, he was assassinated at Ancona.

[35] William A'Court, Baron Heytesbury (1779-1860), had been appointed Ambassador to Russia in 1828. He had been British minister in Naples between 1814 and 1822.

27 March 1829. My time is occupied in Gardening. Sir Wm. is gone &
I begin *à me faire* to the loss of the whole society.

Yesterday, we had 16 people at dinner, 7 Ladies & our odd Minister. I
like Mr Canning very much. He is stiff but very clever, & I thought
Mrs Canning looked triumphant justly when I said that Ly Warwick
had twice over married a Fool.[36] It seems that she married Ld W. as
Charlotte did Albert[37]: "par inclination et par l'ordre positive de Mme
sa Mere." Ly Warwick is very facinating in manner, clever & *naturel,*
& like Ly Lovaine[38] when the sun shines. She was dressed a strange
figure when she came to dine here, just as if she had taken off her
night cap, in the midst of the *tiré a 4 epingles*[39] of the Naples women.
She hates foreigners, how right of her, but I never shall forget her little
black head in the midst of theirs.

28th March [1829]. We met them at dinner next day at Mr Hills. She
is very amusing & asked me what we did here in society. I said what is
true "slept a great deal". She & Ld W[arwick] quarel too much. She
makes great fun of Ly Strachan[40] who was boasting to her that she
never was made so much of as at the present time & said "There is
your prudish friend Ly Lovaine who comes to me & Mrs Cadogan,"
on wh. Ly Warwick said "Mrs Cadogan, why, she's as bad as yourself." I sat next Capt. Cadogan at dinner.[41] Poor Man, why are half the
Men martyrs to their wives? Ld D[o]uro was there who looks silly
(one fool in a family, see Johnson[42]) & Ld Ch. Wellesley, who is said

---

[36] Lady Sarah Elizabeth Savile (1786-1851), eldest daughter of the 2nd Earl of Mex-
borough, had married the 4th Lord Monson (1785-1809) before marrying Henry Richard Greville, 3rd Earl of Warwick (1779-1853), in 1816.

[37] Reference to Goethe's *The Sorrows of Young Werther.*

[38] Louisa (1781-1848), wife of George Percy, future Earl of Beverley, travelling with
her daughter, Miss Louisa Percy (1802-83).

[39] 'dressed to the nines' might be the equivalent English expression.

[40] Widow of Sir Richard Strachan (1760-1828) and consort of the Marquis of Hertford.
She appears in person later in the journal.

[41] Capt. the Hon. George Cadogan (1783-1864) had married Louisa Honoria Blake in
1810. He became 3rd Earl Cadogan in 1832. She had once been the lover of Henry de
Ros. (See Greville, 1, p.70).

[42] Samuel Johnson is alleged to have said that primogeniture was an excellent thing because it ensured there was 'only one fool in a family', i.e. all children except the one
inheriting had to have the wits to make their way in the world.

to be clever but is very ugly indeed.[43] Mr Hill spit out his dinner enough to disgust every one - with all his strange ways I like; whether any woman would be happy with him is another thing. What a charming little person Mrs Canning is. She gains on me daily!

Readings this Month of March:
Bishop Heber's Journal & Letters, a charming book.[44]
Sorrows of Rosalie, a beautiful Poem written when Mrs Norton was 16. Mrs Sheridan showed it to Ld Holland[45] who was charmed with it but requested that it might not be published until the young Lady was married![46]

1st of April 1829. We called on Mrs Canning, a gentle amiable person who has drawn a better lot in life than Ly Warwick has, notwithstanding rank, beauty & riches. She was telling me about the Turks & Constantinople. Their rigid fasts during three weeks till sunset, their dress & their baths. The effect upon the looker-on[?] of all a population falling on their knees to prayer, at the calling.

Today we dined with Mr Hill for the third time this week. It was very stiff. Mme de Budna (Ly Kinnairds Mme de Budna)[47] was there with a husband 15 years younger than herself. She has no good looks left but an agreeable countenance, & a young husband don't make a woman look more charming. Pr'ss Tre Casi & the D'esse d'Ascoli dined

---

[43] Arthur Richard Wellesley, Marquis of Douro (1807-1884), was the Duke of Wellington's elder son, Lord Charles Wellesley, his younger son.

[44] Bishop Reginald Heber's *Narrative of a journey ... and letters written in India,* had been published in two volumes in 1828.

[45] Henry Richard Fox, 3rd Lord Holland (1773-1840) had married (1797) Elizabeth Vassall, who had previously been married to Sir Godfrey Webster. Their son, Henry Edward Fox, was to succeed to the title in 1840.

[46] The advice was heeded. Caroline Elizabeth Sarah Sheridan (c.1809-1877) married George Chapple Norton in July 1827. *The Sorrows of Rosalie* was first published in 1829.

[47] Countess Bubna (1790-1840) was the widow of the Austrian general Ferdinand, Count Bubna von Littitz who, after the Napoleonic war, served as military governor in Lombardy. The Countess seems to have become acquainted with Lady Kinnaird in Milan (see Lady De Clifford, *A short journal of a tour made through part of France ...in 1817*, Richmond, n.d., p.65). After the Count's death in 1825, the Countess married, in 1828, Gustav, Prince of Bathyány-Strattmann (1803-83).

there. The last was as silly as nature & satin & feathers cd make her.[48]
Pr'ss Tre Casi looked very pretty & Mr Hill told her that P'ce Cassaro[49] did not look as if he came from the country of Punch[50] - wh. her
intellect could not take in - Mr Hill complains never will. If he marries
Ly Drummond, he will have something to cry for. How she will enjoy
bringing her trousseau, & when she asks him how she looks, what will
he say? It is said that Miss Percy is to be a Catholic![51] We went to
Mme Dupont where was a dinner for Ly Drummond, Ly Mary Deerhurst & Mr Hill & Ly Lushington & Maria. What fools foreign
women are. Such a *seccatura*[52] it is to support a *tete a tete*.

Sir Wm. Gell sends me a gay letter enclosing the Cardinals Ticket for
electing a Pope.[53]

6th. [April 1829]. Our Plans are made - we have had many a pleasant
day this winter & shall have many a pleasant one next Winter. We are
going to Switzerland in June to stay there till my Father comes from
England.

We spent yesterday quietly. Today we have been a long spring walk
with the Langford Brooks & Lushingtons. We all talked only foolish
gossip. Mr & Mrs Langford Brook admired each others wisdom &
wit. We went to the Solfatara & round by the terrace walk & Ruffo
Villa. The bright blue sky, the budding green on the Vines, & the various charms of Spring enchanted us. The ground so hollow of the crater of the Solfatara, the water boils that runs from it. There is a manufactory of Solfatara for wh. the proprietor pays Gov't a 100£ a year.
Sismondi gives an account of a ball & *course de Char* in the Crater

---

[48] Carolina Berio di Salza (c.1793-1856), the wife of Sebastiano Marulli, Duke of Ascoli.

[49] Antonio Statella, Prince of Cassaro (1785-1864), the diplomat who, in 1831, was to
succeed Luigi di Medici as Minister for Foreign Affairs.

[50] i.e. Italy, the country of the *commedia del'arte* figure of Pulcinello.

[51] See note 38.

[52] According to Stendhal, *seccatura* had become an 'in' word of the period. He suggested it might be defined as 'the annoyance provoked by a fool when he arouses a passionate soul from reverie to deal with something which is not worth the bother.' *Promenades dans Rome*, p.377. It could be translated more easily as 'bore'.

[53] Cardinal Castiglione had been elected Pope on 31 March and had assumed the name
of Pius VIII.

given in 1452 by Alphonse King of Naples to Frederick the 3d of Germany. It was by torch light on the occasion of a royal wedding.[54]

8th April. Today's post brought the account of the dual between the D. of Wellington & Ld. Winchilsea.[55] Last night was a party at Mr Bisses. Here is one the Mr Hills speeches - I had on a yellow hat with Marabouts & Birds of Paradise, & very pretty it was - an old hat of Herbault's new done up.[56] "Well", says Mr Hill, before the Master of the house, "I'm quite surprised to see you put on such a Hat as that to come to such a place as this."

Some talked of the Devils own scrape[57] - I asked Sir H. L[ushington] what it meant. He asked Mr Hill who looked as if he not only knew but felt: this Mans oddities surprise me, & his indecision of character. I don't know any thing so bad as indecision, even in a Dog, wh. I was witness to today.

10th April [1829]. Walked up to P'ce. Scaletta's[?] with Mr & Mrs Canning. I like her more & more. "She yields her charm of mind with sweet delay."[58] Last night there was a small assembly *chez elle*. Mme Dupont is trying to make Mr Hill & I good friends, but it wont do, I can't swallow his manners & we have met probably for the last time. Ly Dry has got a new Nephew who is very much of a Shoemaker & very little of a gentleman.[59] Babillard has a quarel with the Duke de Blacas[60] on the subject of ancient families & putting his own before

---

[54] See J.C.L. Simonde de Sismondi, *Histoire des Républiques italiennes du Moyen Age*, Vol. VI, Paris, 1840, pp.242-3. The text makes it clear that it was a hunt by torchlight and accompanied by music which Alphonse had organised.

[55] The duel between the Duke and the 9th Earl of Winchilsea took place on the morning of Saturday, 21 March 1829. Neither participant was injured.

[56] Herbault had been for some time the most fashionable milliner in Paris. Attending a wedding in 1828, Apponyi describes the sensation caused by a Herbault hat in Italian straw with white feathers which had cost 1800 francs. (Apponyi, I, p.127).

[57] Presumably 'marriage'.

[58] See Edward Young, *Love of Fame, Satire VI, On Women*, first published in 1728.

[59] One of Thomas 'Babillard' Stewart four brothers, sons of Sir George Stewart and his wife Catherine, Sir William Drummond's sister.

[60] Pierre, Duc de Blacas (1770-1839), French diplomat who had negotiated the marriage of the Duc de Berry with Princess Caroline of Naples. He had been appointed ambassador to Naples in 1824.

all others in Europe & having a seal with 60 quarterings - we expected him to be the Ld Winchilsea of Naples.

11 [April 1829]. Saturday E'g we went with Mr & Mrs Canning to *Mosé*.[61] We begin to get very tired of it. It is as dull & dignified as an E'g at the Duc de Blacas. Mr S. Canning is a hero of a diplomate throwing up 12,000£ a year because his opinions differ from his employers.[62]

Sunday [12 April 1829] we took a walk to the newly discovered grottoes with the L[angford] Brookes. We had torches carried in. There is a curious passage cut in the rock to the right, which opens at the top of the Mountain like a door overlooking the sea.

Mr Canning is a high minded Man. He told Ministers some time back that if such & such Measures were pursued, he could not stay at Constantinople & he has resigned his situation as he did his first wife's fortune. In England abilities & high mindedness meet its reward. Mr R[ober]t Gordon is coming out with the old Castlereagh & Metternich principles.[63]

Today, we took a charming walk with the Cannings, Lushingtons, & L[angford] Brookes to Puzzuoli & the Tombs where we lost each other but met again at the Lago d'Agnano by Astroni - the beautiful woods covered with violets & anemonies, the verdure, the distant sea & Vesuvius, & Camaldoli. Papa, G[eorgina] & Mr Canning lost their way & G[eorgina]'s acc't of the two Fidgets was amusing enough.

15th. [April 1829]. Sir Henry [Lushington] came - we talked of the Cannings, of the horse *Eclipse* who was turned into a Paddock &

---

[61] The première of Rossini's operatic drama *Mosè in Egitto* had taken place at San Carlo in 1818.

[62] A conflict arising from how firmly the boundaries of the Greek state proposed by the Poros agreement were to be imposed on Turkey and exacerbated by misunderstandings between Canning and the Foreign Secretary, Lord Aberdeen, had led to Canning's resignation.

[63] Robert Gordon (1791-1847) had been appointed to replace Stratford Canning in the negotiations with Turkey. He was the younger brother of the Foreign Secretary, George Hamilton Gordon, the Earl of Aberdeen.

never used again,[64] & of Pr. Buttera[65] washing the feet of the Apostles - of whether it was right or whether it was wrong to go in a steam boat of a Good Friday, of Sir P. Malcolm, of his being double dealing & a fidget, & disliked by the Navy, &c.

Good Friday, 17th. [April 1829]. Heard a good Sermon, conversation on the Catholic religion bringing all others into disrepute; of no carriages & no noise being allowed on that day; of the soldiers saying Jesus Christ must not be disturbed.

The L[angford] B[rookes]s came. It rained & no carriage cd come so they staid & dined. He is the dullest of all dull Men. She is good-humoured, but silly & not more so than other women.

Everyone is taken up with Catholic speeches. Mr Sadler is a lawyer of 50 whom the D. of Newcastle has found out.[66]

Called on Mrs Canning. Mr C[anning] not used to Ladies & uncomfortable with them. Papa hurt himself - if a Man has no pursuits, the deprivation of liberty of limb [is] terrible.

Mr & Mrs C[anning] came in; she is a nice gentle person whom I would willingly have to reign over us. Mr C[anning]'s reserve don't wear off; he is impenetrable. Whether you mention the Sultan, or Mr Sadler, or the Catholics, he seems to think it his duty not to commit himself. Withall, one looks up to him - his Star is a brilliant one, depend upon it. Apropos, of brilliant stars, Mr Fox is at Rome,[67] & Mr Cornwall says has packed off his valuables for Buonos Ayres & is

---

[64] The racehorse *Eclipse* was so superior to all opposition in the season 1769-70, that he was retired and became a stud.

[65] Prince Butera (1790-1841) was born Georg Wilding, the son of a Hanoverian officer. Having served in the Neapolitan army under Murat, he married Caterina Branciforte (1768-1824), the eldest daughter of Prince Butera, and, in 1822, was allowed by the King to take her father's title.

[66] Michael Thomas Sadler (1780-1835), a long-standing opponent of Catholic emancipation, had been put up for the seat of Newark by the ultra-Right-wing Fourth Duke of Newcastle (1785-1851). Sadler had no legal qualifications.

[67] Henry Stephen Fox (1791-1846), nicknamed Black Fox, had already served as a diplomat at Palermo, Naples and Turin. Appointed in 1828 to be British Minister in Buenos Aires, his departure was delayed, and he only reached Argentina in the autumn of 1831.

coming here. Mr Cornwall[68] came in last night, Mr Canning too, and they both looked as if they hated each other & would willingly show it. I don't like him, or his jokes against religion, unseemly very much in the son of a Bishop; I am anxious to see his wife after all that one has heard of the marriage. He says that the people in Eng'd are all against the Catholic question, "but it being a comfortable religion to die in, he does not know why it sd not be a comfortable one to live in, &c. &c. &c." The Russian Legation have been assassinated in Persia!!![69] Ly Westmorland has written I don't know how many Letters to the Duke of Wellington on the D'Orsay subject.[70] Getting no answer she sent to say that she feared he had not go[t] them - The Duke, who had no mind to answer her but in her own style, said "that the jealousy of the French Gov't had intercepted them."

22d April [1829]. Mrs Canning sat with us on the Terrace covered with Roses & flowers. How beautiful it looked & what a nice little person she is. I wd rather have her to reign over us, than that fierce old idiot L'y Drummond. She has a great deal in her under that quiet manner. She says that she was six months confined to the garden of the Palace at Constantinople, every person & every thing round them being constantly fumigated. She had her own Boat & Mr C[anning] his ten-oared Barge. She liked it & regrets not seeing it again.

24th April [1829]. It was a maxim of Catherine de Medici: "Cover your face before you disturb the hornets nest." I say it of Fools, who are the hornets nest, for I have remarked that in life every one suffers from Fools, whether as lovers, friends or acquaintance. Avoid them & fly from them as you would Poison. This is the difference between Mr Hill & Ld Heytesbury's way of going on. Ld Hey[tesbur]y kept fools at a distance, Mr Hill loves them & tho' an Original & a humorist & a

[68] Frederick Hamilton Cornewall (1791-1845), the son of Folliot Herbert Walker Cornewall (1754-1831), bishop of Worcester, had married Frances Henrietta Caulfeild (1803-1887) in 1827.

[69] The event had taken place on 11 February. An account of it is given in Peter Hopkirk, *The Great Game*, London, 1990, pp.112-3.

[70] Jane Saunders (c.1779-1857) had married John Fane, Earl of Westmorland in 1800. They had five children, but then separated around 1811. As a long-term resident in Rome, Lady Jane had involved herself in the controversy over the Comte d'Orsay's marriage to Lady Harriet Gardiner, daughter of the Earl of Blessington. Outsiders considered that the marriage had been forced on Lady Harriet in order to cement the close relationship between her father and step-mother on the one hand and the Count on the other. The marriage was a short and unhappy one.

good deal wiser than Mr Tom Steward & his wise Aunt, yet they have managed to turn the Tables upon him. Tom Fool says he has put a stop to his paying his addresses to her, & I believe he has, for he was not making a joke of her (his manner of making love) at the ball on St George's Day. I am amused at the look of T. Steward. I think I might have more Epistles like those of 1825 - he is very coming. The only idea[s] I brought away from this dull ball were the prettiest black velvet hat with French feathers & a pink *gros de Naples* gown[71] upon Mrs Cornwall, fresh from Paris. I met that Rose of June Mr Mellish at dinner today. He told me that he knew Charlotte in Germany, but she liked Albert. Göthe made two stories into one.[72]

26th April 1829. A great day in our lives. It was the most lovely day that ever was. Papa was lame & hated the thing. So off we set as happy as possible to Vesuvius with the Langford Brooks & Cannings, Capt. Thompson[73] & Sir H. Lushington. We left the carriages at Ressina where the usual scene of noise, scramble & quarel took place with the Lazzaroni. The best view that I know of the bay of Naples is from the church at Ressina where cypresses & vineyards break a view rather too extended in all the splendour of Ocean, coast, Islands & City - the foreground is so rugged in brown & barren Desolation that the contrast is the greater with the distance. The remains of so many erruptions & streams of Lava are all around - & out of this grow these scattered Cypresses & festooned Vines. It is not like any thing to be [seen] elsewhere.

The Sun was very hot. With large bonnets & umbrellas, on Muleback, we began to ascend the Mountain at 2 o'clock as far as the Hermitage, where we four Ladies were put into four Chairs & carried up the Mountain. The ascent became then perpendicular & abrupt. The Men sunk every instant up to their *Genu* in Lava.[74] However, as they said

---

[71] *gros de Naples* - a heavy silk material much used in the making of dresses and hats.

[72] Charles Richard Mellish had been born in Weimar and Goethe had attended his christening on 21 May 1801. Mellish's father, Joseph Charles Mellish (c.1769-1823) knew both Goethe and Schiller and had done translations for them. Charlotte and Albert are characters in Goethe's *The Sorrows of Young Werther* which combined aspects of the writer's relationship with Charlotte Buff and her fiancé Christian Kestner along with the suicide of Karl Wilhelm Jerusalem, a young official, who shot himself with pistols borrowed from Kestner.

[73] Possibly Captain John Armstrong Thompson of the Bengal Army.

[74] i.e.knee-deep in lava.

that they had carried up Ly Northampton & the Duke of Buckingham,[75] we must have been light weights to them, as there were eight
men to each chair. After much labouring against the ground, we
reached the summit thro' a scene of barren desolation that prepared us
in some degree for the magnificent sight from the summit. We looked
immediately down into a valley or large Crater on the other side, in
the centre of which rose the present crater. It was like looking down
into the Solfatara, having a large & enormous *Bocca*[76] in it out of wh.
came volumes of smoke, flame & red hot stones & from which pro-
ceeded various little streams of Red Lava which circulated like small
rivers in the ancient Crater, all the ground without, being streaked &
spotted with various coloured sulphurs, yellow, green, red, &c. Every
now and then, an explotion like thunder took place & then the red cinders spread in the air & flew about all round. We would have looked
for ever & watched each change & each explotion with gt interest as
we lay on the ground rolled in our cloaks, but E'g was coming on, &
on looking towards Naples & the Campagna, we beheld a scene almost equal in magnificence to that wh. attracted us so forcibly: the
most brilliant & deep-coloured sunset came all over the Ocean & the
Island, while the Campagnia & the country up as high as Terracina
seemed thrown into shade. It seemed a sight almost too fine for mortal
man to look at, one that defied Painters to copy or Poets to describe,
one that made one feel one's littleness & the certainty of a God & a
Heaven & a Hell. The Sun sank gradually & the picturesque figures
about us wrapped in cloaks & rags, called to us to look on the other
side again at the flames that we[re] issuing which gained in colouring
& grandeur as night came on. The dark shadows of the mountain became more dark & the red flames & stones became more vivid. It was
an impressive & awful sight - the most awful one can imagine - we
could have looked on for ever. The red stones were thrown up at a
great height & then rolled down the sides of the dark crater. Mr Canning called to us all to go as the wind grew cold. The Torches were
lighted by the Lazzaroni & we tore ourselves away - and with guides
supporting us walked down sinking a foot into Lava at each step.
When we got a little way, the air was soft & mild as in summer & by
torch light we reached the Hermitage where Mr Canning had had a

---

[75] The guide Salvatore told Charles Greville that the Duke 'was carried up in a chair by
twelve men, and the weight was so enormous that his shoulder was afterwards swelled
up nearly to his head." (Greville, I, p.450). The Duke's own description of his ascent
can be found in *The Private Diary of Richard, Duke of Buckingham*, Vol.I, pp.305-12).

[76] 'mouth'.

good supper brought from Naples. We all enjoyed the day exceedingly, were all pleased & satisfied & only agreeably tired. Mrs Canning seemed to have her way in everything - yet to be the most perfect of wives. From the Hermitage to Ressina we rode, & there getting into our Carriages got back to Naples by 12 o'clock at night - it was the pleasantest day I had ever past.

27th April [1829]. Mr & Mrs Canning called. We went to Mr Uwins to see his drawings.[77] We talked of Ly Byron - I can't help thinking that Mr C. was a suitor to her - a guess! We talked of her reforming Ld Byron. He said "Ladies were presumptuous and attempted impossibilities". I think if she had taken years she might, & had never let him know that he improved, & thus cheated him into morality. Every thing but a Gambler may be reformed I think, as where there is spirit or understanding, Truth acts sooner or later.

28th [April 1829]. Mr & Mrs Cornwall dined here, both very disagreeable. He is wasping, cross & clever, she is well dressed but *mauvais ton*, & nothing that betrays good blood or good nature - now one or the other is desirable. Mr Craven dined here - if he was unstiffened, he would not be so very disagreeable. I am amused at the fuss that Foreigners make about signatures though I doubt whether they often themselves, from what the Legations say, would not turn them to a bad purpose. M. de Sass[78] writes a note of Bombast enough to sicken one of russians & courtiers in wh. he tells me that I may look on the name of Alexander & see what the Russians say about the Grand Duchess - what a fuss about a little royalty.

29th [April 1829]. A great dinner, bored to death between Mr Langford Brook & Mr Strangways.[79] Lady Dal. Hamilton dined here;[80] she is come brimfull of Roman gossip - Miss Percy is a great admirer of Bishop Baines, the Catholic Bishop,[81] & is to be a Catholic. Ly Westmorland had been so deep in the d'Orsay affair that Ly D. H[amilton]

---

[77] The painter Thomas Uwins (1782-1857) took up residence in Naples in 1825 and left late in 1830.

[78] Baron de Sass, a member of the Russian community resident in Naples.

[79] William Thomas Horner Fox-Strangways was Secretary of the British Legation in Naples between 1828 and 1832. He was a keen amateur botanist.

[80] Lady Dalrymple Hamilton (1778-1852).

[81] Peter Augustine Baines (1787-1843) had, for health reasons, spent the period 1826-9 on the Continent, mostly at Rome.

wishing to keep clear of it had only sent her a message on leaving Rome. Ly West'd wrote to her that whether she left PPC on a card,[82] or sent her God's Blessing by a Laquais de place, came to the same. Ly W. has been going about asking whether she knew any handsome young man who wd not object to wearing very tight Pantalons for a Saint Michael.[83] She is as mad as the winds, it seems - for she was one day let into the Vatican by a new door, she said "I know what this means, Lord Westmorland is become a Cabinet Minister; my Coachman knows it, My Chasseur knows it, everyone knows it but me. That's the way I'm used!"

May the 1st 1829. Mr Hill has asked me to dinner at the Vomerò. I got Papa to write that I had a cold. We dined at Mr Cannings. Ly Kenmare[84] called on Wednesday & I returned her visit without our meeting - so that is happily ended.

2d [May 1829]. Yesterday we dined with Mr Craven a snug old Bachelor; he has everything very comfortable, *mesquin* & in bad taste. The day was a pleasant one, tho' Mr Str[ang]ways was on one side. Mr Canning was talking away on intellectual women & quoted some lines from *Don Juan*. He advises me to turn my Spanish Proverb from "a wise man changes his mind, a fool never," into "a fool changes his own mind, a wise man other peoples."

Walked in the Capo di Chino Villa.
The German Post is too large to buy - Sixties [*possibly* 'Sistres'] may do.

Today (Sunday) every one who dont go out on Sunday dines with Mr Hill. I was proud, as he is a bear, & would not go. Pretty little Mrs Canning would not & was an hour with Ge[orgina] & I.

Monday [4 May 1829] was a bad day. Sir Pulteney Malcolm sailed into the Bay.

---

[82] PPC - *pour prendre congé*, i.e. to take leave.

[83] Lady Westmorland was, as will emerge, a great enthusiast for *tableaux*.

[84] Augusta Ann (c.1799-1873), daughter of Sir Robert Wilmot of Osmaston, Derbyshire, had married Valentine, 2nd Earl of Kenmare in 1816. She was the sister of Foley Wilmot, so recently turned down by M.T.

Tuesday [5 May 1829] - we took Mrs Canning to the Villa Gallo[85] - & we walked back thro' the woods. How lovely it looked with verdure & flowers. Summer is fast coming, & we are all going. We talked on some painful subjects. She seems very happy with her husband, yet there is 20 years of difference of age & they suit. At first she said she sd just as much have thought of marrying her own Father. She is all gentleness & he all knowledge. It is evident that he proposed on a blush.

Mr Gordon, or rather Sir Robert Gordon, is come, for the Order of the Bath was sent to him yesterday wh. was rude enough by Mr Canning. I hear that he is very black & orange after his Brazil Mission.[86]

Friday [8 May 1829] - the weather & the people are so changeable that all is arranged for the Party to the Camaldoli & put off always. In the E'g we had a Party of 30. Mr Gordon is stiff & Spanish, dignified & very good looking. The Cannings & Sir Pulteney were with us. Ly Drummond had had Mrs Canning to dinner & she was left to walk in last - almost bad taste.

10 May 1829. Sir Rt Gordon brought me a sad letter from dearest Charlotte, scrawled off in haste. I trust that all goes well by this time. She sends me Chalmers's *Sermons* & *The Sorrows of Rosalie*.

We exchanged company today. Mrs Canning came to dine with us & Papa went to a great Diplomatic dinner at the Palazzo Torella, after wh. Mr Canning, Sir Rt Gordon & Mr Strangways came & drank Tea. We talked of Mr Hill & his oddities, of Sir Pulteney & his audience & caprice[?], about P'ce Charles,[87] of Lord Nelson, of America, of Chess & Adams, & of Mr C. having been so warm on a question[?], as to threaten a discussion. I find Mr Canning writes beautiful Verses. History of the Ribeaupierre[88] dinner wh. is quite Russian - that is every

---

[85] Built in 1809 for the Duke of Gallo, its main attraction was 'the view, especially towards Naples, which is nowhere seen to more advantage.' (Murray's, *Southern Italy*, p.159). The Blessingtons had lived in the villa between April 1825 and February 1826.

[86] Robert Gordon had been British Minister in Brazil between July 1826 and August 1828. He had just received news of his knighthood. Stratford Canning had to wait another twenty years for his service to be similarly acknowledged.

[87] Presumably Charles, prince of Capua (1811-1862), the second son of Francesco I.

[88] Count Aleksandr Ribeaupierre (c.1781-1865) belonged to a French émigré family in Russia. He had arrived in Constantinople as Russian ambassador at the end of 1826.

thing that is mean & low. Sir R[obert] G[ordon] did not seem half as formal I thought as he used to be. "Il sabio munda conscio, &c."[89]

At last we did get to the Camaldoli & a charming day we had of it. The ride is charming, thro' a paradise of yellow broom & wild roses, with such openings to views of Capri & the Campania, amongst wild flowers & verdure. How beautiful is Spring in Italy. (I thought of Grey's *Ode to Spring*.[90]) Nobody who has not known it or seen it can know what Spring really is. The Men went into the Convent. The origin of the vow of silence is that men sd pray for the souls of others & retire from the world for that purpose. Some of the Camaldulites are called *Padri Chiusi* & never go out. We Ladies had a Luncheon spread by our servants on the ground in the woods, where we must have looked a very pretty looking picturesque set sitting under the Trees, like Stoddarts print of the Ladies in the Florence Garden.[91] "I like not your prison feasts!"[92] We were a happy party & had left our townliness behind us. The more I see of Mr & Mrs C[anning], the more I like & admire them. I see that they hate Foreigners & representation. In fact his tastes are literary. It must be disagreeable to dine three times a week with your natural enemies. The longer I live abroad the more I hate foreigners. Foreigners & English are so different in their nature that they must end by being like cat & dog to each other.

Tuesday, 12 May 1829. Mr & Mrs Canning, Mr Mathias[93] & Strangways & Langford Brooks dined here yes'y - we sd end in being great friends. I have got two beautiful Poems of Mr Cannings writing, one of wh. he very amiably put into my books without my asking. I wish he was Minister here. He seemed quite happy with old Mathias & they talked over Grays Latin Ode to the G'de Chartreuse that I wanted to get translated.[94] Mrs L. Brook is too noisy. Her dull husband gave her

---

[89] 'Il sabio munda conscio, il nescio ne.' (A wise man reflects, a fool does not.)

[90] Thomas Gray's *Ode on the Spring*, first published 1748.

[91] Thomas Stothard, R.A. (1755-1834). The engraving referred to must be an earlier version of that reproduced on page 113 in the first edition of Samuel Rogers's *Italy*, published in 1830.

[92] The final line of a six-line verse prologue to Chapter 8 of the second volume of Sir Walter Scott's novel, *The Abbot* (1820), lines written in praise of picnics.

[93] Thomas James Mathias (c.1754-1835), writer, poet, and long-term resident of Naples.

[94] Thomas Gray had originally written this Ode into the guest book of the monastery of the Grande Chartreuse in 1741.

a set down wh. she bore with gt good humour. Sir [Robert] G[ordon]'s speech about me surprised me a good deal. He is going to Turkey to say we must be good friends because you're our ancient Ally - but we must take away part of Turkey for Greece & we will not defend you from Russia. This must be difficult.

13th May [1829]. We had a large party to Baia with the Lushingtons & Langford Brooks & took our dinner with us. We were all in high good humour & Sir Henry is a perfect *Cicerone*. We first went to the Sybils grotto on the Lake Avernus & then on Donkeys to Baja & to the Campi Elisii where we dined under the Pergola ajoining the Cottage that commands a view of the Cape Misenus & Ischia. As E'g came on it was delightful: the sea was smooth as glass with long long shadows on it & the festoons of bright green Vines & wild Roses hung from Tomb to Tomb & Ruin to Ruin. They all came home to Tea, but Mrs L[angford] B[rooke] went to wish Good by to Mrs Canning.

14th [May 1829] San Carlo. Ld Augustus Hill,[95] Sir Rt Gordon, Sir R. Acton, Ld Dunlo[96] came into the Opera Box with many others. Sir R. [Gordon] strikes me as grave, handsome & *distingué* but Londonny - but not as clever as Mr Canning. They none of them like going to Constantinople where Ladies & resources[?] are wanting, they say.

17th May [1829]. It seems that our time lately has passed in a series of degustations. Yesterday we had 16 people at home & today 18 at the L. Brookes. The Constantinople Embassy: They are a curious set for the purpose, & they say that they shan't succeed in what they are going about - to make peace. Ld Yarmouth[97] is a mixture of Mr De Ros & Ld Alvanley,[98] people say, in his morale. He gave a wonderful account of his friend Mr Fox's leaving his Paris lodgings regularly in a Hackney to ask the way before the quarter expired carrying off his valuables with him. What Honor - but a name! Ld Dunlo seems a

---

[95] Lord George Augustus Hill (1801-79), youngest son of the 2nd Marquis of Downshire, brother of Lady Mary Hill, and an attaché in Naples.

[96] William Thomas Le Poer Trench (1803-72), subsequently Lord Clancarty. Later in the year, Lord Dunlo joined George Keppel for a journey in European Turkey. See George Keppel, *Narrative of a journey across the Balcan*, London, 1831.

[97] Richard Seymour-Conway became 4th Marquis of Hertford after the death of his father in 1842.

[98] William Arden, second Lord Alvanley (1789-1849) friend of the Prince Regent, beau, gambler and member of White's.

good sort of unpolished person, Mr Grosvenor London all over[99] - Mr Parish[100] looks vulgar & ill-tempered - Mr Mellish a true attaché & Sir Rt. G[ordon] - the only one who looks fit for the purpose - like a Spanish Grandee, a dark grave Man of the World - not like Mr Canning who it is evident is not a man of the world. He is reserved, has pride & tact, & I never saw that reserve vanish except one moment that he was talking to Mrs Canning & me when it seemed to me that it might be shaken off. We had altogether a curious dinner. They say Ld Cochrane & Sir Sydney Smith are to command the Turkish & Russian Fleets. The next day was equally curious - for Mr Hill took me into dinner & discoursed in one of his most wonderful ways - Good Gracious, What a Man he is! decidedly an original of the first water, to wh. no copy cd do justice - & how he talked of Ld Clare & of Mrs Fitzherbert,[101] saying that none of the Girls wd have him. I said, no wonder, for he was one of the old Ladies. Certainly every one is partial to Mr Fox. Ministry to the S. A[merican] States will shortly be done away with. Surely Destiny is a curious & a real thing - perhaps I might have been now the wife of a Gambler, a man without principle or honor, whom every one likes. Ld Barham[102] dined with us the other day. I don't like him - tho' he came puffed in a letter from Sir William Gell & a high character with him - but he is riche[?] & vulgar & affected.

18th [May 1829]. There was yesterday a dinner at the Vomerò - not a dinner for me. Mr Hill said he had the 4 ages: Golden, Iron, & Brazen, were there, but the Silver failed. I would not go to the *Diable Boiteux* where Fodor[103] sung, but went to Ly L[ushington] - where Sir H[enry]

---

[99] Robert Grosvenor (1801-93) had visited Naples with Robert Gordon in 1823 when Lady Blessington described him as 'the liveliest Englishman' she had ever seen. (See *Idler in Italy*, II, p.124). On this occasion, he may well have been reserved because he had just discovered that his father had learnt about his debts and indicated that he would not pay a farthing on his son's behalf. (See Grosvenor Diary, Bodleian M.S. Eng. misc. c. 667).

[100] Henry Headley Parish (1801-75) had acted as Stratford Canning's private secretary in the 1820s.

[101] Maria Anne Fitzherbert, the widow who had become the long-standing companion of the Prince of Wales, later George IV.

[102] Charles Noel Noel (1781-1866) had inherited the title of Lord Barham in 1823, and subsequently became Lord Gainsborough.

[103] Josephine Fodor (1789-1870), a famous soprano, had sung in Paris and London, before moving to Naples. The opera *Le Diable boiteux* was based on the novel by Lesage, with music composed by Charles Favart in 1782.

came & we talked reasonably. I wd rather be hanged than go to the ball tonight, but must. It will be very disagreable.

20th May [1829]. The ball was a fine one; & every one beautifully dressed. I never saw such a scene as the Russian Mme Zamuloschka made - about David, the singer,[104] whom she, a Russian of beauty, birth & fortune, is passionately attached to. When the people who came from the Opera said he had been hissed, she cried. I came home early. The next day Sir R't G[ordon] came to wish us Goodby - - - - - - - - - - - - - - - [105] He told us that Mr C[anning] had carried his find to see his first wifes Monument in Switzerland[106] - how very german & yet it is just in Mr Cannings character. He said he was suspicious & I saw that at his care with Mr C[anning].   Georgina say[s] suspicion was one of the duties of the Profession; he said not to show it. More passed that I don't write. They embarked at 5 - !!

We had people at dinner. Mr Hill & Ly Drummond, his future, whom he abused like a pick pocket, & said every thing to her the most disagreeable & provoking. He talked of the Cannings & of the Minister, Mr Canning, & of his good heart in getting Ld Erskine to be sent to Studgard.[107]

22nd of May, a horrid storm. The Constantinoples cd not sail, & came to the Gala after tossing about all day in the Harbour. We may see results - we can never know motives. Today is Friday & they have all sailed in a bad ship with a Captain half affronted with them all already.

---

[104] Countess Yulia Samoilova (1803-75) was an extremely well-born and rich Russian widow who settled in Milan in the 1820s. Henry Fox notes her infatuation with David, while scorning the notion that she was a beauty. (*Journal*, p.343). Apponyi relates that she paid off Mme David with a large sum of money to prevent her creating scenes (Apponyi, I, p.275). Giovanni David (1790-1864), was a leading tenor of the time. In July, he was to sing the lead role in the first performance of Donizetti's *Il castello di Kenilworth*.

[105] The dashes suggest that this was not a routine parting, an interpretation confirmed by M.T. inserting a note at a later date: 'This visit unlocked in me many a long year of misery.'

[106] While living at Lausanne, Stratford Canning's first wife had died in childbirth in June 1817. Her monument was in the cathedral.

[107] In 1825, George Canning, as Foreign Secretary, had appointed David Montagu Erskine (1776-1865) to become British Minister in Stuttgart.

The Season, or what is vulgarly called so, is done. It has been a very pleasant year. No plagues, much amusement & many curious people. Belhavens, Cannings, Mr Terrick Hamilton, Mr Wilmot, Sir Pul. Malcolm, Sir Ed. Stopford, Mr Elphinstone, Ld & Ly Warwick, Sir Rt. Gordon, one proposal & several half proposals smothered in their birth. The next I suppose will be from a Callender son of a King[108] - I am really very happy & cured of liking by the silly & degrated light this had put him in, but he was Mad & has a Hump - great things. He likes me now & I don't him. Take a woman when she is in the mind. 'Was' is not 'is'.

26 May[1829]. Yesterday we went by the Aqueduct to Caserta with that silly man & good natured woman Mr & Mrs L[angford] B[rooke] & Mr Strangways who is not pleasant. Eat dirt at the Inn, were disgusted by the beggars, saw the Jardin Anglais, & the Muratte[?] Palace[109] & came home tired to death.

Reading this month: Chateaubriand's Works
Johnson's Works,
Pope & *Loves of the Angels*.[110]

1st of June [1829]. G'l Toledo's ball was put off on acct. of the death of the Queen of Spain.[111] He cried - & sent the supper to the Hospital.

2nd [June 1829]. We went to dine at the Vomero where the host[112] is nearly or quite mad, spits out all his dinner. After dinner the Men all played & he sat down to rave to a circle of women who were audience. He was so *buffo* & extraordinary that we laughed till the tears ran down our cheeks upon the Court dinner: the Sardinian eccuyers,

---

[108] See *The Arabian Nights*.

[109] The building of the Royal Palace was begun in 1752 under Charles VII. Possibly M.T. is recollecting the time when it was occupied by Joachim Murat, Napoleon's brother-in-law, installed as King between 1808 and 1815.

[110] A poem by Thomas Moore.

[111] Maria Josepha of Saxony, the third wife of King Ferdinand VII, had died on 17 May. General Pedro de Alcántara Alvares de Toledo y Palafox (1803-1867) was the Spanish ambassador in Naples.

[112] William Noel Hill.

Mrs Daltons Curtsy & her long stays,[113] old Bisse in a hot summer day, Pr'ss de Sanguisko[?], her donkey & her son running away with Ly Drummond out of the bath when her Nephews went away - quite equal to his *ton*; to me he was very entertaining but whether he was very clever is quite as difficult to decide as whether Hamlet was really mad or not.

Rome June 1829. Sir William Gells house is a wonderful abode. His garden he moves about in in a wheel barrow[114] - it is all picturesque knooks & odd bosquets & his Court of Lions with flowers & a fountain - we went to him in the E'g. He sent Ly Ruthven to fetch us & next Morn'g, we breakfasted with him off of Maccaroni & Mutton chops during wh. Banquet, wreaths of flowers after the manner of Pompeii being spread from Pillar to Pillar in festoons & then the Dog sang, & the Organ was played & some of the Tower of Babel society, consisting of some Greeks (one in a real costume) came in. Sir Wm. is quite a person who stands alone as to cleverness, gaiety & fun. With regard to his want of religious feeling, I don't think it as g[rea]t as people suppose. It proceeds from lightheartedness & never having felt anything deeply or bitterly. He is full now of Ly Davy, who is come & found Sir Humphrey better than she expected, but, Sir Wm. says, don't wish him to live in his present state,[115] & full of Crazy Jane[116] whom he now sees & whose motto is "Those who are not with me are against me."

---

113 Mrs Dalton was living in Rome. Henry Fox described her as 'a handsome, dashing Catholic widow looking out for a husband.' 'The widow is good-nature itself, and enjoys nothing so much as being attacked about her lovers and her admirers, one of whom (Mr Rookwood Gage, an old man) came in after dinner. It is said that once at dinner he was pouring soft nonsense into the widow's ear, and she replied, "Talk if you like, Mr Gage, of truffles, but not of love".' (*Journal*, p.268 & p.368).

114 Because of his gout, he was thus wheeled around.

115 Sir Humphrey Davy (1778-1829) had spent the winter in Rome, but had suffered a stroke on 20 February. He had left Rome on 30 April for England, but died in Geneva on 29 May.

116 i.e. Lady Westmorland.

Florence June 1829. I was too tired to go out. Papa found Lord & Ly Burghersh divided between all the joy at the success of Ld B.'s Opera & sorrow at the supposed death of Lord Wm. Bentinck.[117]

Campagne Grosjean, Geneva July 1829. In this solitude my mind is calm, my thoughts are healthy. The passions are the Curse sent upon us. I thank God I have none whatever. Ly Lovaine & Ly L. Percy[118] have what is called 'found us out.' They are the pleasantest & most unreasonable people I know, formed to be better than they are & sadly angry with the world. Miss Percy has all the misery of an unhinged mind - better had she married at 17.

Papa [from England] writes the word that the Copleys are coming.[119] I suppose they will come out of Vesuvius with a noise & in a cloud of red hot cinders. *Quand on ne sait pas hurler avec les loups, il ne faut pas vivre avec eux.*[120] We read all day - have a fine view of Mont Blanc, an enclusure to walk in where are Cherry Trees & Vines & plenty of industrious people & healthy children, a cheerful & happy scene, neither beggars or dirt, luxury or riches. It is Agar's Prayer verified.[121] What a contrast to Italy!!!

Anne of Geierstein[122] will make several good Melodramas. Charles of Burgundy's conversation & manners ressemble Mr Hills, le bon Roi Renée is like Ld Guildford,[123] & Annette's account of a poor marriage

---

[117] John Fane, Lord Burghersh (1784-1859) was British Minister in Florence between 1814 and 1830. He was an active amateur composer, including of operas. On 27 May 1829, one London newspaper had erroneously reported the death in India of Lord William Bentinck.

[118] Presumably 'Miss', not 'Lady', Percy is meant. See note 38.

[119] Sir Joseph Copley (c.1769-1838) and his two daughters Maria and Elizabeth. Henry Fox describes them in 1823: 'Sir Joseph is very agreable; his sarcasms are biting, and he gives great effect to his jokes by never joining in the laugh. Maria Copley is one of the most remarkable girls I ever met with, full of talent, full of knowledge, and quite free from pretension....Miss Copley is also clever and very well informed, but extremely lengthy and explanatory, and, what I mind still more in a woman, full of cant, slang words and phrases.' (*Journal*, p.179).

[120] 'If you can't howl like wolves, don't live with them.'

[121] See *Proverbs*, Ch.30, vv.8-9: 'Give me neither poverty nor riches; feed me with food convenient for me ...'

[122] Sir Walter Scott's novel, largely set in Switzerland, had been published earlier in the year.

[123] Francis North, 6th Earl of Guilford (1772-1861).

is worth attending to. *Gertrude* is a bad wicked book.[124] Leigh Hunts book on Ld Byron is worth reading, tho' the book of a vulgar Man.[125] His account of Ld Byron reminded me of Ld Durham,[126] one phrase particularly: "It was difficult in his most serious moments to seperate what he spoke out of conviction, & what he said for effect. It was by fits [only] that he spoke with any gravity or made his extraordinary disclosures, & at no time did one well know what to believe."[127] Ld Byrons marriage appears to have been a very common place proceeding: he wanted money & was piqued at being refused by an Heiress - she thought better of it & that she cd reform him. Ladies, as Mr Canning says, are very presumptuous.

I have improved in nothing but health & looks, spend my life in alternate sleep, eating & exercises, like the industrious Swiss whom I watch all day, excellent people without imagination & with four meals a day - happy people who do their duty & bring up all their children well & make all ends meet. In the E'g we look at the Sun setting upon the white Glaciers in majesty & glory.

The sect of Mommiers at Geneva makes great progress.[128] Ld & Ly Tweedale are of it. Those soured spirits the Lovaines amuse me. Miss Percy is not now a girl to fall in love with. She is 40 as to the world & more. Lady Charlemont[129] was here nearly as lovely as ever the other day, but her blue stocking propensities are increased. She said to Ly. L. "Have you read Mrs Marcet upon Political Economy?"[130] I begged of Ly Lovaine to ask her if she had read Mrs Bridget some one's book (an old Maid) on population. The King is rude to the D. of Wellington,

---

[124] A four-volume French novel by Hortense Allart de Méritens (1801-79), published in 1828.

[125] Leigh Hunt, *Lord Byron and some of his contemporaries*, 2 vols., London, 1828.

[126] John George Lambton (1792-1840) created Baron in 1828.

[127] M.T. has brought together two separate sentences from p.85 and p.90 of Vol.1 of the Leigh Hunt work - see note 125.

[128] 'Mommiers' was the nickname given by Calvinists to a strongly evangelical group who dissented from them in 1818.

[129] Anne Bermingham (c.1780-1876) of Rosshill, Co. Galway, had married the Earl of Charlemont in 1802. Byron was bowled over by her beauty: 'I would, to be beloved by that woman, build and burn another Troy', but not by her intellect calling her 'that Kashmeer Butterfly of the "Blues".' (See Marchand, Vol.3, p.215 & p.171.)

[130] Jane Marcet's *Conversations on Political Economy* had first appeared in 1816 and had reached a 6th edition by 1827.

never asks the Duke or Mrs Arbuthnot to his parties. Ld D[o]uro, speaking of his father this winter at Rome said "he is so close, he never tells us any thing, he never tells anything to Mrs Arbuthnot even." Lady Lovaine says, we begin to like fools - is this true, I wonder. It is certain we begin to have patience with them - living in the world has brought us to this.

Geneva 1st Aug. 1829. *Le Livre des Femmes* is a clever book, particularly the chapters by Thomas & P. Lambert.[131] Coopers *Pilot*[132] has one fine storm in it - and that is all. Manzoni's *promessi Sposi*[133] I have read in French & am enchanted with - it makes a great impression - the village scenes are just such as we now see in the unfrequented places of Amalfi or la Cava or out of the high road in Italy. He is equal to Sir Walter Scott often in beauties of Description.

Georgina & I are very happy in our solitude - she particularly who writes her novel which, taken from real life, is excellent, blinds her eyes with politics, & enjoys liberty, & an absence from bores, foreigners & *suggezzione*. We have never in one Month passed the gates but twice to take a walk; & here we walk under the Cherry Tree avenue every E'g looking at Mont Blanc.

Papa's letters full of accounts of Fêtes & dinners make us think ourselves female solomons for not having put ourselves into the Caldron.[134] Ld Hertford & Ly Strachan will shame & show the world guided by love of amusement. The Lowther Ladies[135] say that Ly Strachan is a quiet, good sort of little woman & they don't see any harm in her - an extraordinary style of praise. I asked Ly Lovaine what they did about them at Rome. She said: "we all put our virtue in our pockets & went to dinner, for you know Ld. Hertford lives better than any one." What a miserable family they are: *esprit*, & worldliness -

---

[131] This two volume anthology on the 'character, habits and nature of women', published in Ghent in 1823, included a historical summary by Thomas (I, pp.1-98), and some 'new reflections on women' by Mme de Lambert (I, pp.207-231).

[132] James Fenimore Cooper's novel *The Pilot: A tale of the sea* had been first published in New York in 1823. English editions followed, including one by Thomas Allman & Son, London, 1829.

[133] Alessandro Manzoni's classic novel had first appeared in 1825-7. A French translation entitled *Les fiancés* had been published in 1828.

[134] i.e. London.

[135] Daughters of the Earl of Lonsdale.

disappointment. I did pity Miss Percy today. Destiny blights a womans sense.

Papa's letters give me no wish to be in London. How wise we are! This E'g Ly L[ovaine] & Miss P[ercy] came; they left a disagreeable impression. They talked "light winged hope destroyed," talked world, a bad world, fashion, intrigue, malice. Then they talked in the most abbandoned way of the Protestant Religion, treating it as a religion of lies & deceit & abbandoned at the country of Cant; in short, they were like those possessed by evil spirits, & the figure of the boy in the Transfiguration haunted me after I thought of it in bed.[136] Miss Percy is in the high road to be a Catholic, & I told her if I was Ld Lovaine, I'd take them out of a Catholic country as fast as four post horses cd carry them.

Geneva. Augt. I want them to read the 2nd Vol. of *Les Soirees de Neuilly*,[137] which is a pretty picture of the intrigues of a Priest at Paris sowing divisions in families, & the scene of the "Examen de Conscience" will show the evil of Confession for children. It is a curious scene of falsehood & duplicity. To hear Ly Lovaine, we Protestants have no chance of being saved, & these Ladies say that the only reason that they are not Catholics is that they are not good enough. I think with astonishment of two such clever women being so infatuated, imposed upon by Jesuits, such people as Le Pere Joseph & many of the characters shown up in Leclerq's *Proverbes*.[138]

I like this peaceful life, I profit by it mind & body. My mind is calm. I am happier than I have been for Months. Georgina calls it her honeymoon. What does one want in summer but quiet, good air, liberty & books. Poor Papa wd have been bored to death here, & we bored too. We had a visit from Mr T.H. who found us much improved & the three Miss Fanshawe's looking like the three Fates.[139] For the first time I

---

[136] M.T. was probably thinking of Raphael's painting of the *Transfiguration* in the Vatican. See *Matthew* Ch.17, vv.1-21.

[137] Hygin-Auguste Cavé and Adolphe Dittmer, *Les soirées de Neuilly, esquisses dramatiques et historiques*, Paris, 1827.

[138] Théodore Leclercq's *Proverbes dramatiques* published in Paris in several volumes and editions in the 1820s.

[139] The three Fanshawe sisters, Penelope (1764-1833), Catherine Maria (1765-1834) and Elizabeth Christiana (1777-1856) resided at 15 Berkeley Square, but frequently travelled on the Continent. Catherine Maria had achieved some renown as a poet.

think with Ly West[morlan]d "It is a great trial being a single woman" - but all is a trial to woman, youth & beauty &c., & old age & ugliness. Nothing stands still - look at nature; while I speak, a leaf falls, a cloud passes over.

Ly Charlemont is here, still like Psyche, *c'est dommage qu'elle soit un peu pédante*.[140] In conversation she is a Cul de Sac. Ninon said 'la beauté sans grace, c'est un hameçon sans appât,'[141] wh. is her.

Poor Miss Catharine F[anshawe] - so clever, so good. How much better if she had married, left her sisters, kept her fortune & her friends - & she could not have been more tyrannized or more unhappy than she is. In general I am Anti-marriage. This changes me.

We went into Geneva to Maunoir, the famous occulist at Geneva.[142] Georgina's eyes are very bad. He sends her to Dr Buttigni.[143] Old Dr Buttigni is really a picture in his velvet Cap, looking like one of Rembrants old Men - & his Anti-room is crowded with Patients, of every nation & age - it is a scene not to forget - that Anti-room.

We went to see a Collection of Autograph[s] at Geneva belonging to Dr Coindet upon which he reasons philosophically, even on their signatures. Louis 16 - he says was *bon homme amiable* but weak, all full of *mesquinnerie* - he has letters of Rousseau upon various sujects & the original of *Emile* written in a small Italian hand. Voltaire wrote a little hand. The[re] is an amusing Letter from Garrick to Colman - Queen Charlotte of Naples, Letter to Carraciolo (why Charlotte?) - one of Ld Nelsons - one of Oliver Cromwell - Ld Byron, Mlle Mars, Sismondi, Koscius[k]o, Göthe. The most curious ones are framed & glazed.[144]

---

[140] 'a pity she's a bit pedantic'

[141] 'Beauty without grace is a hook without bait', Ninon de Lenclos (1620-1705).

[142] Jean-Pierre Maunoir (1768-1861), Genevan surgeon and oculist. His wife was English, and two of his three daughters married Englishmen.

[143] Pierre Butini (1759-1838) had a Europe-wide reputation as a medical practitioner.

[144] Many of the items in the collection of Dr Charles Coindet (1796-1876), including the manuscript of *Emile*, were bequeathed to the Bibliothèque de Genève after his death.

Geneva & its Environs please me. The *campagne[s]*[145] of the C'te de Selon & the Duc de Clermont & Sir Francis d'Ivernois's at Aire, are all charming.

Ly Bath['s] luck in getting her daughter, who is not good looking, married to the Duke of B[uccleugh], merely because she paid him no attention, sets all the maneuverers wild - Ly Lovaine says it is only that she has manoevered better than them.[146] We regret going away. I wrote to Papa as follows:

18 Aug't 1829. My dear Papa.
We shall have been here two months next week & have been very happy & comfortable. Georgina & I have been to an Occulist once, & twice to a Dentist. We have been to visit two Physicians & have seen the Church-yard at Geneva. We had a letter from Ly Belhaven. What lives of gaiety & amusement those Scotch have. Dear Dear Hammy[147] & Lady Ruthven too.

Papa writes me word it is the fashion to praise & be excessively good natured. Puffing is now the thing.

Paris. Hotel Meurice 25th Aug't [1829]. We arrived yesterday having had a delightful journey, the first we ever made alone - five days the two last of which we came at a Gallop - 12 hours a day - with good Serv'ts. I like travelling without a Man tho' I sd not like walking down rue Villon or going out to dinner without one. These are shynesses & helplessnesses of kinds - I heard Mrs Canning say how glad she was to be alone & without Mr Canning on a journey. Papa was dining with Ld Stuart.[148] When he came home, I was so shocked at his looks & alteration that I had difficulty in not showing it.

30th Aug't [1829]. I believe there is neither peace of mind or calmness to be had for long in this world. I am seriously uneasy about Papa.

---

[145] i.e. country villas - often rented out to foreigners for the summer season.

[146] Lady Charlotte-Anne Thynne, third daughter of the Marquis of Bath, married the Duke of Buccleugh on 13 August 1829.

[147] Presumably an affectionate diminutive of Hamilton, Lady Belhaven's first name.

[148] Charles Stuart, created Baron Stuart de Rothesay, had been reappointed British Ambassador in Paris in 1828.

We spend the whole day with Milliners & Mantua Makers, come home tired to death, dine, & go to a Theatre.

Friday, we saw *Marino Faliero*, a tragedy by Casimir Delavigne.[149] The wife avows her guilt which scene is excellent, & the death of the lover is well managed. The dresses are splendid, furs & velvet sleeves & *traines*.

At Feydeau,[150] they give an English story, *Les deux Nuits*[151] - some English officers dine at a dinner which costs a trifle 200 guineas. After talking much of eating, the hero, Sir Edward Acton is called My Lord, he leans familliarly on his servant's shoulder (a Footman in livery) & asks & follows his advice as to his affairs & conduct. These are in 1829 french notions of english manners. Mme Prader[152] looked very pretty in black with a white wreath on - there was a certain black velvet hat with blue *plumes de Coq* wh. struck my fancy.

At the Academie, there is Rossini: *Cte Ory* & *Guillaume Tell*.[153] This last is fine[ly] got up - it cost 18,000 Frs. Mlle Taglioni's dancing is perfection of grace & repose.[154] The whole is like the scenes in Woovreman's Pictures[155] - so bright & gay, & there is a scene of a *Chasse* by a Lake that is quite beautiful.

---

[149] The tragedy by Casimir Delavigne (1793-1843) on the subject of the 14th century Venetian Doge Marino Falieri was staged in 1829 for the first time. Byron had written a play on the same subject (1820).

[150] Popular Parisian theatre in the rue Feydeau, first opened in the 1790s.

[151] Opera by François Adrien Boieldieu (1775-1834) first performed on 20 May 1829. The Duchesse de Maillé did not rate highly the text by Scribe. *Souvenirs*, p.271.

[152] Félicité Pradher (1800-76), popular soprano and wife of the composer Louis-Barthélémy Pradher.

[153] *Le Comte Ory* was first performed at the Théâtre de l'Académie Royale on 20 August 1829 and *Guillaume Tell* at the beginning of the month on 3 August.

[154] Marie Taglioni (1804-84), famous dancer of the period, born in Stockholm, the daughter of an Italian choreographer and a Swedish dancer. John Waldie, perhaps attending the same performance, described her as 'perfect in ease, grace, elegance, and finish, and is truly exquisite and delightful.' (See *Journal*, 26 August 1829).

[155] Philips Wouwerman (1619-1668), Dutch artist who specialised in hunting and landscape scenes.

La Muette de Portici is still finer.[156] La Muette by Mme Noblet is not equal to the Nina of Biggottini, but near to it.[157] Fenella is a young girl, deaf & dumb, the Sister of Masaniello - she loves the Son of the Viceroy, without knowing him until the day of the public marriage. The Music is beautiful, the scenery & action Italian complet[el]y, the dancing & dresses Spanish as belonging to the Viceroy's Court. Such Bolleros & Tarantellas danced; it ends with the revolt of Masaniello[158] - this ballet will last for years.

At the Francais we saw a new Play, *Le Protecteur et Le Mari.*[159] It is in a new style, modern manners & a modern hero who utters language imitating[?] an english MP - Mlle Brocard, his wife is beautifully dressed & *manieré* - & he wants her to make up to the Prime Minister to get him a place - this is the plot. I hear many of the Actresses are always drunk - this pretty graceful Mlle Brocard & Mlle Le Verd;[160] Mme Henri I found so, & I thought she was mad, as it never came into my head.

Dress at Paris is now a triumph for them; they make deformity desirable & ugliness beauty, & every thing that they wear graceful - The Petticoats are short, the sleeves like pillows, Gaiters are worn of a Morn'g & the *tournure* is that of the hottentot Venus,[161] & yet if any tolerably pretty woman puts it on, she is lovely.

---

[156] *La Muette de Portici*, 5 Act opera with music by Auber and words by Scribe and Delavigne. It was first performed on 29 February 1828 with Lise Noblet (1801-52), a dancer, in the part of the dumb girl Fenella.. According to Gronow, Lord Fife had much admired Mlle Noblet and had spent nearly £80,000 on her.

[157] *Nina*, a three act ballet with music by Nicolas Dalayrac (1753-1809) based on a play by Benoît-Joseph Marsollier, first performed in 1813. Emilia Bigottini (1784-1858) had created the role and it was subsequently associated with her. For instance, Apponyi attended a benefit performance in 1827 at which she returned to the role and was received with enthusiasm by the dancers and singers as well as the public. (Apponyi, I, pp.61-2).

[158] Masaniello, a Neapolitan fisherman, had led a revolt against the Spanish in 1647, thereby becoming a folk hero of the common people of Naples.

[159] A play by Casimir Bonjour which received its first performance at the Théâtre Français on 5 September 1829.

[160] Mlle Suzanne Brocard (1798-1855) and Mlle Emilie Leverd (1788-1843) were leading actresses on the Parisian stage.

[161] The black slave of Dutch farmers near Cape Town, Saartje Baartman was brought to Europe and, because of her unusual shape, was exhibited in London and Paris, and came to be known as the Hottentot Venus.

We dined with Mme Delmar who keeps a good deal to her own style of dress. Her Husband has decided to live - she is very amiable & has every thing in the world except Happiness. M. de Schann was the wit;[162] their Hotel in the Champs Elysée is charming. Another night I went with her to the Italian Opera, in her box. I saw that wit & beauty M. de Flahaut (with grey hair) an old Man; he speaks English with grace & taste wh. struck me. Mme de Flahaut is really hideous.[163] The Duc de Guiche asked her if she was with child. "Je suis etonné connaissant les usages anglais, il a peut [pu] faire un pareille question," M. de Delmar said.[164] The person now at Paris who turns the heads of all the women is a certain C'te Valeski, a son of Napoleons by a polish Lady.[165]

We went last night to see Mlle Mars[166] in *La jeune femme colere* & *L'Ecole des Vieillards*[167] - in the last she was not so good; her figure is heavy - "Et ton ami Bonnard ne se remariera pas" is all I remember, wh. line amused me - because .... In *La jeune F[emme] C[olere]* she is still exquisite, having the open french quick manner of a young French woman; her skin is gone & her figure too, tho' she is certainly more the woman of fashion than anyone, tho' Jenny Vespré's nods &

---

[162] Niklaus Georg Karl Tschann (1777-1847), Swiss chargé d'affaires in Paris between 1814 and 1847.

[163] The Comte de Flahault (1785-1870), had been educated in Britain, acted as aide-de-camp to Napoleon, and taken refuge in England after the Hundred Days. In 1817, he had married Margaret Elphinstone, the daughter of Viscount Keith, who, dismayed at the match, disinherited her. She made over her own £4000 a year to her husband. (See *Correspondence of Charlotte Grenville, Lady William Wynn*, ed. Leighton, London, 1920, p. 202.)

[164] 'I am surprised that, being acquainted with English custom, he could have put such a question.' The Duc de Guiche (1789-1855), brother-in-law of the Comte d'Orsay, had held a commission in a British regiment and had lived several years in England. His sister was married to the Earl of Tankerville.

[165] Alexander, Count Walewski (1810-68), the illegitimate son of Napoleon by Marie, Countess Walewska. For a detailed description of the Count at this period, see the Duchesse de Maillé. *Souvenirs*, pp.272-4.

[166] Mlle Mars, the stage name of Anne Boutet (1779-1847), the leading actress of her day. Neumann affirmed that she had 'no equal in portraying sentimental character' (Vol.I, p.188), and for the writer reminiscing in Fraser's Magazine in 1860: '... in the *rôles d'ingénues* and the *rôles des grandes coquettes*, Mademoiselle Mars stood apart so far above all rivalry as to be beyond all envy.' (Vol.62, p.580).

[167] Plays by Charles Guillaume Etienne, first published in 1804 and Casimir Delavigne, first performed in 1823.

becs & wanton smiles, are as amusing & more.[168] We saw the other night *Le Bandit*,[169] a gentlemanlike brigand - as I am going on the road, I did not fancy it - & *l'Elephant du Roi de Siam* is quite charming for an Elephant.[170]

We were five weeks at Paris & thought but of dress - & theatres. Mlle Sontag in the *Barbiere di Seviglia* is enchanting - such a pretty woman, such a manner, such finished coquettry, such voice, execution & tones - she is too enchanting.[171] I carried away a quantity of things from Herbaults; providing the feathers, for sixty £ we got twenty four Hats, bonnets, berrets, caps &c.; a black velvet hat with pink feathers & a Pink crape with white Marabouts are pretty; a green bonnet like the Q. of Spains with green & white Esprit & a pink satin cap are beautiful. I saw a *Oiseau* satin hat with birds of Paradise going to the Brazils for the Empress. It was beautiful.

I love Paris dress - Victorine made me a yellow silk with blond sleeves *a la Sontag*, a good yard across the back "Mon habit, que je vous remercie."[172]

We saw sights at a great rate. It is curious the effect of the Diorama on the mind. It transports one to the vallies & mountains of Switzerland & the illusion is so complete that it takes away ones senses - & like

---

[168] Jenny Vertpré (1797-1865), one of the most talented and popular actresses of the period.

[169] Emmanuel Théaulon's operatic drama was first performed at the Théâtre des Nouveautés on 12 September 1829.

[170] This act formed part of the entertainment at Franconi's theatre, otherwise known as the Cirque olympique in the Boulevard du Temple. John Waldie attended a performance on 8 September 1829 and praised the elephant's performance above all others.

[171] Henriette Sontag (1803-54), one of the greatest singers of her day, was at the height of her career and fame. Perhaps attending the same performance, John Waldie wrote that 'Sontag was in glorious voice, and sung Rode's variations most delightfully, twice. I never heard any thing so exquisite, except her singing it once before.' See Waldie, *Journal*, entry for 24 September 1829).

[172] 'My dress, how I thank thee,' a line from the poem *Epitre à son habit* (1752) by Michel-Jean Sedaine (1719-1797).

the *Ranz des Vaches* makes one sick for the love of the country.[173] We have often gone to the Louvre. Charles 10 has taken some of the Pictures into his private collection, amongst others the famous Titian of which it is said there are three. The persons represented are Alphonso, Duke of Ferrara who married Laura Bianti who had been his Mistress. There is also a Titian of a d'Avalos who was General in Ch's 5th armies in Italy. There is a Berghem, a great favorite of mine - Animals passing a Ford, a woman on horseback with several figures in the foreground.

For some years, such crowds of English have not been at Paris. 3 Chapels are full of a Sunday. Mr Ways Chapel is fitted up with blue velvet sofas - ormulu - & looks like a Pavillion in the Champs Elysee wh. it is.[174] Over the pulpit in letters of gold are "Go forth & preach the gospel". Ld Stuart[175] asked us to go with him but I would not: he is much too amusing to go to church with, & I went to Mr Ways, or to the dirty Oratoire in the Rue St Honoré. We bought at all rates at Paris - prints I cant reprint; 165 Francs we gave for *Un An à Rome* by Thomas.[176]

Left Paris.

France is a country to open one's mouth & shut one's eyes in.

---

[173] 'This is one of the prettiest exhibitions in Paris. It consists of two paintings so disposed as to present the most complete illusion ...The two views are presented alternately for a quarter of an hour and the room in which the company are seated turns upon a pivot, from one view to the other.' *Galignani's New Paris Guide*, Paris 1830, p.562. The two views on show in the summer of 1829 were the Alpine scene entitled 'Mount St Gothard, from Faido (Ticino)' by Daguerre and 'The Grand Canal', by Bouton. The *Ranz des Vaches* was a melody sung, or played on the Alpenhorn, to call cattle, and the hearing of it, when on foreign service, was said to induce extreme homesickness amongst Swiss soldiery.

[174] The hotel and café adjoining the Jardin Marboeuf had been purchased by the Rev. Lewis Way who converted the café into a chapel and the hotel into a parsonage.

[175] The British Ambassador would have attended the chapel attached to the Embassy.

[176] Antoine Jean Baptiste Thomas, *Un an à Rome*, Paris 1823 - a folio-sized volume lavishly illustrated with coloured lithographic plates.

We went into Switzerland by Lausanne & passed the picturesque Castle of Joux on the frontier wh[ere] Touissant[177] was confined & died. We arrived at Vevey, a bright autumn sort of holyday Sunday.

Sunday-night at Vevey in the Inn I passed the most miserable fortnight of my Life - from intense anxiety of mind. Two days after we arrived Papa was taken very ill. All feelings but those of anxiety for his life were lost. Ld & Ly Minto who were in the house were most scotchly kind about their Physician. They went however the very day he was at the worst[178] - but a good Swiss Physician attended him day & night - & came on with us to Milan. To add to all this, the Snow fell & became every day deeper & the difficulties of surviving the intense cold of the house was such, added to the climate, as I had never felt before, & that view from the walk near the church has left such an impression of misery upon me of lake, mountains, cold & snow as never can be effaced. We had a sad anxious dismal journey down to Florence - with terrible weather. I wanted to return northwards from Vevey but the Physician said his complaints required a warm climate so we came on. Oh that horridly glorious view from Vevey!

Parma, Oct. 1829. What a break in my life! no wonder I cd not write. Papa is going on well but now I have another misery, one that makes me wretched, but on this family misery, I will never write, for the sake of the feelings of those who may read this. I must bend to it. All, all have their private miseries as well as their public miseries.

Florence. The first thing that I saw was Hortense, the D'esse de St Lieu [Leu][179] at the window in a pink silk pelisse, & the second thing, Hortense bargaining in a curiosity shop. French chatter & french fuss is *not* manner, thought I, manner admired by Europe too.

---

[177] Toussaint Louverture (1743-1803), the charismatic leader of the revolution in Haiti, seized by the French in 1802.

[178] Lord and Lady Minto left Vevey for Paris on Saturday, 10 October. Their physician was a Dr Williams.

[179] Hortense (1783-1837), daughter of the Vicomte de Beauharnais and the future Empress Josephine, married in 1802 Napoleon's brother Louis. Her youngest son was to become Napoleon III. In 1814 Louis XVIII created her Duchesse de Saint Leu but, as a result of her support for Napoleon during the Hundred Days, she was subsequently banished from France.

The first feeling of sunny gay Italy after snow & frost & cold & misery was this day on looking down into the Vale of Florence. How beautiful it is after a summer of winter. Papa is better. The gallery is shut & the curiosity shops are all we have seen. There are 6 Galleries of *Tableaux à Vendre* of wh. the english has [have] raised the price. Portrait of Leo 10 - ten guineas. We have bought a little Cabinet & a chess board & some Indian china. Ly Isa[bella] St John is here - a sad specimen of a marriage without consent of friends.[180]

Sienna Oct. [1829]. I am ill or rather going to be ill. I never close my eyes but nerves & fever & misery follow me. We hear every where of the King & Queen of Naples & his journey with 120 post horses & his servants who steal Knives & forks & spoons & other things. We met Medici & exchanged Horses with him.[181]

Sienna. Oct. 1829. I lay awake the other night thinking of Smiles, of all the different sort of smiles I had ever known, of the power they have over one, & how few are satisfactory, a slight tinge of Folly or Sarcasm shocking all. A serious persons smile is seldom pleasant; like Mme de Stackelberg['s] smile, it is against nature. Smiles should be the expression of a joyous mind. Mlle Mars ten years ago had the most perfect & refined smile I ever saw. It was so amiable an expression, but not *prodigué* over & above; it came so from the heart that one cd have exclaimed:

> "Loose now & then a scattered smile
> And that I'll live upon." [182]

Ly C. Cavendish tho' never a beauty had the most lighting up smile I ever saw. When she first came out in the world, it really was "Il lampeggiar del angelico riso,"[183] & almost ended in a laugh. All the greatest beauties looked *fade* by this smile & those laughing eyes. Ly

---

[180] Lady Isabella Fitzroy, daughter of the 4th Duke of Grafton, had married Joseph St John on 29 August 1829. Her family had not approved the engagement. M.T. doubted the marriage would be a happy one (see below).

[181] The King and Queen were accompanying their daughter, Maria Cristina, to Spain for her planned wedding with Ferdinand VII of Spain. Luigi di Medici (1759-1830), chief minister of Francesco I, had set off for Spain slightly later.

[182] Silvius in *As you like it,* Act III, Sc.5.

[183] See Petrarch's sonnet *On the Death of Laura*: 'Gli occhi di ch'io parlai sì caldamente.' 1.6.

Mansfields smile was sentiment itself & as if it was in consequence of forgettfulness of matters of feeling; Ly W[h]arncliffe's was the most refined smile, a smile of pleased assent & nothing more. The smile of an italian woman is to me the most disagreeable expression possible - it is always in scorn, never from the heart, but always from some lurking unexpressed feeling. Mlle Sontags smiles are still in my head, what a lovely expression! that *soit peu coquette*! certainly, but so pretty, "such becks, & nods, & wanton smiles", so taking, that if I were a Man, & a man to fall in love with an actress & a foreigner, she wd be my Lady. At this time of day, I don't think I sd fall in love with an actress. I sd like something more refined & that did not smile to multitudes, those that had not in their hearts, millions of mischief. Then a smile is worth having. See Woman - & Jenny Vertprè.

"Then does the smile of woman stamps our fates
And consecrates the love it first creates." [184] (Barry Cornwall)

Amongst the smiles there is the affected smile of Miss Pulteney & Miss Hope. "For this hands, lips & eyes were put to school & each instructed features had its rule." These Ladies make "practised smiles as in a looking glass." [185]

Sienna, Oct 1829. I am very busy with plans of book making.

Protestant burial ground at Rome & Tombs
Colloseo. Martyrs. Devotion & preachers. 12 Stazzioni - preach successively at each.
Via Cruxis - what are the Sacconi? Cross.
Is the preaching obligatory?
The Bonaparte's - what they were & what they are!
Palazzo Doria - Genoa - now & formerly.
Villa Ricciardi, Naples.
Giorgione - his works.
Campo Santo, Bologna.
Voyage autour de ma chambre.
Cardinal Bembo - the love letter & lock of hair at Milan.
Manzoni - his works.

---

[184] *The poetical works of Barry Cornwall*, Vol. 3, London, 1822, p.39. The first two words of the quotation should read 'Even so ...'

[185] See George, Lord Lyttelton, *Advice to a Lady*, 1731, and Leontes in Act I, Sc.2 of *The Winter's Tale*.

Portraits of Painters at Florence.
a Snow Storm in the Alps.
a night on Vesuvius.
La Grande Chartreuse.
Glamnius Castle.
Westminster Abbey.
Rubens & his wives - Antwerp & Munich.
Ly M. Wortley Montagu in her Turkish dress. Constantinople then & now.
"She has lied, but no more than other women would have done."
Sir Walter Scott & Abbotsford.
The His'y of China & Japan.
The His'y of Boul[e] & Marquitry.
The latter end of Statesmen, viz. Wolsey, Burghley, Bacon, Stafford & Clarendon, Shrewsbury, Bolinbroke & Marlbro., Sir Rt. Walpole & Ld Chatham, Fox, Pitt, Castlereagh, Perceval, Canning.

Sienna, Oct. 1829. Lying awake the other night I thought over the different things that have made me as I am in this life. First my grandmother was the cause.[186] I loved her & who did not? She was so sensible & clever & good a woman & she with her goodness & her cleverness & her plain matter of factness gave me an early sense of right & wrong, what is called principle, & nature furnished me with such a portion of obstinacy of character that once imbibed, there it staid, notwithstanding bad example & precept; still that wd not have saved me from follies & sillynesses & their consequences (I don't mean that I never had any), but looking back Miss Edgeworth's writings have had a powerful influence over my life. Yes, certainly they have, the *Letters to [for] Literary Ladies*, *Practical education*, *Belinda*, the *Moral tales* have saved me from loving Fools, from thinking frivolity better than solidity, & gave me a distaste for Fashionables & preference of a strait to a zig-zag path. My next formers were the Drummonds.[187] All I saw in that happy family, all those evenings passed at Charing Cross, all those Sunday Nights, made me know

---

[186] The Talbot children spent most of their childhood in the Bath home of their grandmother Mary Preston (c.1734-1817), daughter of Hon.Henry Hamilton and widow of Rev. Nathaniel Preston.

[187] In the book *The Drummonds of Charing Cross* (London, 1967), the authors describe Andrew Berkeley and Lady Mary Drummond as 'a perfect couple, simple in their life and beloved by the people in their neighbourhood'. Could they have been M.T.'s friendly hosts?

what a happy home was. Alas! more bitterly from its contrast with my own. Then reading of Mme de Stael constantly did not improve my unsettled intellect - they are poison to wh. the world gives no antidote. Then I fell in love with a superior Man, or one I chose to imagine so - a Man highly gifted by nature & education & quite Mad. This saved me from fools, from wise Men, from foreigners, from bores, from good husbands, from excellent parties - & from a variety both of good & evil. I never after liked but the same speccies of excentricity, or something *très distingué* - all copies from the same picture of superiority over the multitude, or rather what I imagined to be so, for what does poor woman know of the real character of a Man, until experience teaches her, what can she know of his sins & faults & follies, of his caprices or of his virtues?

Rome, 4th Nov. 1829. Rome I love & regret; it smiles into one's soul, yet it is a place that neither inspires cheerfulness or satisfaction, because here the mind ponders too much on the past. The beautiful & picturesque objects are lighted up with a clear sky & quiet atmosphere, not with that broad glare of light & joy with which nature is decked out at Naples. It is the City of recollections & regrets & tho' now the great rendezvous of the vulgar & would-be genteel English, the sight of them in parties together does not alter the romantic & sentimental feelings that surround Rome. As a residence I don't know whether I don't prefer Naples - the want of cares & the idleness there make people happy & agreeable, but it is a chance how characters turn out there, as sometimes people take to Gambling for a stimulous, but the every day life is one of even leisure. The D'ss of Devon[shire][188] who was the most prosperous woman of the age had here contrived a life of perfection divided amongst acts of charity, the fine Arts, having the cleverest & handsomest of her cotemporaries for a respectful Adviser (Cardinal Consalvi), Pius 7 for her friend, the Romans for worshippers, the *corps diplomatique* for supporters, & the most cultivated of the English paying her homage. Her house comprised all the comforts & the productions of the North & South of Europe, & her society was composed of Artists, Antiquaries, Politicians, Poets, Musicians, all endeavouring to please her, who had the gift of pleasing so many. Her secret was obligingness; she never omitted a kind word or action, & now for my Moral - I really can't find it - Life is short & if she was a good Catholic, which I believe she was, she had no Sins, according

---

[188] Elizabeth Cavendish, Duchess of Devonshire (1757-1824), was resident in Rome for the last eight years of her life.

to their doctrine. How unlike her rival Ly Westmorland who brought anarchy & confusion every where - & is dreaded with powers so great[ly] superior to hers.

We went sight seeing - first to Palmeroli's, Piazza Barbarini. His Father is lately dead at Dresden where he was employed in the Picture Gallery.[189] His son has things to sell, old Pictures, a good ancient Copy of a Holy Family 30 Scudi - a beautiful thing he was busy in cleaning up for Shrewsbury![190] as he calls him - old Cabinets cheap. The son seemed terribly overcome with recollections of his Father.

Thorwaldsen Studios are glorious. He has now things going to Copenhagen fine indeed. A colossal statue of Copernicus. He has such Basso-relievo - still the Night & day are the finest of any.[191] There are figures for the Tomb of Pio 7 going to St Peters, a Bust of C[ardinal] Consalvi, a Baptismal fount for Ld Caledon.[192]

We went to the Protestant burial ground - of which I have written a full account. There shall I lie if I die in Italy. I wish it - & what do a few years more or less avail one, of checquered good & evil.

Went to the Colliseum - my other favorite haunt.

Ld & Ly Lovaine are here. Miss Percy has a good story amongst hundreds of others of Ly Westmorland. There is a Mr Petre whom they all think very clever - but also is supposed to be an Atheist - but who is a great friend of Miss Percy's.[193] Ly West'd said to her: "but you don't know how wicked he is - & what sort of conversation he holds" & she ran on with a list of his sins. Miss Percy said: "He never talks to me in this way!" "Oh, but you shall hear him: Come home with me Saturday & I'll make him talk."

---

[189] He had been called to Dresden in 1827 for a fee of three thousand ducats principally to restore the Sistine Madonna. (See Anna Jameson, *Visits and Sketches*, London,1834, II, p.107).

[190] Charles Talbot, 15th Earl of Shrewsbury (1753-1847).

[191] Reliefs executed by Thorwaldsen in 1815.

[192] Du Pre Alexander, 2nd Earl of Caledon (1777-1839).

[193] Probably William Thomas Petre (1796-1858).

Naples Sunday [15 Nov. 1829]. We came here Friday se[ve]nnight; it has poured dogs & cats since. No doubt Rome is more attractive, more amusing & more reasonable than Naples.

The King is gone to Spain[194] & Medici after him. They come back in a year. Meanwhile the D. of Calabria exercises the Troops.

Lady Drummond has a new set of eyebrows. La Contessa Matta[195] as all the servants call Ly Westmorland is here on her way to Sicily. She has a chance of not arriving, as they say the steam boat will not weather a Storm. Sir F. Hanbury says he can save but one of his family - I don't think it will be his greatest burthen - "only think what a weight she'll be," he says.

Sir Wm Gell is the only Notbore. Lady M. Deerhurst has taken to ride like a Man & her daughter too, a girl of 16.[196] Poor Ly Emily Caulfield died at Nice!! the other day.[197]

17th Nov. [1829]. I am very nervous & unwell. Music, the least sound or noise, totally overcomes me. Peace of mind is not to be had long. I feel as if I had lived a long life, seen & felt every thing & now should prepare for eternity! prepare with fear & trembling. For many years I have not felt so serious minded, & as if all was finished & done. The cause of this is too grevous a cause of domestic misery to write about & so enough of it.

25th Nov. 1829. I have heard a variety of strange things lately but forget them all. Sir Wm Gell [who] is the only person worth seeing I see; the rest are mere people to fill up gaps & dinner tables, who can eat &

---

[194] The King's son, Ferdinand, Duke of Calabria, stayed behind as regent.

[195] Contessa Matta - Crazy Countess.

[196] Lady Mary Beauclerk, daughter of the 6th Duke of St Albans, had eloped with the 7th Earl of Coventry, Viscount Deerhurst, in 1811. Her daughter, Lady Mary Augusta, had been born on 11 May 1812. Henry Fox mentions 'Lady Mary and her daughter riding astraddle to court the censure and malice of the world.' (*Journal*, p.370). He was subsequently (in 1833) to marry the daughter.

[197] She had suffered a broken blood vessel on leaving a ball in Turin. (See Charles de Montalembert, *Journal intime inédit*, Paris, 1990, I, p.329). Aged 21, she was the younger daughter of Francis Caulfield, Earl of Charlemont and Lady Anne. Her three siblings were already dead.

drink, & say tiresome things. We stay at home sick. Mr Ponsonby[198] & his nephew came from Malta last night. That Malta is now the gayest & most charming place in the world. Mr Nugent[199] is M[aster] of the revels, provides their Opera & Champagne in *vin ordinaire*. Mrs Nugent is very ugly & never speaks. 'If you cd see her mind,' he says. The recantation of that mad Tom Stewart occupies gossip here. He has gone into a Convent at Palermo & has had his head shaved, & if he had a dozen of leaches put on it, it wd do him good.

26th [Nov. 1829]. Sir Wm Gell told me a good saying of Medici - witty to those who know Italy. Talking of the *chambre des Deputés* in Paris & London, he said, that there were but three places to live in: Paris, London & Apragola (a retired village near Vesuvius), for that where there was not Camera, there was always Anti-Camera.

27 [November 1829]. I had a visit from that good, excellent, civil, cold victim, Mme de Stackelberg. The Contessa Matta makes great sensation here. They have got some excellent stories of her. When C'tess Blucher came for the first time to visit her at Rome, she said: "You would just suit me for an Angel & C'te Blucher for John the Baptist in prison."[200] He said in his broken english: "My wife could not be an angel, it was quite impossible for she was in the family way." Ly West[morlan]d however insisted on her getting up on a Ladder & then she placed the C'te as John the Bap. & Ly West. surprised them with a *feu d'artifice* which enveloped this poor Angel in the family way in smoke. Another story they have of her is about a Servant who left her & came to Ly Airey to be hired. He said that the reason

---

[198] Possibly a relative of Sir Frederick Ponsonby who was Governor of Malta from December 1826 until May 1835.

[199] Nicholas Nugent had married Mary Whitmore in 1827. That same year he had been promoted from the official post of Collector of Land Revenue to Treasurer. According to Buckingham, he 'occupies himself entirely with the opera, and takes great pains with it.' (*Private Diary*, II, p.81)

[200] It was a popular form of entertainment to place family and friends in *tableaux* depicting some religious or historical scene. Buckingham noted, in 1828, that Lady Westmorland (the 'Contessa Matta') 'is just now mad about acting *tableaux*, and she drags everybody she can lay hold of to partake in this amusement. If a handsome woman or young man arrives, she seizes them to make a *tableau*, and if they resist she quarrels with them.' (*Private Diary*, I, p.255). Countess Blücher was the second daughter of Sir Robert Dallas (1756-1824), a former Lord Chief Justice, by his first wife. Madeline Dallas had married Count Gustavus Blücher von Wahlstadt, the grandson of Field Marshal Blücher, in Florence, on 23 September 1828.

he left Ly West'd was that he did not like to walk by moonlight in a field with Buffaloes, where Ly West'd had taken him, as she said, to try his courage.[201]

Society now is one great Cheshire Cheese - we dined with them at Mrs L[angford] Brooke. The women are all vulgar dress & expense. I am better - Sir William [Gell] is the only Fun going.

28th Nov. [1829] Went last night to Castle Dry - crowds of English & pretty dressed italians. Mr Ponsonby had had five hours discussion with Ly Westmorland, he said, of every thing since Adam & Eve. I said I was sure she put Adam in the wrong.

I had a letter from that pretty, nice person, Mrs Canning - as pretty as she is - containing astonishment of our old Ladies dress & flirting - & the english weather. Saw Paccini's Opera from Sir Walter Scott. Bocca Badati, uglier than Ly Dr[ummond] & as great an Heiress.[202]

3d Dec. 1829, Naples. Our Cheshire cheese society is very dull. Mr Canning is talked of for Lisbon. Quadri the Occulist[203] is to cure a Lady here by pulling out all her eye lashes. Ly West[morlan]d never ceases talking of the quarels of 1822; she wants to make up with the Palazzo Seracapriola[204] - just to make use of us. Public affairs are going on very ill; people are clapt into prison here for 4 or 5 years, without knowing why or wherefore. Mr Grant[205] got an order to see the Jail which they entreated him not to make use of. A story of Kernot the druggist[206] & the King is told such as in cheating could only happen at Naples.

---

201 Sir William Gell told this story to Henry Fox. (Fox, *Journal*, p.338).

202 The opera *I fidanzati ossia il contestabile di Chester,* composed by Giovanni Pacini (1796-1867), was based on Sir Walter Scott's novel *The Betrothed*, and had its first performance at San Carlo on 19 November 1829. One of the leading sopranos of her day, Luigia Boccabadati played the role of Evelina Berengaria. At the death of her father in 1819, Lady Drummond had inherited over £500,000.

203 Gianbattista Quadri (1780-1852), celebrated Naples physician, widely consulted.

204 It was in the Palazzo Serracapriola that the Talbots were residing.

205 Possibly Macpherson Grant, a British attaché in Turin about this period. In 1829, there was also a Dr Grant, army surgeon based in Corfu, travelling in Italy.

206 Kernot's English pharmacy had been established in Naples in 1826.

Sunday 6th [December 1829]. We have made it up with the Stacks - they are very civil & even kind to us as formerly. There dined there: Le Duc et La D'esse Dalberg avec Mlle leur fille,[207] P'ce & Pr'cess Dolgeruki, Mme de Ribeaupiere, & Sabouroff, the image of Ld. Alvanley, who plays & sings. Foreign society might be pleasant if you had confidence in them. *Au reste*, this year of English, there is not a single person of talent or distinguished here except Ly W[estmorland] who is much too mad to have anything to say to - but who I dare say wd amuse us, &, was one once used to the society in Bedlam, every place wd be flat after, as Ld Robert Seymour used to give us to know.[208] We had a nice vulgar dinner. Papa has changed his look: & the present great Man is I think less aristocratic in his dinner than Roger was. Mme Falconnet looked beautiful - dressed in a Red shawl gown & a large white muslin Turban, but she is Falconnised already.[209] Ly Glenorchy's beauty I am disappointed in.[210] Mr Irby of old London days dined here - & Lord Fordwidch, the image of both Mother & Grand-Mother.[211]

8th Dec. [1829]. Yes'y we dined with Yorkshire wh. we like better than Cheshire. They lie awake at night thinking of Newmarket. That species ought to stay in Eng'd. So Ly Tyrconnel has found out that her fortune is in her own power[212] - & the wicked have not prospered. I dare say that Ld Tyrconnel says to his dog: "Get you gone you nasty cur! I wish you were married & settled in the country."

12th [December 1829]. I caught a bad cough in Yorkshire & have never been out. We had yesterday a little dinner at home, at wh. P'ce

---

[207] Emmerich de Dalberg (1773-1833), German in origin, had served under Napoleon who created him a duke. In 1808 he married Marie Pellegrine of the Genoan Brignole Sale family. Their daughter Marie Louise (1813-1860) was to marry Sir Richard Acton in 1832 (see below) and subsequently, in 1840, Granville Leveson-Gower, 2nd Earl Granville.

[208] Lord Robert Seymour (1748-1831) had, as an M.P., been an advocate of the creation and regulation of Madhouses for the specialist and caring treatment of the mentally ill.

[209] Isabella (née Pulteney, b.1807), the wife of the Naples banker François de Palézieux Falconnet. They had married in Paris on 12 October 1829.

[210] Eliza Baillie (1803-61) had married John Campbell, Lord Glenorchy (1796-1862), in 1821.

[211] George Augustus Frederick Cowper (1806-1856), subsequently 6th Earl Cowper.

[212] Sarah Crowe (c.1800-1868) had married John Delaval Carpenter, 4th Earl of Tyrconnel in 1817. The following year, on the death of her father, she had inherited Kiplin Hall in Yorkshire, where the couple took up residence.

Butera was so gay & Sir Wm Gell so amusing that Mr Irby buried his *ton* & stupidity & Ld Fordwitch his shyness & Mr Craven his deafness in it. They were full of curious stories, priviledges & precedencies. The Town of Naples is a Spanish Grandee & can wear its hat before the King - on seeing it arrive in procession wearing its hat, the Spanish Grandees put on their hats; then the order of St Ferdinand, and then the Duc de Blacas. It was an odd scene, they said, to see.

Monday, Dec. 21 1829. It is 8 days since I have taken to my bed. I have been very ill with a spasmodic cough. Roskilly[213] gave 12 grains of Calomel, 21 of James's Powders, besides draughts & blister[s] on my chest - the whole in 24 hours. I knew I sd be ill this year, having been in a state of inflammation since I left Paris - my mind, thank God, is calm & resigned to anything. What does it all signify - Life is such a speck in comparison of Eternity - & what does my existance - a single lone woman signify, who wants me? Should I die here, I hope to be buried at Rome - various are the silly & serious thoughts that this week have past thro' my mind. My will I mean to make.

Thursday there was a great dinner here wh. Papa wd not put off. Georgina says Old Stack behaved a praise-God-barebones[214] or an old French beggar, saying "Je prie Dieu pour la princesse Christine," who being now Queen of Spain is worth praying for. Mme de Stackelberg is always *très distinguée*. How does she come by such vulgar screaming daughters who have a *ton d'antichambre*.

Mr Irby succeeds here. It is impossible to guess how a Londoner will turn out abroad. Ly West'd jointly with Ld & Ly Glenorchy is going to take the Torella.[215] There will be nothing found of them but bones & tail like the Kilkenny Cats. Ly. Glen'y is a silly beautiful woman with pretentions of various kind[s] & no manner. I often think over my intimacy with Ly Westmorland. I long, yet dread, coming across her. She wd have made an admirable lawyer. I once wanted her to sit for her Picture, as Portia. "The womans no heart my dear, don't vex yourself about her," as Ly Belhaven said.

I had a letter from Ly Belhaven & another from Charlotte.

---

213 John Roskilly (c.1789-1864) had long been practising medicine in Naples.
214 i.e. hypocritically.
215 i.e. rent a suite in the Palazzo Caracciolo di Torella.

Xmas Day 1829. I have read & written on serious matters till my head turns round - books & serious thoughts occupy me. I am fast recovering; my mind is calm & contented. I never felt so seriously inclined for many years, therefore I thought God intended I sd die, & that my wish of being buried at Rome wd be indulged in. I have however set out again upon the journey of life. I tried to make a sketch of my Will the other day in bed - but my head was so confused with hemlock - So much for procrastination of Wills. I have thought over my friends. Hammy & Charlotte I love best, rare person[s] are they. I have been reading Addison constantly lately. Upon cunning & discretion particularly I thought of them. They shine, Addison wd have thought. Charlotte must have my journals.

26th [December 1829]. Like all persons recovering I hear quantities of Gossip. The way to get confidences is to stay at Home & then every one comes & puts in some thing as they do into a poor box. Our minister [Mr Hill] is a curiosity. Papa dined there yes'y. He called across the Table: "You expect the Red Rover.[216] Miss Talbot gave him that name. The best name that ever was given." When Mrs L[angford] B[rooke] & P[apa] were going away, he said "Now don't go, let's have some Tea to fuddle our noses." Lord Fordwitch asked him if the Queen shot! Yes, he said she cocks her old eyes & kills the pigs.

Sir W. Scott's Old Lady in the 1st Vol. of *Ch[ronicles] of the Cannongate*[217] is an imitation of Addison. It is beautiful.

Visits. Ly Glenorchy called - her house & kitchen miseries with La Contessa Matta. The Lushingtons all honey, airs & graces, & with them a great Traveller, Mrs Ch'as Lushington,[218] a handsome woman of sense who looks as if she ought to be pearls & diamonds all over. Mrs L[angford] Brooke understands how to go on with the Lushingtons better than we do. She reads the riddle. Ly West[morland] is determined to re-knew with us & Sir Wm [Gell] that she shall. I won't.

There is a wonderful deal of charity & goodness in the English. 3 per cents looking up; gave Roskilly *carte blanche* to give what he pleased

---

[216] i.e. Lieut. Gen. Sir Edward Stopford (1766-1837).

[217] Scott's *Chronicles of the Canongate* first appeared in 1827.

[218] i.e. Sarah Lushington (c.1785-1839), the wife of Sir Henry's younger brother Charles who was serving in the East India Company. Her travel account entitled *The Narrative of a Journey from Calcutta to Europe by way of Egypt* had been published in 1829.

to the poor. The lower classes here must be much like the Irish, living off of nothing, or gormandizing & feasting when they can get it, good natured, & neglecting their affairs to nurse a sick neighbour. Roskilly tells me that he often attends a sick person or a dying person, with the room full of company or friends or relations, many of whom are playing at Cards near the bed. The Marquis del Vasto, the proudest Spanish grandee here, was told that his Coachman's wife was dying in the Alley near the Palace; he would not give any money to keep her alive, but he sent for the King's Confessor who with his fine Equipage & his two footmen went down into the dirty little *Vico*[219] to confess the woman. She died - & the neighbours in the alley made up money to pay for her funeral - this is very italian - the whole of it - & an Epitome of the ways of going on from the Alley to the Kings Palace.

Thursday [31 December 1829]. The Red Rover arrived yes'y; he says that Sir Joseph is horridly cross. He gives a ridiculous & melancholy acct. of Ly Lovaine who is in the dolefuls at Rome; when he spoke of the marriage between her niece & Mr Talbot, a Love match, she exclaimed, & mine was a love match.[220] He said Mr R. Percy was on the coach coming to Rome. "I hope he'll be lost in the snow," she said. The Red Rover is grown very deaf & additionally dull. He is good natured, vain, well bred, *militaire*. Oh, but they are all most honorable men.

Last day of 1829. The Ther. fell to 57 on the drawing room table. They all went to the Galla. I had the best of it staying at Home; how I love staying at home.

All men except clever men ought to be married - *Ils ne suffissent pas a eux-memes*[221] - no one wants them. Sir Ed. Stopford ought.[222] There is a curious story of jealousy come from Genoa - I forget the name of the Husband - he has just married a Bringnole [Brignole], a girl of 15, a niece of Mme Durazzo's - The husband took some jealousy of a ser-

---

[219] It. *vicolo* - Eng. *alley* is meant and not Vico the small township south of Naples.

[220] Hon. Caroline Jane Stuart-Wortley was the daughter of Lady Lovaine's brother, 1st Baron Wharncliffe. She married the Hon. John Chetwynd Talbot on 30 August 1830.

[221] 'They are not self-sufficient.'

[222] Sir Edward Stopford never married.

vant. He called him & shot him dead. The police came but he had barricaded his house so effectually that they cd not get at him.[223]

Mme Delmar writes from Paris to me to say that she has made the enquiries I wished & that the P'cess of Radzivill is not countenanced by Pozzo di Borgo or visited by the Polish Ladies!!! It ends our correspondence: I thought it would be the end of her Theory & her practice.

Somery's follies would make a volume. He told me with a long face today of Mlle Esterhazy's death. I was so near laughing - he had a *Pensée* capable of containing the hair of 5 Ladies in the leaves as I told him, & he has *la pauvre* Miss Gwynne's picture in his Album for the good of the public.

The first day of 1830. It seems that Pr'sse Christine has been magnificently received.[224] The public entrance was beautifully Spanish according to old Etiquette. The Queen was alone in her carriage, the King riding by the side & he got off to open the door to assist her out of the carriage. Marie Antoinette, they say, married Don Miguel, who will cut her up like the Oger.[225]

Sir Edward gives a horrid acct. of that poor wretch Sir Joseph. He says he was like a child at a dismal story & he was found with the Dictionary crying over the *Promessi Sposi*.

2nd [January 1830]. Yesterday was the 1st day of the Year wh. gives one cause to think a little. Owing to circumstances latterly, I am become more serious. I have thought often of my latter end, & that it is now high time to prepare for it. I have read over my journals. What surprises me in them is the warm interest I took in trifles, & the violent *engouments* I took for both men & women. Now, it is not often that a person pleases me, tho' a book often does. There are a number

---

[223] Maria Brignole Sale (b.5 April 1811) had married Raffaele De Ferrari (1803-76) in January 1828. On 7 November of that year, Raffaele had killed a servant named Francesco Morgavi, provoking widespread popular condemnation. Maria's mother Artemisia, née Negrone, was the sister of Luisa, wife of Marchese Gaetano Durazzo. In 1815, Lord Glenbervie had reckoned the latter one of the beauties of Genoa. (*The Diaries of Sylvester Douglas*, ed. F. Bickley, London, 1928, II, pp.139-40).

[224] As Queen of Spain.

[225] Don Miguel (1802-66), while acting as regent in Portugal during the minority of his niece Maria, had, in 1828, seized the throne.

of idle frivolous things in these journals. I am ashamed of them & amused with them, & my heart aches sometimes at reading them - but on the whole I will let them remain. Then the way I felt my unhappy home (for that I am changed & my home too, for staying still in one place has mended it.)

There was a ball at Ly Drum's,[226] & we had a[t] dinner old Mathias who talked for four; Ld Fordwitch handsome, not pleasant; Mr Craven whom Georgina says was sold by his wicked Mother to the Devil & at 1/2 8 becomes of a horrid form; the Langford Brookes - he dullissimo, she good-natured; Mr Irby who takes prodigiously here - his motto in society is "Calculation" I guess; the red Rover. They all went away & Sir Wm staid & was very agreeable to Georgina & I. Mr Mathias says they torment him here about his writings - they objected to print *Sta Minerva*.

The snow is so deep - three mails are due. Poor Ly Mansfield, I little thought ever to hear her called an Old Housekeeper. What changes & chances in this world. Ly Sandwich's stingyness has made such sensation that Mr Poyntz wrote as Ly. C. Montague's Guardian to desire she might have a wad[d]ed Pelisse![227]

8th [January 1830]. Poor Me! Last Thursday I was well & happy; since then I have passed two such nights & two such days from mental misery that I look as old as Methusalah.

10th [January 1830]. I have taken to the world, went to Old Stacks childs ball, saw Ly West'd who has had her first quarrel with Ferdinand, dined at Mr Vansitard's, went to Mme Falconnet's ball where I saw Mr & Mrs & My Lord & My Lady, all bodies & no souls. Society here is a perfect Cheshire cheese, quite as heavy & they say as rich.

We had a pleasant dinner today, tho' a foreign one.

---

[226] i.e. Lady Drummond

[227] Lady Catherine Montagu (1808-1834) was the daughter of Lady Sandwich (1781-1862). Her father, the sixth Earl of Sandwich had died in 1818, and William Stephen Poyntz (1770-1840) was one of the guardians of his children appointed in his will. Lady Catherine subsequently married, in December 1831, Count Alexander Walewski - see note 165.

The newspapers give an acct. of Sir R. Gordons Fête at Constantinople & the Queen of Spain's Entrance at Madrid.

14th Jan'y [1830]. What have I done lately. We had a great dinner. Mr Hill was shy, odd & original, spit out his dinner enough to disgust a dog, let alone a woman. We talked of the Cannings; he does both him & her entire justice. The Duc d'Alberg, whom I now see every night is the man who had the quarrel at the congress of Vienna with Mr Canning. I am inclined to believe it was a trick on the part of Mr Canning to fall into a fury, not being able to get the better of the old diplomate. The duke was Amb'r at Turin & is clever & *rusé*. Mr Hill says he smuggled some thousands of Fr[ancs] of french gloves - he talks like an old gentleman of the ancien regime. He is a liberal; his wife is an overpowering woman, *très grande dame*, a Bringnole,[228] & his daughter, the new style of french girl, the *Oui Papa & Non Papa* being now wholly exploded. La Contessa Matta says that we don't bear her the affection she does us. What a piece of humbug.

15th J'y [1830]. I seem to be amazingly gay if gay can be living with whom you don't get a new or amusing idea. Never was a stupider season, heavy as the weather wh. is like a London Nov'r.

The first bad news from Pisa was the 13. We dined at the Langford Brooks where there were Neapolitans & it was dull to extinction. The Neapolitans are *les sourds et muets de la société*.[229]

18th [Jan. 1830]. A dinner at home. Sir Wm says that Mme Dupont bullies her husband & that all englishwomen do who marry foreigners. He is right. Alas! poor dear Georgina.

19th [Jan.1830]. There is much to do & to say - tho' I am a poor catch cold thing, forced to retreat into my shell. Never was such a season of coughs & colds. We laughed at Ld. Aylmer[230] for saying that once in the N. of Ireland Farenheit was at 9. But todays papers say it is at 7 at

---

[228] The Duchesse Pelina Dalberg (1787-1865) was the daughter of the Marquis Antonio Brignole-Sale of Genoa.

[229] 'the deaf and dumb of society'.

[230] Matthew Whitworth-Aylmer, 5th Lord Aylmer (1775-1850) had married Louisa Anne Call (1778-1862) in 1801. In 1824, he had plunged twice into the Tiber in a vain attempt to rescue Rosa Bathurst (see Madden, II, p.385). In 1830, he was appointed Governor General of British North America..

Paris & that *Traineaux* are *la grande Mode dans les Rues*. Meanwhile here we are threatened with the plague. We pine for news as Letters & Papers are stopped & fumigated & are 3 posts in arrear.[231] I had yes'y a visit from Ly Ashburnham. She is an agreeable woman, a true Percy.[232] Mr Irby pays I guess her truly in saying that she was just the sort of woman who does not like having 1/2 a doz. daughters. Ly Lovaine says: "To be sure Ly Ashburnham is a tiresome woman but she has one good point about her: she is very anxious to marry her daughters." Sir Ed. loves her & cats, Custard & Apple Tart. His nephew laughs at him as all nephews do.[233] What a character the Red Rover gives of Mr Fox. That he wd sell his dispatches for Money, that he can't be trusted. What escapes women have!! He is writing the history of Calabria. He will shine more in imagination than fact. Those who believe not in truth cannot write his'y. The Red Rover is wanton but honorable, vain but to be trusted. How many military resemble him. I had an indigestion opposite from Mrs L[angford] Brook. Ly Conyngham[234] is dying & several Ladies are fattening for the situation. They say that she consulted the Bish. of Win[chester] as to the propriety of her retiring from court & quitting the world & he dissuaded her, saying "somebody worse would take her place." How like something in Louis 14th time!!! We had a great talk over the fire the other e'g with the Red R. & his nephew, a rising Gent in the F[oreign] O[ffice]. Ld Stuart's forte they say is dispatch in business. They say his dispatches are obscure on purpose. The King & him have always been in correspondence & he receives all his information from him. No one know[s] how Ld Stuart gets his information. It is better than anyones. Pozzo di Borgo wants him away - he is too much for him, but he cd manage Ld. Granville.[235] Mr Fox I always thought forms himself on Ld Stuart's model. The French, the most fickle people in the world, are tired of Ly Stuart. It seems that Mr Mellish's sputter did not do with Sir R[ober]t G[ordon]. He & Ld Yar[mouth] are come back. They

---

[231] The 'plague' was an infection which had broken out at Ferrara and which resulted in letters from the Roman States to Naples being opened and fumigated. (See *The Times*, Friday, 5 March, 1830). The censorship of letters was in any case widespread.

[232] George, the third Earl of Ashburnham (1760-1830) had married Lady Charlotte Percy (1776-1862) in 1795. She had 13 children including 7 daughters.

[233] William Bruce Stopford (1806-72), the son of Sir Edward's younger brother, Rev. Hon. Richard Bruce Stopford.

[234] The mistress of George IV; she was over 90 when she died in 1861.

[235] Granville Leveson Gower had replaced Sir Charles Stuart as ambassador in Paris in 1824. However, Stuart had returned to the post in 1828.

are all turned Turks in dress & habits. I asked Mr Stopford for the last english cant words - being in my speech 2 years behind hand. I left people talking of intellectual Men - a gifted manner - an attractive girl - of turning a person over. I had promised to send me the new Vocabulary.

I have been looking over & burning old journals - some of first impressions in life are curious. I find some resolutions odd enough on coming into the world: "Not to marry (supposing I am asked) but those who possess principle, sense, agreeableness, good nature & temper, wealth &c. that is to say, not to marry at all, but keep out of the scrape, step carefully & avoid falling in love as one should avoid falling down stairs." Resolutions. Not to marry a fool. It wd be troublesome. Solomon wd hold a woman cheap, a middle aged man marries for convenience; he is blasé & selfish; a young man's love is soon over; a[n] old Man is out of the question; a good humoured Man is led by every one; a bad man leads you - to the Devil.

The red rover is going & his nephew, a good looking young man who feeds here occasionally. The Abbé Campbell is dying - God rest his Soul!! He used to read the Letters & now I suppose they can't get anyone to do it fast enough & this plague of fumigation is sent in consequence.[236] It sounds alarming by the Paper sent us by Sir H[enry] L[ushington]. The deaths of P'cess Pozzo di Borgo & all her servants brings us back to the days of the *Promessi Sposi* . The news is a Ther. at 7 at Paris. Mr Fox is writing a His[tory] of Ca[la]bria; all his facts will be imagination & his imagination facts. I went to the great Drum[mond]. Ld Glenorchy sat down to talk of the mad C'tess, would I meet her? I gave an ungracious Yes & trembled. He says if she ain't with you, she is against you. His lordship begins to feel his thraldom. She is an awful woman & has conjured up a literary quarel between Sir Wm. Gell & Mrs Starke,[237] & she sent to Mr Hill to ask him to invite Ld & Ly Aylmer, afterwards saying, when he made excuses for want of time, "Does he think I want them, it was only to teach him his duty." If Ly W[estmorland] had had one spark of dignity, she wd not

---

[236] The abbé (Henry) Campbell (1754-1830) was widely believed to have been employed by the Neapolitan Government to censor letters sent by and to the British community.

[237] Mariana Starke (c.1761-1838) had in 1820 published *Travels on the Continent* which was more guide book than travelogue and as such enjoyed enormous popularity. A large section of the book, which runs to over 800 pages, was devoted to Italy

have gone to Mr Hill as they had a quarel years back, but she is a shabby person. There was a little soirée at Old Stacks & a Harp player Labarre,[238] not a good gown but my own tune. There is a story of Sir R[obert] G[ordon] & the Emp. of Brazil in wh. a determination of character comes out wonderful.

28th Jan'y 1830. And now a sweeping out of *Les habitués de la maison* has taken place. Mr Rbé,[239] as they spell him, & the R. Rover & his nephew are gone. The nephew is steadier than the Uncle & is like a pleasant young man in a novel. I shall not be sorry to be quiet & left to my books - my dear books - we have had five days dinners & company - perpetual company - Monday we dined with Psyche, dear fat Psyche[240] as Sir Wm Gell calls her. P'ce Butera was there in gt spirits & there was much fun about Ly Ash[burnham] & her 7 silent daughters whom she is dying to marry. As we all prophesied - the madness of Ly West[morland] is come. There has been a scene unique they say about bills & housekeeping in wh. she abused the husband[241] & said of the Wife "Is that a person to look over butchers books, & settle household acc'ts." In short like Ophelia, she has scattered "Here's rosemary & here's Rue." Roskilly says it must end in madness or dropsy. She lives off of Walnuts & Lacrymachristi - & her love of investigation carries her far below the dignity of a Cabinet Minister's wife. It is said that when she & her amiable atheist Mr Petre begin to discuss, they call for Tea & a bottle of Claret. We dined at Mr T. Parkers.[242] The dinner was cold & Mr Hill sulky, Sir Wm. ill, & Sir Ed. & Mr Craven deaf - the spell was broken as Mr C. staid past the hour.[243] Yes'y though 15 we were very merry. Sir Henry tried to make P'ce Butera & I quarel, but failed.

29th Jan'y [1830]. I often read old Journals; to judge by them few have been more miserable. It is too late. I write this blotted by Tears of a renewal of discourse unavoidable. Mine is the character I would not have a woman be for her own happiness & that of those about her.

---

[238] Théodore Labarre (1805-70), harp-player and composer.

[239] i.e. Irby pronounced *à la française*.

[240] Lady Sykes (c.1795-1861), née Mary Anne Foulis, had married Sir Tatton Sykes in 1822.

[241] Presumably Lord Glenorchy.

[242] Robert Townley Parker (1793-1879), his wife Harriet, née Brooke (1798-1878), and family, seem to have resided in Naples in 1830-1.

[243] See entry for 2 January 1830.

What have I been - irresolute - irritable. What am I now, subdued yet irritable. I make a set of resolutions for my own sake & my duty to God. I live with one whose passion is praise - whose fault is irritability of temper - & whose virtues are many - whose life & manners[?] have been so injured, that to humour her is a duty. To do this I ought completely to change my own character, at my age difficult, but it is right to do so - I sd be rewarded by my conscience if by nothing else. Heaven knows, except books & quiet & an armchair, Happiness for me cannot be looked for, ever, & yet I am not so badly off as some of my fellow creatures (I mean those who have food & raiment). This misery is therefore Human Life, a Trial for another life, & sent to detach us from all [&] every thing on this Earth, comfort, friends, & confidence. But Alas! why sd I go on agitating myself with these dreadful thoughts. To live well with Georgina I ought to say what I don't think, let every thing pass. Now I am naturally open & sincere; my opinions are positive & unyielding; my manner is decided - My manners I must change - my opinions I ought to give up - would I had the softness & gentleness of Mrs Canning, who having to say to a violent man never shows she rules - I am dreadfully unhappy. The overturn of my whole nature, of my whole comfort is come now.

2nd Feb. [1830] I am better, not so deeply & internally wretched. I have staid two day[s] alone - & quiet in my room. Poor Mrs L[angford] Brooke, she is a person so happy by character & disposition - & happiness is so rare. She thinks Mr L[angford] B[rooke] clever, whereas he is prosy & sensible only & dull - she was telling me that Ly West[morlan]d said of Sir Stratford Canning: "That is a man of whom I dare not ask a question." "Now I dare say," said Mrs Langford B., "she feels the same with Peter - because there is a great deal like Peter in Mr Canning."

Dined with that fine specimen of a woman's tongue, Ly Aylmer. Her prattle is unceasing & eternal. She says accordingly to Sir Wm. nasty little things & her husband don't mind her wh. is odd. We meet everywhere at dinner the Duc & D'esse d'Alberg & their daughter. They are thorough French. I don't know so universal a favorite as Mrs L[angford] B[rooke]. Her Husband is still alive but hardly any hopes remain. Hers is the goodhumoured character to please generally. Mr Hill is gone to solitude & what he calls shocking. I sometimes think him as mad as Ly West[morlan]d.

I am reading Massillon & Bourdaloue;[244] religion & death are often in my thoughts. I never thought so much of them. If I die here I hope to be buried at Rome. Many things make me low & nervous. I wrote a long letter to Mme Delmar, another to d[ea]r Ly Belhaven. Ly West[morland] begins to excite great sensation. She told Ld Glenorchy to be in the way if Mr Hill insulted her - she was in a fury at his telling her it was too late to invite Ld & Ly Aylmer to meet her. "I did it to teach the man his duty. Did he think I wanted them," she said!!

5th [Feb.1830]. What an extraordinary thing is Neapolitan society. At P'ce Gerace's dinner I was looking round & listening, for seated between old P'ce Gerace & Francavilla, what could I do. The company were the best born, best bred & best instructed at Naples. First their way of eating, the quantities of Trash & *zucc[h]errini* they swallowed, wh. they call *Porccheria*, & the sons say of the old P'cess "Mamma mangia sempré Porccheria." Then their gestures, in good humour, but absolutely like the Lazzaroni, with manners as if they wd tear each other to pieces; their conversation, if such it can be called, about San Carlo. All the women, beautifully dressed & in the best style - & the dinner too beautiful. Mme de Gioja[245] was hard on Mr Ch's Acton's gambling! I had been reading Massillon on the sins of others.

Sir Wm Gell sat here last night. He was particularly agreeable, as he is when he is rational & set his speech aside. He was giving an account of his having read Mr Auldjo's *Mont Blanc*[246] the night before, in a fit of Gout, stretched on a mattrass before the fire, with a lantern suspended over his head to give him light.

8th [Feb. 1830]. Two Mails are due in consequence of bad roads. There are 40 Bachelors (Babies mostly) giving a ball at Rome, many recommended to Papa, to feed & house them I hear - tiresome ac-

---

[244] Jean-Baptiste Massillon (1663-1742) and Louis Bourdaloue (1632-1704), French preachers, whose published works would have been easily available..

[245] Teresa Gioja was the widow of the Neapolitan choreographer Gaetano Gioja. Her first husband had been a French aristocrat who had bequeathed her a fortune on condition she did not remarry. When she broke the condition, she was thrown into a convent, but was liberated by Queen Marie Caroline. Her daughter Marietta married the baritone Antonio Tamburini.

[246] John Auldjo, *Narrative of an Ascent to the Summit of Mont Blanc on the 8th and 9th August, 1827*, London 1828. This account with its landscape illustrations, smaller lithographs of the climbing party at various stages in the ascent, and its maps and diagrams, brought the feat of climbing Mont Blanc to the attention of a wide British public.

quaintances those are. Sir William is very funny about his Spanish friends. When he goes away at Genl. Toledo, he says in Spanish "O Terrors, O Horrors, & thus ends the play," which it seems is the end in Spain of both Tragedy & Comedy.

10th Feb'y [1830]. After all I go thro' of wear & tear of mind & nerves I wonder that I exist or look anything decent, tho' I am aware that I am excessively changed this year. Music or Verse has such effect on me that I am obliged to come home in the middle of the Opera. Roskilly gives me Valerian. I pity her, pity her from my heart - to have made her sole resource by temper & folly, her companion ill at ease with her. I am resolved to go, go out & go everywhere, & so I went to Mme Falconnet's ball. Medici is dead![247] - he had begged to remain at Naples, but the King said he must resign & so he went & died at 72, of Spain & fatigue & cold. All his dear friends were there. The duke de Cassaro succeeds him, as one might see by the entourage round his daughters.

13th Feb'y [1830]. I am low, wretched & nervous. Went to Capo di Monte!! Ambition at 72!! how terrible. Medici died of worry. I returned ill, but dined comfortably with Ld. Augustus [Hill], Sir Wm. & Col. Stuart. The next day, the mad C'tess & them being two we dined at Ld Glenorchys. We are all in black for that exemplary Queen of Portugal.[248]

18th [Feb.1830]. Ill. Gardening & *en solitaire*. Mr Rich[?] says Mr Lyton Bulwer was married in black, because he thought he looks best in black wh. rather spoils the story. Since the 13th I have been worried to death - of the matter of my misery, I shall not write. My head is puzzled. I garden. I have read thro' the *Spectators* & made extracts from them. I pass my time in crying & wearing my nerves by thinking of the past, & anticipating the future. No one interests me - &, except Sir Wm Gell, everyone bores me.

Monday, we dullified at Genl. Toledo's. A black bore of Neapolitans. Why is it that Foreigners chuse the worst english as intimate associates. The *ton* of an English boarding school is what they seek & like -

---

[247] Luigi di Medici had died in Madrid on 25 January 1830.

[248] Queen Carlota, the wife of the former monarch Joao VI, had died on 7 January 1830.

Andersons[249] - Taylors - Sophia Lushington - & prefer these to Ly Canning or to Ly Durham. There was a fine ball last night at M. de Stackelbergs, & here they all forget the old Q. of Portugal in favor of pink gowns & lighted Rooms. Sir Wm Gell told the D'ess of Eboli[250] how like a fat old Turk she is. Pr'cess Tre Casi, her sister Eleonora Spaccaforno & Mme Statella were the beauties there[251] along with Ly Glenorchy who wore a turban with birds of Paradise fantastically placed in - & if it was not for a little peevish expression about the mouth, she wd be beautifully lovely. Mme Statella is a grandee kind of beauty, stormy, & fine coloured. I felt very ill & near fainting & worse in nerves since my last visit here.

P'ce Buttera went off yesterday with Letters for Engl'd & Ly Westmorland to Rome with her carriage full of Oysters. She was obliged to go, everyone's door being shut against her, & she was cut entirely. Ferdinand said, while dressing my Hair: "It shows how mad she must have been to go away the night of such a ball!"

19th Feb'y [1830]. We had 17 at dinner. Made myself up by Eiltier[?], P'cess Tre Casi's Lover, Saubouroff sat next me, & very clever I found him. He is like Ld Alvanley in wit & figure too. M. de la Passe[252] was as usual a bore on the other side. He found 14 flaws in the Seve [Sèvres] china plates & 5 faults of spelling in the Menu. It is paying him a great Compl't to listen to all the trash he is going to read to us of his writing. They staid at Ecarté till 4 in the M'g. The say is

---

[249] Warren Hastings Anderson had married Mary Dewar in 1820. He was a partner in the merchant house of Robert Anderson & Co. of Edinburgh.

[250] The Duchessa Maria Luisa d'Eboli (1782-1854). According to Greville, she received 'a few people every Monday with dancing and a Pianoforte, Whist and Écarté.' He also described her as 'poor, but she was a beauty, and has had adventures of various sorts.' (*Memoirs*, Vol. 1, pp. 467 & 435). A French visitor (*Souvenirs de voyage en 1832 et 1833*, Vol.2, Paris, 1834, p.136) described her in more kindly fashion as one who 'remains young and beautiful, whose charming mode of conversation is inimitable and holds you under a spell which resembles happiness.'

[251] Princess Tricase, née Maria Felicita Statella, was the wife of Giovanni Gallone, Prince of Tricase. Her sister, Eleonora Spaccaforno, was using another of the Statella titles. Mme Statella, née Stafania Moncada, daughter of the Prince of Paternò, was the wife of Antonio Statella, Prince of Cassaro, and therefore sister-in-law to the other two ladies.

[252] The Vicomte de la Passe had served as a French diplomat in Hanover and Bern before being appointed Secretary at the Naples embassy in 1829.

much about Ly M. Deerhurst riding *en Cavalier* at Rome - her daughter too, poor thing.

20th [Feb. 1830]. Dined at C'te Stacks. He was dreadfully civil, but gave me a lesson on Etiquette with regard to Ly Ash. & P'cess Gerace. His daughters are vulgar & noisy. Gl. Toledo is like a fine Spanish picture & the D'esse Fernandina frozen.[253] I am sure they are good, duller than any thing dull. M. de Sass makes a regular Predica[?] in company, to the Monte St Angelo & others who listen. Ly Drummond thinks herself too young to wear a black velvet gown. Ch's D.'s Letter is full of the horror felt in London at Ld. Graves's end. Ly Louisa Murray sent him the caricatures that brought on the Catastrophy. What a state of immorality we are got to.[254]

28th Feb. 1830. I hate everything French - & that Coxcomb of a Man M. de la Passe; his reading is vanity in wholesale & his Sicilian journey is like the Frenchman's *Voyage d'Italie* in *Les Pensées de Felicie*.[255] We all behaved as ill as possible. The D'esse Fernandina played with a dutch toy & half of us laughed. Mr Nugent has sent me from Malta such a head of a grand Master, de Rohan by name, such a grinning Jesuit of a French Priest I never beheld - it is too ugly.[256]

1st of March 1830. My poor nerves are cruelly racked. I have been staying at home. The Thema's of society are: 1st Ly West[morlan]d. - she & her Oysters met a french Lady at Terracina, Mme de Richmond, & the moment Ly West. heard that she was *la belle soeur d'un Ministre d'Etat*, M. de Villele,[257] she writes to Ly Ashburnham to know her here. Mme de Richmond is rather a tax on Ly Ash. & complained of

---

[253] The Duchesse Fernandina (1802-1876) was the wife of General Toledo.

[254] Thomas North Graves (1775-1830) had committed suicide on 7 February allegedly as a result of seeing caricatures which cast aspersions on the character of his wife from whom he was separated. Lady Louisa Murray (1777-1842) was the wife of Sir George Murray.

[255] *Les Souvenirs de Félicie L****, by Madame de Genlis, (new ed., Paris, 1821, pp.84-9) contains the humorous outline for an empty and self-centred account of a tour to Italy.

[256] Emmanuel de Rohan (1725-1797) was Grand Master of the Knights of Malta from 1775 until his death. M.T. later gave the picture of him to Sir Walter Scott (see entry for 2 February 1832).

[257] Joseph, Comte de Villèle (1773-1854), an ultra-royalist politician during the 1820s. He had married Barbe Desbassayns de Richemont in 1799.

her having left Rome because "Il n'y a pas de refronces",[258] which Ly Ash. looking puzzled at, she said "Mais il n'y a pas de Modiste."

We had little *jeux* at the Lush[ingtons], it is too like schoolgirls, with *jeux* & *ton* to match; of all dull things under the sun, a recommended set of people in Letters are the dullest, as what they are never coming out & they might just as well be a set of Neapolitans. We had that bore yesterday, Ld Russell,[259] a fine picturesque face, might as well *be* a picture from any life he shows. Mrs Cuthbert[260] lady-like, her daughter a black tall impudent girl sat next Ld Russell & pulled him by the sleeve at dinner to get his attention from his other neighbour Ly Ch's Ashburnham - style too bad for decent company. Sir John Mordaunt pompous & conceited.[261] Mr Brand hideous but looks clever.[262] In the E'g the stupidity increases; will people not cease with their tiresome recommendations. Col. & Mrs Fitzclarence came.[263] I have heard much good of *him*.

December is come again. It snowed & I brought home such a cold from Ly Glenorchy's dinner. I was very tired & left them playing little *jeux* at 11 o'clock. I was much amused at dinner by the Duc Dalberg & Mr de Sass talking english politics of wh. they seemed completely in the dark. Ly Glenorchy looked beautiful in a Turban put on by Ferdinand of divers colours. She does not please, why I can't tell, for she is not wanting in sense or civility, but she has a supercilious look, *ma la Statella mi piace piu*.[264] M. de Pourtalès[265] came to say Good-

[258] A *fronce* means in dressmaking a 'gather', so the whole phrase must mean 'they don't do regathering' - Lady Ashburnham might be excused for not comprehending!

[259] Lord William Russell (1809-1872) became Duke of Bedford in 1861.

[260] Sophie Cuthbert (née Smith) was the widow of James Ramsay Cuthbert (c.1776-1821). Her daughter, also Sophie, was to marry Admiral Hon. Henry John Rous in 1836.

[261] Sir John Mordaunt (1808-1845) was MP for South Warwickshire.

[262] Thomas Brand (1808-90), nephew of Baron Dacre, succeeded to the title in 1853. He was the travelling companion of Lord Russell.

[263] Col. George Fitzclarence (1794-1842) was the eldest son of the Duke of Clarence (later William IV) by his mistress Dorothy Jordan. In 1819, he had married Mary Wyndham, the illegitimate daughter of the 3rd Earl of Egremont.

[264] 'but Mme Statella pleases me more'.

[265] James Alexandre de Pourtalès (1776-1855), brother-in-law of Naples banker François Falconnet, and himself the son of a Naples banker.

bye. I like him, he is so good. Mme Beneker de Grudisberg[266] - he is banker all over.

12th March [1830]. Poor Ly Ash[burnham] who dined here Wednesday & went home to see her youngest child[267] has lost him thro' mismanagement; he died Thursday - so much for Ladies doctors. I have cold nervous attacks, low spirits & unhappyness of mind. Poor Ly Ash[burnham] with 7 daughters. We have received Moore's *Life of Ld Byron*.[268] I have dipt into it & it makes my poor weak heart & still weaker head ache, puts me in mind of things & persons & places that when I was happy I cared not for - but now, everything I read hurts me, & I put away the book unable to read more.

Ill, but get up to a large dinner. There is nothing for effect like green & gold & pictures & light & plate, & all the world are smitten then. The small green dining room takes the eye amazingly. Mrs FitzClarence who seems a dawdle tells me that Ly [*4 lines crossed out:* West. says Ld Glenorchy wanted her to .....that she was a woman of ... character to .... !!!]

14th March [1830]. The sort of society we have here is very tiresome - Strangers & boys, every body sends here their Cousin & Grandson. We dined at Ly Drummonds on Sunday & eat dirt there. Son Altesse Le P'ce de La Tremoille was there - his is the finest blood in Europe. He makes claim to the Crown of Naples; he has a Star & Red Ribbon, but has not *l'air noble*.[269] In the E'g were the usual set of vulgar Todies & dress play. The present nephew[270] is worse than the mad monk, he being only mad whereas this one is a Shoemaker in sole & *ton*. Mme Dupont sat with me by the fire & abused the Lushingtons & their Sunday balls & said as how they set at Sir Rich. [Acton] & Mr Craven & as how he ridiculed them in return for their attentions. *Ainsi*

---

[266] Marie Louise (b.1786), daughter of Etienne Du Titre, silk merchant and member of the French colony in Berlin, and his wife Marie Anne. The Du Titre children had had the clergyman brother of poet Adalbert Chamisso as their tutor. In 1808, she had married the Berlin banker Wilhelm Christian Benecke von Gröditzberg (1779-1860).

[267] Hon. Reginald Ashburnham, b.3 February 1819.

[268] Thomas Moore, *Letters and Journals of Lord Byron*, 2 vols., London, 1830.

[269] Prince Louis de La Trémoïlle (1767-1837). The claim to the throne of Naples went back to 1521 when François de La Trémoïlle married Anne de Laval, the direct descendant of Frederick, King of Naples.

[270] i.e. the newly arrived nephew of Lady Drummond, brother of the 'mad monk'.

va le monde. Mr C[raven] is a snug old Bachelor who keeps himself in his independence. She ended by saying I was the proper wife for him to wh. I said Thank you & a *triste* life we sd have of it without gaining Love or Happiness & both losing independence. After all what is a woman's independence - it is a coin of nominal value that rises & falls according to circumstances - & when she is not in love, is always in her head. Enough, but this made me laugh. He with his *mesquin* ways, looking like a dancer or actor, I with my love of the Grandioso in style or looks. What I like is an old Picture walking out of its frame in looks & something peculiar. To turn to vulgarity - & *mauvais ton* - I think I know what they are now, having seen Mme Beneker de Grudizberg - a *posé* quiet manner, no gestures, a calm voice, no bruskerie of *ton* or manner - saying enough & not too much, this is good *ton*. For any thing *recherché* see P'cess Sanguisko[271] whom I recollect at Vienna & at the Tuilleries - a little girl - such grand elegance - but she don't succeed here like many other charmers; they prefer at Naples their own home-bred charms to any others. We dined at M. de Falconnet's - That wont be long a good menage. She speaks her mind too much & too roughly & loudly.

We had a large dinner & soiree on Saturday; the duc Dalberg I sat next, a charming old *rusé* diplomate - looking so clever & cunning - I remember hearing of his & Sir S. Canning's quarrel at the congress: & Sir C. falling into a fury with him. Mr de Stackelberg has got the cold of a true Courtier who chuses to die in the Service. It seems that the Emp. of Russia is in love with the Gde D'ess Helène, his sister-in-law, who was sent here last year to be out of the way. Her brother of Wurtemberg[272] is here & the cold was got in a Party for him to fish at Fusaro - The Duc Dalberg seemed so delighted at this cold that it won my heart.

19th March 1830. A dull day at Lushington Castle. The Lush. society is like children in a nursery playing at hide & seek, hunt the slipper - Neapolitan fools & foreigners & yet wiser than me. Mme Falconnet's & Sir R. Acton's childish quarrels amuse me. Ld Russell is a mass of affectation - can't speak for it. Gl. Toledo told Papa that Marie Lou-

---

[271] Princess Klementyna Sanguszko (1780-1852) was the wife of a Polish general.
[272] Prince Frederick of Württemberg (1808-1870).

ise[273] has refused Leopold Saxe Cobourg. What a destiny is reserved for the agreement about Greece is that it is to be seperate from Turkey. He is expected on his way to his Kingd'm. I cd draw him as Macbeth saluted by the witches. I can't imagine this *rangé*, money-saving, near-sighted Man Thane of Greece - for King he never will be, it is said, owing to *la jalousie* de S.M. le Roi d'Angleterre: what a destiny married to the Q. of England, refused by Napoleon's widow - they say that in all Greece there is but one house belonging to Mavrocordato at Napoli di Romano - imagine this *posé*, *rusé* prince putting his crown on to keep off the rain, to reign over Barbarians.

We dined yes'y at Ld. Glenorchy's - she looked lovely. I went with Ly Isabella St John to Ly Drummonds where it was amusing because some things hit my fancy: Gulnare, who is a wonderfully impudent woman, & she has taken the Corsair who has just landed.[274] Mme Falconnet who talks & scolds & reminds me of La jeune femme colere, or Shakespeare's Katherine, all the time I like her. The St John is an unpromising marriage - as everything of that name must be. He stays playing & betting till 5 in the M'g. The Duke has forgiven her[275] - Poverty without love.

Today I took a set of silly women to the Santangelo collection.[276] I was quite ashamed for them & for the good-natured proprietor. They yawned, looked at nothing & understood nothing. I admire the Giorgione in preference to any picture I ever saw. The portraits are supposed to be a duke of Bracciano married to an Orsini. He seems pondering upon state matters & she is trying to persuade him to something he is averse to - a minister or conspirator & his too fond wife. The colouring is deep, rich & magnificent.

---

[273] Marie Louise (1791-1847), daughter of Archduke Francis of Austria and second wife of Napoleon, had been made Duchess of Parma at the treaty of Fontainebleau. She entered a relationship with the Austrian Count Adam von Neipperg and married him after the death of Napoleon. Neipperg had died on 22 February 1829.

[274] Gulnare, queen of the harem, and Conrad, the corsair, are the two central characters in Byron's poem, *The Corsair*. There is no indication as to whom Marianne has affixed the appellations.

[275] i.e. her father, the Duke of Grafton.

[276] A collection made by the Santangelo family and displayed in their Palazzo in the Strada di S.Biagio de Librai. It contained sculpture, paintings and an extensive collection of coins and medals, and was subsequently purchased by the city of Naples in 1865.

Mrs Fitzclarence is the greatest dawdle I ever saw for a man to be blessed with for a wife. Col. F.C. dont mind her but oppressed[?] the children, & settled the ménage. She sleeps with her heels higher than her head wh. may acct. for the heavyness of her intellect. Ly Hadding-ton[277] calculates her friends by the quantity they pick up of marble, & her styngyness I hear is wonderful. Sir Joph has made her his *but* at Rome. There are crowds here come from Rome. Ly Burghersh is going on doing the g[rea]t Lady at Florence. She rec'd the Grand Duke in a sort of night cap lying on her Sofa & when tired she yawned & turned round. Her children are music mad & composers. Ld Dunlo is here returned from Constantinople. They are all now come away & the acting & dancing man told me yes'y with g[rea]t importance that he staid at Naples, to wh. my assent was more than cold, I believe.

20 March [1830]. Sir Rufane Donkin,[278] a regular story teller, spirited, ill tempered & well read, is amusing. He is full of the Niger, & has offered Govt. to go & look for the source. I think he gives the same account of the decrease of the Pyramids & the Nile that Mr Hill does of Pero: Ears, poor dog, poor dog, his ears grow smaller & his tail shorter every day. The P'ce of Calabria sent for him & was very civil & offered him a review of his troops. Sir H. L[ushington] has got a beautiful picture of the cave at Amalfi. We dined there; little *jeux* a bore. I came away next day - they were cross & I gave them honey & butter.

26th March [1830]. These are curious times. P'ce Leopold refused by Marie Louise comes here on his way to Greece, & Napoleon's Capt. Maitland is the person appointed to take him.[279]

I am better & go out everywhere. England is now, to believe Letters & Travellers, anything but a moral nation. Ld Holland preaches morality they say to the Duke & D'ess of [& Ly ... *2 lines crossed out*].

---

277 Lady Mary Parker (1781- 1861), only daughter of fourth Earl of Macclesfield, had married Thomas Haddington, ninth Earl of Haddington in 1802.

278 Sir Rufane Donkin (1773-1841), a professional soldier and founder member of the Royal Geographical Society, had published a *Dissertation on the Course and probable Termination of the Niger* in 1829.

279 Sir Frederick Lewis Maitland (1777-1839), as captain of the *Bellerophon* patrolling off La Rochelle in 1815, had negotiated with Napoleon, and subsequently conveyed him into English waters. In 1830, he was commander of the *HMS Wellesley* in the Mediter-ranean.

27th [March 1830]. The St John's & Ld Dunlo dined here &c., & we went to the Accademia where Fodor sang & screamed a French air horribly, by way of its being french I suppose.[280] Ferdinand had put Turbans on everyone; the blue ones were hideous & mine a large white one I thought the prettiest. P'cess Sanguisko was over dressed & looked *mauvais ton*. Ld Dunlo amused us with his Constantinople stories & of the Reis Effendi being so enchanted with Mlle de Guil[le]minot's[281] french squared waist, that he went home & put all his Harem into the same dress. The women lie with their feet in a pan of Charcoal & a large Quilt drawn over them as if they were in bed. He was diplomatic & reserved as to what he said of his Miss[ion], described the climate as enchanting. He told us of the slave market - they are walked up & down like animals. They love trinkets & beauty spots, petticoats hang in the inside of the leg & they are squared in in the waist.

Yesterday we went to San Jorio[282] to see Mrs L Brooke. She is a well tempered, well intentioned person - but what a curse is a stupid husband. The place with its grand terraces might be charming & the thunder of Vesuvius just over their heads is sublime.

5th of April [1830]. Mr Hill is often sick of himself thro' very selfishness. He stormed & laughed about the very unaffected woman having found the chairs settled for the Sunday E'g party. It was broiling hot at dinner *chez lui*. There were the Duc & D'esse D[alberg] & their daughter, the St Johns, the silent Ld Russell & many others. Ly Isabella reminds me of Ly Clarendon & [Ly] Maryborough in her style of conversation. She deals, like them, in stories, & has one of the atrocities & loud & shocking oaths of Ld Southampton who was brought up a Methodist.[283] Mr Hill has got some good Caricatures: one of his Majesty reading the N[ews] Papers by the light of a single candle, another of the superannuated Politicians, & many of the D. of Wellington.

---

[280] Joséphine Fodor was now at the end of her career. (See Felix Mendelssohn's *Letters from Italy and Switzerland*, ed. Lady Wallace, 3rd Ed., London, 1864, p.144.)

[281] Her father, Armand Charles, Comte Guilleminot (1774-1840) served as French ambassador in Constantinople between 1824 and 1831.

[282] Now known as San Giorgio a Cremano.

[283] Charles Fitz-Roy, Lord Southampton (1804-1872) belonged to a collateral branch of the ducal house of Grafton.

7th [April 1830]. This letter of Ly Byrons is written *très sagement*, not saying more than is necessary but merely vindicating her friends. We had a large party at dinner. Mr Hill was very original & nice, except in the article of eating his dinner. He says Ly L[ushington] never went out of a Sunday except to the Opera when the King of Prussia was there. The Captain is his Mother's true son, a puppy.[284] We talked of Ld Byron. He said he was the most suspicious of mortals, but behaved kindly & well to him at Genoa. The St John marriage is a sad promise, already Play[285] - & is it - jealousy -.

8th [April 1830]. We went to the Portici yes'y.[286] There is a china room very pretty manufactored at Naples in Charles's time: Chandeliers, wainscoat & frames for glasses all china. The curtains are white silk spotted with gold. There is a Room of Pictures; one of Napoleon by Gerard, two of Murat, Massena, King Joseph & his wife. The rest of the house is uncomfortable trash.

Ch's Greville & Mr De Ros are coming,[287] that same Mr De Ros whom Mr Fox cannot teach the difference between right & wrong.

Easter Tuesday, April 13th [1830]. Easter has passed quietly without any thing to mark it. It is an extraordinary [thing] that in so bigotted a county, it is a perfect Carnival. Good Friday is passed by all the beauties of Naples in going from Church to Church & walking in the Toledo dressed in most becoming Caps & Veils - making a public promenade, no carriages being allowed in the Str[eet]s.

Saturday we dined with that queer man Mr Hill who sends his porter to invite his company by word of mouth. 'Il trouve son compte a être

---

[284] Captain Stephen Lushington, R.N. (b.1803) was the second son of Sir Henry Lushington.

[285] i.e. gambling.

[286] The seat of a royal palace built in the mid-eighteenth century by Charles III. The so-called porcelain room was moved into the museum of Capodimonte.

[287] Charles Greville (1794-1865) moved in the highest political and social circles of his day, with the result that his memoirs, when published in the 1870s and 1880s, were read avidly for their revelations as well as their insights. His friend, Henry William De Ros (1792-1839) succeeded to the baronetcy on the death of his mother in 1831. Greville described him as 'the grand purveyor of women to all his friends'. (Greville, 1, p.319).

original,'[288] I begin to think, with the foreigners. Dalbergs, St Johns, D'esse d'Eboli.

Sunday, 18th April [1830]. I have gardened until my arm is dreadfully sore, & a Note from Sir Wm enclosing the real original Haji Baba[289] came. I heard men in the drawing-room, suspected who it was, & gathered courage to go into the room & found Mr Greville & him. He looks open & good-natured & clean, tho' I suppose joke & gibe are his province. They dined & we had a pleasant day of it, & had much amusement with Haji Baba & Ly I. St J[ohn] across the Tea table with good stories of Ly Haddington & the piece of buckram & the pot of marmalade & all the various styngynesses. 123d.[290]

All over Europe now, *on est revenu du prestige* of the charms of foreign society; Ly Wm Russell,[291] Mr Morier says, & all the puffers of its charms are. He asked me if we were not dullified. I said Yes - like the Man who slept for show in Q. Anne's time. The first year we yawned, the 2nd we dozed, & the 3rd we slept.

We dined with Mme Falconnet in her Paradise - what vulgarians - when solitude succeed to grieve!![292] Such a Man & Woman as are Mr & Mrs Webster,[293] so forward & vulgar, he dressing sauces on his plate. I was too beautifully dressed, all Paris & Herbault, had on a bonnet that Herbault made me like the Q. of Spain's. Asked at 6 & got to dinner at 8. Horace Vernet[294] sat near me. He is a little sharp looking man, looks clever & artist-like, & swallows his Champagne in a

---

[288] 'It suits him well to be original.'

[289] i.e. the author of *The adventures of Hajji Baba of Ispahan*, James Morier (1782-1849). He was travelling with his wife Harriet (née Fulke Greville).

[290] Presumably some allusion to Lady Haddington handing over pennies when pounds might have been more appropriate.

[291] Lady Elizabeth Russell (née Rawdon) was the wife of Lord William Russell (1790-1846), the second son of John, 6th Duke of Bedford. The latter happened to be in Italy at the same time as Lord William Russell, son of the Marquis of Tavistock (i.e. John's grandson). Apponyi described her as the most witty and most learned woman he had ever met. (See Apponyi, I, p.80).

[292] cf. Lord Byron, *The Giaour*: 'If solitude succeed to grief, Release from pain is slight relief.'

[293] Major Henry Webster (1793-1847) and his wife. He was the son of Elizabeth Webster, subsequently Lady Holland, and she the daughter of Irish M.P. Samuel Boddington.

[294] Horace Vernet (1789-1863), French painter best known for his battle scenes.

curious sort of way. One neighbour, Sir G. Temple, I took for a German,[295] the other I shant forget in a hurry. As to Mr Hill really he has his company as the Tigers & Lions. Come in Ladies & Gentlemen, come in & see the show.

Tuesday [20 April 1830] we had a Whist party.

Wednesday [21 April 1830] we took the uncertain Ly Glenorchy to the opera. She is halfbred, neither fine Lady, or any natural, one or the other I like. Ly Isabella [St John] is amusing, tho' in animal spirits a tone too high for me.

24th [April 1830]. Yesterday a hot late dinner & not gay, tho' I was between Mr Hill & the D. Dalberg whom I like. They are a pleasing set. The D'ess has best manner in the world, the best *ton*, a little *trop sucré*. How difficult to attain is that charm of world & good breeding that French women study but seldom succeed in, because a shrill voice, a harsh manner of expression, & an inordinate love of dress spoil them. Her civility however distressed Georgina for Mr Hill was standing near & she said: "M. Votre Pere est vraiment representant d'Angleterre, il fait les honneurs de Naples a ses compatriotes."[296] I dare say it made him very angry. The daughter is a nice natural girl. Mr Hill grows more odd daily; he is an unhappy being. Then I pity at large all ill regulated hearts & heads, all uncontrouled tempers. They are the most to be pitied in this world. They & all connected with them *ne font jamais fortune,* & are never contented or happy: vagabond habits or irritation of temper kill happiness. Ly Isabella rattles away. She is too masculine & don't interest me. She is spoil[t] & clever, but, like her Aunt, Ly Isabella screams like a Mackaw. I wrote a long Letter to Ly Canning.

28th [April 1830]. We took a charming walk with the Lushingtons & St Johns: to the Cappucines over Pozzuoli where on the liquefaction of the Miracle of San Gennaro, a stone drops blood, this Chapel hav-

---

[295] Sir Grenville Temple (1799-1847). In 1829, he had both married Mary Baring and succeeded to the baronetcy.

[296] 'Your father [i.e. Sir George Talbot] truly represents England. He does the honours of Naples to his compatriots.'

ing been the scene of the martyrdom[297] - we walked by the high terrace over the Hill which commands views of a Paradise decked out in spring attire, but staring on the Island of Nisida are the deep dug dungeons where chained prisoners are confined & from whence their cries for mercy cannot be heard.

Dined with the Lushingtons, a pleasant day; abused selfish Husbands, & settled a Pic Nic to Astroni[298] for the 1st of May.

29th [April 1930]. Dined at Sir Rich. Actons. He is a *très aimable* Amphytrion.[299] The Glenorchy's & St Johns, & Mr Craven who is going a Tour with the D'esse d'Eboli. The Barone who has running horses, as Statella[?] said to Sir Richard, "Ho due Passioni: I Macaroni e i Cavalli." Lady West[morlan]d was told by Ly Wm Russell of Ly Northampton's dependants' lamentations at her death & said "Rome howl'd when Nero died."[300]

1st of May 1830. Our Astroni Party was perfection. - a pic-nic - 17 or 18. I tired myself terribly & overwalked myself. The views from the walls are charming - & we dined in the wood of Ilex *a la Turque* on the ground hid in Firn - delightful pastoral days - when a little makes one pleased or gratified.

5th May [1830]. We had yes'y a party to Cuma & Fusaro - dined after the manner of the ancients lying on the grass - we laughed & had an excellent dinner. Mr Greville & Sir Richard [Acton] & St Johns. Haji Baba staid with his wife. If Sir Richard has tried to marry Mlle Dalberg that wd have been something worth having - but the Lushingtons are making up a match with him & Mlle Galiati.[301] She is in looks a pretty little soubrette - not a good *ton* & P'cess Dentice gets the benefit of his attentions meanwhile. Who will be ungrateful, every one!!!!

---

[297] The church had been built in 1580 in honour of S. Januarius who had been martyred on the nearby hill of Solfatara. The stone in the chapel named after him was supposed to be that on which he had been beheaded.

[298] A large extinct crater, 4 miles in circumference, just north of Pozzuoli. It was surrounded by a wall and used as a royal game preserve.

[299] i.e. dinner host.

[300] Lady Northampton had died at Rome on 2 April 1830.

[301] Charles Greville considered her 'remarkably pretty.' (Memoirs, I., p.455)

7th [May 1830]. We yes'y went to dine at the Belvedere, the finest thing in Europe.[302] The French Garden with a Fountain, roses & orange Trees, the Pavement & marble balustrade - below are Gardens & Naples & beyond the calm deep blue sea covered with boats. Round the corner of the balcony is another view finer still of the Camaldoli, stone pines, churches all lighted up with the rays of the setting sun, & I imagined the Old Monks blessing us as they look[ed] down upon us. The loggia at the end of the Gallery has other views equal in beauty. While the company assembled for dinner, the Sun went down & the Moon rose & we all dined at near 8 in the Gallery where the Statues are; & after dinner marched back thro' the Moonlit gardens filled with roses to the suite of rooms above, where Tea & singing finished this pretty day. What fools half the Men are! Our aristocracy calls Shame upon us. Some pretty poetry has appeared on Ly Ellenborough.[303]

8th [May 1830]. Yesterday the Talbots, Moriers & St Johns dined with us. Sad things old marriages are & people who do well at home in their own country coming gandering abroad amongst those who neither know who or what they are.

12th [May 1830]. Walked in the Villa Gallo. How fresh & peaceful & beautiful are these spring walks at Naples. I never can again be thus happy. Ly Isabella is improved, wonderfully improved. Sunday Mr Greville went away. He was quite affected at going & nearly cried. Mr Morier speaks of him as a very different person from what I sd suppose him, a poetical, eloquent, high flown person full of enthusiasm & a love of nature. What a different character his London friends give of him, of the blazé man of the world, half gamester, & half newmarket, absorbed in such pursuits there, here admiring the Moon rising upon the sea & writing verses on the Cappuchins at Rome. If any one cd know their real character or their powers, what a curious his'y the real life & the *manqué* life wd be! "Some village Hampden."[304]

---

[302] The Villa Belvedere belonged to the family of Carafa di Belvedere and was situated on the Vomero hillside. The Blessingtons had rented it between 1823 and 1825.

[303] It had been in a Brighton hotel in February 1828 that Lady Ellenborough (*née* Jane Digby) had been caught *in flagrante delitto* with the Austrian Prince Felix Schwarzenberg, but it was only in March 1830, with the opening of divorce proceedings in the House of Lords, that the act received widespread publicity.

[304] See Thomas Gray's *Elegy written in a Country Church-Yard*. John Hampden (1594-1643) had been a country squire until projected into a leading role in the English Civil War.

That prettiest woman in London Miss Fox marries Ld Lilford.[305] The Fox & the Goose they are called. A Wedding here! 150 people present in the Prussian Chapel. There were *des Toilettes superbes*: & all the fuss of a wedding wh. charms people. The Discourse was *très imposant*. I never heard a better or more impressive. "Those that are married let them remain so - the rest, let them go to a Nunery." He said in the marriage state every day disputes arose; if you wished for such & such miseries "Dites que Oui."[306] Mme Dupont was ready to rise up & say No & she declared to us that she & her *cher Mari* never had any. Sir Rd Acton who thinks that a woman ought never to be allowed to have an *idée triste* said it was not fair upon the Bride Mlle de Kiel.[307] "Combien de Mari[s] pendus, il y aura demain,"[308] said I. After the wedding we dined at that stiff poker of an Old Maid, Mr Craven - my future *sposo* as the good people here have settled for me. "Dites que Non," thought I. We went to the Opera. Ly He[y]tesbury's lover Mr Dundas came to see us. He is not facinating, but I see is lazy to such a degree that the setting up a flirtation wd be delightful to him. His tone of voice is disagreeable & he seems just as happy without as with his passion. I like Mr Morier. I sat next him at dinner at Mr Cravens. He is an unhappy Man, not the jovial Haji Baba I had expected. There are three menages here that give *de quoi penser* - St Johns, Moriers & Talbots. This last is absolute twaddle - a sad thing at 60 it is to marry below yr situation, to have no love, but past love of the world to live off of. The Moriers are unsuitable, she is a slattern. Mr St John plays - & the St John principle.

13th May [1830]. Last night we went to a splendid ball at the D'esse San Teodoro.[309] The ball room is too showy in decoration & not solid. Her bed, of embroidery over pink, dressing room & bath were exhibited - a crowd oppresses me & low spirits crept gradually over me & I feel crushed. Ly I. St John I like, she can see & understand & talk, & we talked of unhappy marriages - a futile theme. She thinks Mr

---

[305] Thomas Atherton Powys, Lord Lilford, married Mary Elizabeth Fox, daughter of 3rd Lord Holland on 24 May 1830.

[306] 'Just say Yes.'

[307] The daughter of the Secretary to the Russian Legation in Naples.

[308] 'How many husbands will hang tomorrow?'

[309] Maria Luisa Tocco, the Duchessa di San Teodoro (1769-1837) was the widow of Carlo Luigi Caracciolo, 4th Duke of San Teodoro (1764-1823). Their palazzo, renovated and extended in the 1820s, was on the Chiaia.

Morier bored, I think him wretched, & Papa & Mr Hill think Mrs M[orier] going out of her mind. The D'esse does the honours better than any woman I ever saw. There was a new Table for refreshments that was edged with roses & turns round continually with goldfishes & a pond walled in with real stone. "Le caractere fait la destinée" certainly. What a thing is that same destiny, a word, a step, a look, destroys or makes it. The picture of a lazy englishman was Mr Dundas at the ball - "You hate these sort of things, dont you," he said, falling about. I said "Yes," & there was an end of our discourse. I was beautifully dressed, like an old Picture, in a yellow gown & blonde & purple ribbons, diamonds & Pearls.

14th May [1830]. The first hot day. Ther. in the drawing room at 70. Last night a stupid *soiree dansante* up the hill where young & old danced like mad, all but me. Ly Isabella says society is busy marrying me. Mr Morier's shocking unhappy piques my curiosity. How unhappy, Good heavens, how unhappy some people are. This is always the pleasantest time of year.

16th [May 1830]. We took a long walk in the woods by the Lago d'Agnano. The day was so beautiful. Ly Isabella was pleasant, young in spirits & enjoyment, & fully aware of her cleverness. However, it is a sad marriage & probably these two persons walking in the woods will never know more happiness than this. He is good natured but wd bore me. It was yesterday year that the Constantinoplites dined with us. Yesterday I dressed myself nearly the same & here one may be happy always. Will it last? It was a Turtle feast. Mr Hill was in high spirits, full of fun, & laughing at Mme Dupont, who sat opposite eating & drinking, & puffing paté de foie grais, bologna sausages, like a *Marchande de Comestibles*. How odd the Morier marriage is. I can't make it out. He was very agreeable the night before last. Yesterday, he did not utter - his wife was present. Wives, what plagues you are. Husbands, what tyrants you are. Tell me who you see & I'll tell you what you are! True I should not judge a Man by the wife he is tired of or a woman by the person she happens to be thrown with for the time being - but see who these people prefer, see who they seek, whether friends, todies, wits, or fools, & you will get at the secret of their disposition. I am sorry for Ly Isabella, clever, & great & grand as her company & position have been, that she has not found better than Mr St John. Her voice & manner I take it have stood in her way!! & so catching are they, that I find myself screaming up in one Key, & growling down in another from having past two months in her company. Her prospects are sad, but her spirits & health are so good that she is not more miserable than those whose lots are much better. I like Haji Baba, he is a nice lazy person always in company, yet finding time to write prose & poetry & see every thing. Sir Henry Lush. is full of his story, a curious one of Mr Swift & Miss Kelly. They changed their religion to be married. There is a great scandal here altogether. The Mother denies its validity & the Gentleman was taken by the police climbing up the irons of the Palazzo Esterhazy in her bedroom. In short, she is an illbehaved young Lady.[310]

19th May [1830]. The St Johns went this Morn'g without *un salut*!! Poor Ly Isabella, her best year is over. We went last night to Mr Webster's to hear Crescentini,[311] & the Ricciardis & Miss Byrne sing. Miss Byrne sings Bravura like a professor, Mlle Ricciardi as if she had a *passion malheureuse*, wh. they say she has. What people those St Johns are! To say nothing of Lady Bolin[g]broke & of the late Lord. The present Ld.[312] is more than wild, the present Lady has a disowned little boy, one brother who is at Malta, ran away with a married woman - put her into a convent - & left her - & the St John in the mission at Florence[313] is given up to play & luckily has a wife who keeps him on board wages - he sometimes leaves her for a year saying he is coming back in a fortnight & he bets his carriage with his wife in it on the race course so that she is forced to return home carriage-less. Mr

---

[310] Some details of this story of a girl (Elizabeth Catherine Kelly) allegedly inveigled unwillingly into a disguised marriage ceremony in Rome and of Charles Greville's subsequent involvement in it, can be found in Greville, 1, pp.479 et seq. A very different version emerges from the autobiography of the gentleman (William Richard Swift) involved, published in 1878 under the title *Wilhelm's Wanderings*. He asserts that he had married Miss Kelly with her consent, but that his mother-in-law challenged the legality of the marriage and kept him separated from his lawful wife. They were not united again until some six years later!

[311] Girolamo Crescentini (1762-1846), celebrated castrato singer.

[312] Henry St John (1786-1851), fourth Viscount Bolingbroke, had married Maria Mildmay (1790-1836) in 1812.

[313] Ferdinand St John (1804-65) had married the heiress Selina Keatinge on 8 Nov.1826. In his *Memoirs*, Sir James Harris described him as 'a very handsome and clever man.' He also tells the story of the duel fought between St John and Count Coteroffiano, the best shot and swordsman in the country: 'When they met it was agreed they should stand at forty yards apart, and, at a signal given by the seconds, they might advance or not as they pleased, and fire when they liked. Both stood still, and St John fired first, apparently without the least effect. Coteroffiano then advanced, and St John thought himself lost, when his adversary walked half way and fell stone dead, having received the bullet without wincing, and intending to kill St John *à bout portant*.' (I, pp.51-2).

Morier talks & agrees with me about the Lovaines; there is a want of principle, of reason & common sense about them - poor Miss Percy! This day year - This day year. I was reading Chateaubriand in my great Chair!!

Saturday 22nd [May 1830]. A lovely day- Spring - flowers - verdure & pastoral delights. Sir H. L[ushington] & Maria & Georgina & I dined in the woods of Monte Barbaro upon the grass & wild flowers. We had 7 hours pleasure - & the Tombs in the wood have set me Tomb reading.

24th [May 1830]. *The Times* has written on Diplomacy showing us how Mr Hill's ways are undiplomatic & what the duties of a minister are.[314] Sir Henry does all, could do all & this *saute aux yeux*. The Morier, the St John & the Talbot menages disgust one with matrimony - Ennui & distaste, debts & deceit, poverty & bad taste & ridicule, & all of them pity the others!!!! a pretty lesson on life. Mrs Morier's acct. of Ly Mary Deerhurst swearing is good; this fully proper, cold, well-behaved woman.

May 25th [1830]. Ther. 76. Drawing room. London gossip rings of Ly Graves's unfeeling conduct. The king is past recovery - twaddle from Mrs Talbot at Castellamare - histories of Mme Dupont's gourmandise. I never see her or the Lushingtons with[out] a story of one or the other. I have taken to books & pouring night & day over them.

27th [May 1830]. I delight in this time of year here. The Italian spring is so lovely & the pleasure of walking & straying perfectly securely over a whole country is so charming - woods & paths - & precipices & sea & mountains - flowers & vines & solitude, with the look of habitation - we went up to the Camaldoli, dined in the Fern in the woods & then scrambled down to Pianura - & rode thro' the vineyards that are trained in festoons across & across. Any people who are in good humour become charming on these occasions. Sir Henry told us the story

---

[314] In an article of 6 May, *The Times* had drawn attention to the very high salaries given to British representatives abroad and attacked the bundling together of items of expenditure, thereby making them difficult to scrutinize. It suggested that the quality of the diplomatic service would be much improved and the expenditure controlled, if 'men of a high order of talents, but of private station in society' replaced 'men of noble birth but mean capacity.' The theme was taken up again in leaders on 8 and 13 May which considered what duties and expenditure might be appropriate. British representation at the court of Naples was not singled out for mention.

of the Brigands - & of Mr Canning['s] dispatch to Sir Ch. Bagot[315] in verse & how shocked Mr Douglas was at it when he brought it out.

28th May [1830]. Mr Hill is just now very fond of us. We dine there of a Thursday. Why is it Englishwomen make such fig[ure]s of themselves. There was a woman of 60, like a dried walnut, in broad neapolitan daylight, before that glorious bay of Naples, venturing to appear in a *chapeau a la bergere* with roses. Mr Hill was in an extasy, cd not contain himself with delight by winking & nodding, sat opposite to me in fits of laughing - & what an oddity he is, & becomes more so daily. M. de la Passe, my tiresome neighbour, would beat Ly Aylmer I think in talking.

30th May [1830]. M. de Santangelo came into the Opera box to announce the death of his Mother after three days illness!!!!

31st [May 1830]. Went up to that happy *Marchande de Comestibles* Mme D[upont]. A courier from Rothschild in 6 1/2 days. Two dukes inspectors of Police. One duke a pastry cook at Naples. Regina[316] proposed to Mrs Higgins.

9th [June 1830]. I have been leading a solitary quiet life. The heat has set in. The Opera is too bad & society is gone. Went to say Adieu to that pretty Ly Glenorchy. P'ce Leopold has abdicated. He has shown a want of character, quite pitiable; no longer can one say slow & sure. He has set them all by the ears in Eng'd. This change of mind & purpose has suddenly got up a regular opposition. He has put friends & foes into a passion & Charlotte writes: "To think of such a weak fool causing so much trouble to so many wise men," & he appears, as Mr Rose says of the Austrian Cabinet, slow to resolve & quick to alter.[317] Ly Glenorchy is saved by her scotch blood from being a silly woman wh. she is not but wd have been. The little P'cess Vittoria,[318] she says, is sincere & well brought up to play Queen & dont amuse the King. I was much shocked last night at the acct. of Mme Monte S. Angelo approaching death. She is dying of the same complaint her mother did.

---

[315] Sir Charles Bagot (1781-1843), British minister in the Netherlands. He had previously served in America and Russia.

[316] Presumably Don Francesco Capece Galeota, Duke of Regina (1783-1838).

[317] See [William Stuart Rose], *Letters from the North of Italy*, London, 1819, Vol.I, p.172.

[318] Princess Victoria, Britain's future queen.

Made her will yes'y, but put her child from her in an agony at the infection so catching in Italy of consumption. She received the extreme unction. So young, so rich, so beautiful. Her husband adoring her, what a refined look was hers, what a pure smile. She was like a white lily. Sir Rd Acton refused her - she did not please him.

12th June [1830]. I cant help thinking of the Miss Byrnes![319] blue as indigo, pedantic as *les Femmes savantes*, vulgar as parvennus, precise as old Maids & ugly as I dont know what, but clever. I see no one. Ly Isabella disturbed me deep in composition. Queen Godiva is here.

We took a charming walk yes'y evening with the Lushingtons. Such a sky as shown on the Lago d'Agnano, such a distant picture of the Islands, & tones of E'g with silence, but distant sounds of animals & hum of insects. Then the Sun set deep orange & blue on the Lake; even the noise of the millions of frogs in the Lake charmed me; pastoral sounds away from the busy hum of Men does the mind good. I should like to have been alone & thought, & yet what good is thought to one chained & bound by long habit & strong circumstance.

20th [June 1830]. We were to have had *Thé* & Ice amongst the flowers on the Terrace - the night turned out ill & we were driven within doors. The Miss Byrnes surprise & amuse me. They are pedantic & blue & original. Are you a lunatic about the Moon? they ask! do you write verses to Rubini,[320] & in short their style are what we good dull, prosy, proper behaved people & *très distingué* personages at Naples are totally unused to. Mme Toledo[321] & I had a *tête a tête* the other night. She gave me the history of the Duke of W[ellington]s & Ld. Fifes[322] being in Spain. She seems to consider one as great as the other, & Ld Fife speaking Spanish well gained their hearts. The ball Feast they gave him she talked to the D. of W. & she was the Lady who presided & sat next him at the ball wh. cost 8000 piastres. There

[319] It would seem likely that one of the Byrne sisters was the Georgina Byrne to whom Rubini dedicated some songs. There is evidence of Georgina Byrne/Misses Byrne passing from Geneva, through Schaffhausen to Italy in August 1829.

[320] Giovanni Battista Rubini (1794-1854), the heart-throb tenor of his day, who contributed to the initial success of the operas of Bellini.

[321] Maria Tomasa Josefa de Palafox (1780-1835) had married Francisco Alvarez de Toledo in 1798 and been widowed in 1821.

[322] James Duff, who became fourth Earl Fife in 1811, had served with distinction in the Peninsular War.

was an alarm that the cook had put poison in the Duke's supper & so, she said, I sent into my Sisters house in the next street for his supper as I sat next him. She is Palafox's sister - those of all ranks frequent the houses of the great - but these visits are not returned. Mr Greville is half mad at Rome with his Miss Kelly. He has been mad enough to put up *Ex votos* & attend flagelations out of fun & the government would soon shut him up if he staid. Mr De Ros is here, a young Ld Oglevie - according to royal style, he is gracious enough to accept dinners & parties. His heart I suppose is like a truffle, black but soft.

30th June [1830]. I have not written since the 20th. I have read night & day, played on the Piano Forte, sprained my arm in gardening, hearted [hurt?] myself, & sworn the peace against the Mosquitoes - (do I mean the war?). I have seen Sir William [Gell]. Miss Byrnes dined here who are blue & wise, silly & clever. They say that P'ce Butera is European.[323] Mr de Ros I have seen often. I dont like him & yet he is soft & pleasing - & in his young days must have ressembled Tasso's *Amore Fugitivo,* & now he is like St Michel treading on Satan, & Good heavens that so fair a person sd be so bad a Man, but he is sick & not interesting from his excessive reserve, which is not the only reserve becoming a man - the reserve of pride - you feel you dare not, cd not trust him, that he has not a good opinion of himself, conse-quently a worse one of you & others - I never sd like this Man. I be-lieve now what I like is reserve but not to me, *hauteur* but not to me, pride but not to me. Mr Moore says Ld Byron was gentle to women, but he does not say he was so to his wife.

I had a Letter from that dear little person Ly Canning - her picture of herself in London made me cry - cry out past thoughts of what I en-dured & of my future monastic life that is fast coming on. Ly Bel-haven's popularity does not surprise me. I love that woman dearly & Ly Canning too. Ly Canning says Dr Chalmers's preaching charms everyone,[324] though Sydney Smith says he is like a Man in a passion. Mrs Morier tells me Ly Haddington says I am perfect, if I was not so fastidious.

1st July [1830]. It was not too hot, tho' the Ther'r was 84 to the North in a current of air. After dinner Papa & I drove up the Strada Nuova &

---

[323] See note 65.

[324] Thomas Chalmers (1780-1847), Church of Scotland minister who achieved wide-spread fame both for his preaching and for his social work.

77

walked in the Masseria at the end. I never saw the verdure look so fresh & lovely & the long evening shadows & a long line of purple light marked upon the clear bright sky from Vesuvius & the Moon rising, & one bright Star (not mine for it was too bright) over the hills. I cannot say I felt happy, tho' it was so lovely, for gloomy future would intrude upon my thoughts & took possession, & I had neither a companion or energy enough to oust them. I thought of a nunery, I thought of an unhappy marriage, & I thought of an unhappy home. I have finished the first & second vols. of Ld Byron. I keep my journal in the same way; he was a clever bad Man, & I am a well-meaning fluctuating, unhappy yet happy woman. The book has made me think deeply, but to a woman what is the use of thinking deeply. Parts are very clever, parts very natural, & parts so like what one has thought & felt oneself that the book is too interesting to lay aside. His ailment I think was an illregulated mind & temper. His selling his books affected me, & his manner of acting about it was noble. I wd willingly sell my Diamond necklace or any thing that was not like books, meat, drink & raiment, house, wife, children! it is like selling principle, happiness & consolation in all past & future sorrows. The little poem Sir Stratford Canning showed me is the most beautiful & affecting of his compositions "There's not a joy the world can give, like that it takes away."[325] I made many extracts from this book - it amuses me so much.

3rd July [1830]. Yesterday we had a very pretty dinner & very pretty ball at the pretty Mme Falconnet in the pretty villa on the Vomero, & all the very pretty neapolitans came with pretty coiffures. It was hot. I sat next H.E.[Fox?] & we talked of bad Men & good Men, of the evil eye, of diplomacy & insincerity, of wigs & grey hair, of that dear little Ly Canning, of Mosquitoes & Ly Aylmer, of Sinners & Saints, of Ld. Augustus [Hill] & Mr De Ros. He has strong feelings.

4th July [1830]. Today I might add a P.S. to our conversation. I got a seven page letter from Charlotte in wh. she says - That the last scandal is about Ly Mary Hill, who has left her fortune to the Courier to whom she was allied!!!![326] Ld Clanwilliam's modesty for the first time of his

---

325 One of three poems by Lord Byron entitled *Stanzas for Music* begins with this line.

326 Lady Mary Hill, daughter of 2nd Marquis of Downshire, had died on 24 May 1830, aged 33. The courier, Joseph Reitterhoffer, had been in the service of the Dowager Marchioness and her daughter, Lady Mary, since 1821. In 1839, he was to poison himself in Clerkenwell Prison where he had been incarcerated for trying to extort money from the Marquis of Downshire.

life amuses people. He says he dont know what he has done to deserve such happiness as his marriage brings him.[327] Poor Ly Mansfield!

Ly Canning is charming, I am very fond of her. She writes me such a pretty letter. It is evident that her want of courage & her gentleness of disposition unfit her for a London existance & yet she has courage & decision of character to a great extent. All charming people are thrown away in London or Paris. Papa came in from St Michael's & said he had met who, & who was coming! the last man I ever expect to see in these little terrace rooms - Le Noir Fenéant. The mutton eating King.[328]

5 July [1830]. They came & played - Le Noir F. is black & hideous beyond expression. He is full of histories from Sicily wh. is one great Monastery & talks of Monks & Monasteries, M.S.S. cheating & selling out of public libraries. It seems that my *ci-devant* wild Goose, Mr T. Stewart, is in the richest in Europe - where as a penance he was ordered the other day to sweep the Court, & he put the sweepings upon the dinner Table! Mr Fox is very entertaining & clever: look for the secret of his character & conversation & it is this: "All the world are cheats & rascals. I'm a clever man & find them out, & others dont; & to be up to them, one ought to be cheat or rascal too, otherwise one is a Fool!" What escapes women have in life. Why life is one entire escape. I am sometimes bored with Sir Wm Gell's buffoonery. I was this e'g. I was unwell & the Mosquitoes amongst the flowers & orange Trees brought by the Lamp light on the Terrace were insupportable. They are all Ly Aylmers, buzzing & humming without an idea, but now & then a sting.

7th [July 1830]. Last night a gran Gala at S. Carlo, all feathers & turbans, light & show. The Galzerani I am disappointed in.[329] Great sensation was excited by Mr De Ros & his pretty Lady & the black Fox taking the most conspicuous place in the house next to the Spanish Minister & the Count. Till now, no one was *sensé* to know of the connection, & the Lady being dressed plainly in all this finery made it the more conspicuous. He is going to live at the bottom of our garden at

---

[327] Richard Meade, 3rd Earl of Clanwilliam married Lady Elizabeth Herbert, 2nd daur. of the Earl of Pembroke, on 5 July 1830.

[328] Presumably both further nicknames of the Black Fox, i.e. Henry Stephen Fox.

[329] The soprano Antonietta Galzerani sang the title role of Alaide in Bellini's *La Straniera*. The first performance at San Carlo was on 6 July.

Castellamare - to the scandal of many there; a pretty pair he & Le noir feneant are, says Sir H[enry] L[ushington]. I see Mr Hill dont or wont protect him. Mr Hill told me he had a story of him that people of the world dont mind, but I see he does. Georgina says Mr Hill will end in being a Methodist - No, not that, neither.

8th [July 1830]. Sir Henry has been to see the curious Cave at Capri.[330] They lay down in the boat, & were washed into the hole of the Cave by the tide. The inside is all water & a few natural stairs, I understood; overhead Stalactites, & all beautiful blue from the reflection of the water. The Lushingtons are charmed with it, & we talked Ondine & Tritons, & the Tempest - in consequence, we had Tea & the Moon at Mme Dupont's Villa. The Terrace rooms were lighted & the moon rose out of sable clouds surrounding Vesuvius; it was really magnificent to look at. Mr De Ros looked ashamed; his has been the action of a fool & no one wd have interfered with him or his lady, but now *on est tombé en commerage sur son compte*.[331] It is so against the decorum of this place. Mr Greville has fallen in love with Mlle Dalberg & is going home poorly.

Castellamare July 11 [1830]. Quite dying of languor & lassitude & heat, having made the exertion of getting out in the garden at 1/2 7 which I never will do again; if I had courage to get out at sun rise when the sky is one sheet of gold & when the only cloud is one line of white smoke from Vesuvius it might do one good, but I cannot make up my strength to doing as they do here - getting up at five. It is hotter than Naples we think.

George the 4th is dead,[332] & that very day, the Ladies went to see Queen Adelaide, & Wm the 4th appeared in mourning at 12 that day - how disgusting. This will be a fine reign for natural Sons & Daughters - since Charles the 2nd's time they will not have had the like - & here we are again in that same Boccapiano where we were in Sept. 1826.[333] Yesterday I read a paper written then here & it expresses such perfect misery that I felt a pity for my wretched self quite terrible: What a life of struggle mine has been with nerves, feeling, an unsuitable home &

---

330 Although known to the Romans, the 'Blue Grotto' had only recently been rediscovered.

331 'people have started gossiping about him'.

332 He had died on 26 June.

333 Boccapiano - the name of the summer villa in Castellamare rented by the Talbots.

unsuitable situation - but it is over - I have sunk into resignation, indolence & content, & have had much happiness between whiles, but next year changes & misery is again to begin.[334]

14th [July 1830]. Every one is dying of heat but me, who having, according to Wm. the 4th's phrase, nick'd the mosquitoes & left off my last blanket, don't mind anything. I waken every morning at Sunrise; the sky over the plain & Nola is a fine yellow red. Vesuvius is dark coloured with its white smoke & the sea one transparent mirror. I have a mind to keep a poetical journal, by changes in the poetry here & there. Here is Evening:

> Slow sunk the glorious sun, a rosiate light
> Spreads o'er the Mountain from his lingering rays
> The glowing clouds upon Vesuvius side
> Softened in shade ... I could not chuse but gaze
> And now a placid greyness clad the heaven
> Save where the west retained the last red light of even.
> Cool breathed the grateful air & fresher now
> The fragrance of the summer foliage rose
> The passing gale scarce moved the o'erhanging bough
> And not a sound disturb'd the deep repose
> Save where a falling leaf came fluttering by,
> Save the near ocean's wave that murmured quietly
> Is there who has not felt the deep delight,
> The hush of soul that scenes like these impart
> The heart they will not soften is not right.
> But nature's lovers are not hard of heart.[335]

I shall thus begin, & go on to Southey's *Night* & the quiet of still home night & Vesuvius,

> "like the Lava's flood that
> boils in yonder mountain's breast of flame."[336]

---

[334] The plan seems to have been for the Talbots to return permanently to England in 1831. Their departure was postponed by a year.

[335] Essentially derived from Robert Southey's *St Gualberto*, stanzas 36-38 with minor alterations.

[336] Cf. Byron, *The Giaour* : "The cold in clime are cold in blood, Their love can scarce deserve the name; But mine was like the lava flood, That boils in Aetna's breast of flame."

Then sun rise, the night passing off & the fresh breeze, & the work people in the vineyards & then glorious Sun at noon day.

16th [July 1830]. The place is very full. I went out about 7 & met gingham gowns & straw bonnet[s] on donkey back. We are at an average in heat from 80 to 83. At Naples they have been 92. Some parts of the day I feel well particularly after keeping perfectly quiet, but the heat affects the nerves & gives one the restlessness of Bed in a Fever - but the sea to gaze at, & draw the boats on it, is always interesting, & then the G[rea]t storm so soon quelled:

> Then glorious mirror, where the Almighty's form
> Glasses itself in tempest[s]: in all time
> Calm or convuls'd - in breeze or gale or storm
> Ice[d] in the pole, or in the torrid clime
> Dark heaving - boundless, endless & sublime
> The image of eternity - the throne of the Invisible.[337]

We only reckon the heat to have begun the 13th & how much better than cold on a journey.

18th [July 1830]. Mr De Ros is coming here & Mr Fox[338] & Cheyne,[339] the latter they say is a pendant to H. Fox, a copy & I dare say a bad one as all copies generally are, being darker, stronger & tremendous, from the fear of being insipid, or perhaps he is like his name (a tempting one), light & brittle painted, but burnt in, with the mark H.F. Is he French china, or old china, or perhaps a china snuff box mounted in Ormolu or Brass - in short one might be witty upon him for ever & for aye.

Monday E'g [19 July], we went into the Lushingtons. They will be a loss, removing voluntary visits - the only good ones with a Ther. 80.

---

337 Lord Byron, *Childe Harold's Pilgrimage*, Canto 4, Stanza CLXXXIII.

338 Henry Edward Fox (1802-1859) was the son of the third Lord Holland. He lived on the Continent, especially at Rome, for long periods in the 1820s, and took up diplomatic posts in the 1830s which culminated with his appointment as British Minister to Tuscany in 1839. His journal (see Bibliography), contains views, sometimes outspoken or opinionated, of some of the people appearing in M.T.'s Journal.

339 i.e. Edward Cheney. Having misspelt the name, M.T. seems to be playing on the word *chain* (pendant) and *chine* (china).

Ly Acton has a pleasing voice & manner but she is a foreigner & an Acton.[340] She has a dread of having or giving a decided opinion, but she has a little *Moue*[?] way, that I dare say was very engaging when she was young, but there can be neither love or admiration without faith. Give me one whose "thought is speech & speech is truth."[341] Ly Isa. [St John] used to object to Sir Richard Acton for the same reason. We had yes'y a note from Ld. Augustus [Hill], wh. made us ready to cry. He is such an excellent good creature. He is going & it struck us as an eternal action; certainly if he dont return, he will not be long in this world. Notwithstanding his large head & bad looks, he is one for whom one has a real regard. Death is nothing - but disgrace is horrible. So all London knows the secret I have kept here, that Ly Mary Hill has left the 5000£ to the courier to whom she has been married some time. It is such a story for bad people to lay hold of; a saint & a prude, they say!!

How extraordinary are dislikes! I believe instinct tells people of them! Here at Naples are Duponts & Lushing's, De Ros, & Morier, Byrne's & Lushing's, Mme Falconnet & Sir R. A[cton] & Sir Wm Gell, all disliking & hating & ridiculing each other for nonsense, yet seizing on the very bad specks in each others characters. [T]here is an english frigate here & Sir Rt. Spencer going to take Ld Clare & his disagreeable stare to Bombay.[342] I wish I was going, not *with* him. I fear my load star don't point *home* & yet I love some people there: Charlotte, Ly Belhaven, & Ly Canning & with faith, wh. is more than I do of the *buona gente* at Naples. Ly Belhaven says that people grew very impatient at George the 4th lingering. 'Enfin si le Roi ne se decide pas,'[343] the French Milliner said, 'we shall be ruined.' Mr Morier comes in here most Evenings. He is a nice pleasing person full of information. He was telling us stories of a Capt. Roberts who is here, a sort of wild Man who looks like the King of Bavaria & lives in his Yaught, wh. was Ld Byrons, & consorts with all the wild & wilful like Leigh Hunt

---

[340] In 1800, after Papal dispensation, the 13 year old Mary Ann Acton (1786-1873) had married her 63 year old uncle, Sir John Acton.

[341] Sir Walter Scott, *Marmion*, Canto 2.

[342] Lord Clare (1792-1851) had been appointed Governor of Bombay earlier in the year. Sir Robert Spencer (1791-1830) was captain of the *Madagascar*. He died off Alexandria on 4 November 1830.

[343] 'If the King does not make up his mind....'

& Trelawny &c.[344] He was talking over Mr De Ros last night, that lucky man, a killer of ladies & the top of fashion in Eng'd - & of him as a detestible character. His fortune he has made by lucky hits upon the young & the unlucky & the inexperienced & the rich; as to wit, he is not to be named with Ld Alvanley or many others. The best of him I think is a certain Fitzgerald softness of manner. The real deceiver is him who seems to trust you & he dont. Let me see who has that manner: Mr Cradock,[345] Spencer, & Ld Stuart has often a great deal of that openness. Those curious females Miss Byrnes are here. They have the Moon & make the most of it: & twirl & twist their eyes in extasies: & that vulgar Mrs Webster they have with them.

Politics from Eng'd. Queen Adelaide has begun her reign with a golden reputation as Ld Newark would say. Ly Cassillis & the D'esse of Gordon[346] will be excellent real Ladies for her with such an eye to the main chance as will make chance certainty. The Duke of Gordon is to be first fidget to the King. The whigs, they say, cannot come in. One has tied himself to another. Another wants a place for a friend & another can't come in without a pension for his wife's Maid. Lady Holland they fear, & so are afraid of Ld Holland! Sir Edward Codrington to be Ld. Allimore[?] it is said.[347]

21st July [1830]. Got up at 1/2 3, walked two hours about my room watching the Sun rise; went out. The Ther'r fell from 80 to 75. It grew hot at 1/2 6. Was sleepy all day. Sir Wm Gell came to us. We passed the E'g at Lushington House.

22nd July [1830]. A good story of the black Fox: he was taken to a spunginghouse[348] & Mr De Ros sent & paid his debts & went to him.

---

[344] Former members of the Byron circle. Edward John Trelawny had arranged for Captain Daniel Roberts R.N. to supervise the building of Byron's yacht, the *Bolivar*, in 1822.

[345] Presumably John Hobart Cradock (1799-1873).

[346] Margaret Erskine (c.1772-1848) had married Archibald Kennedy, eleventh Earl of Cassilis on 1 June 1793; Elizabeth Brodie (1794-1864) had married George Gordon, the fifth Duke (1770-1836) on 11 December 1813.

[347] Sir Edward Codrington had been commander of the British fleet in the Mediterranean at the time of the controversial Battle of Navarino (1827). He was recalled in 1828. The advancement intimated here did not take place.

[348] A house, often owned by a bailiff, where debtors would be held for 24 hours prior to being incarcerated to allow friends to pay their debts. Accommodation charges were extortionate - hence the term 'spunging'.

Mr Fox said to him: "There's another man taken up - let's send to him & have a game at whist." Now said De Ros: "That was not quite my wish, for I reflected that a Man taken up for debt was not likely to have any money." Sir Wm [Gell] talks of Mr De Ros as a most honorable Man. What is an honorable Man, I can't guess. He says he plays & pays & is as cool as possible in all his proceedings, follows up his luck if good, deserts it, if bad. Mr Morier speaks differently - as to his making dupes. H. Fox says he wd not be left alone with his cousin; they say he wd murder him & have the Title & no money. They all hate him because he is mischivous, a mimic & is in correspondence with eight ladies, received 8 & writes 8 letters frequently & shows them all up.

Sir Wm Gell had a curious letter from Tom Steward out of his Convent, very mad & signed The Monk. Theresa Villiers marries the author of *Granby* - poor Man!![349]

23rd July [1830]. I had a curious breakfast with my Old Philosopher.[350] He was describing the effect the variety of women's conversation has on clever men - the way he began was that he would rather sit down to dinner with Andreo del Sarno, the cicerone at Pompeii, or any one out of the failed who knew their profession, than with Camposuele[351] or a man who knew nothing. We likened Camposuele to a cake with sugar on it or trifle - upon which I said how can you bear the company of women who know nothing, the most learned knowing less than a man of moderate education. He said women were so quick they were always amusing & the variety had such a charm. We talked of this sad business of Ly M. Hill, this sinking of birth & pride, this lowering of womankind. He thought a red waistcoat & gold lace were irresistible to females. To the Maids, I said, - but *not* to Ladies, & that if the Apollo of Belvidere was a Courier, he would cease to be a Gentleman. He said, Ld Erskine asked him, "You, Sir Wm Gell, who are a man of the world, did you ever see any thing between the Queen & Bergami to lead you to think he was any thing more than the Courier.[352] Sir Wm said he had only heard the Queen order the

---

[349] Maria Theresa Villiers (1802-1865) married Thomas Henry Lister (1800-1842) on 6 November 1830.

[350] i.e. Sir William Gell.

[351] Probably a member of the family of Vera d'Aragona, Prince of Caposele.

[352] The nature of the relationship between Queen Caroline and her courier, Bartolomeo Bergami, was central to the court case against her in 1820.

posthorses & the carriage. He wrote a Letter to Eng'd to he does not know who about it, and then gave it to me - high fun to us - having repeated some lines from Metastasio & saying Ly Downshire[353] & her daughter [Lady Mary Hill] have been long addicted to spirituous liquers. All this is very amusing but I am sorry to say that my knowledge of human nature makes me know that morality without pride will do little for women & that preaching humility to women is a bad thing for them.

24th [July 1830]. We had last night a very entertaining E'g. Mr Fox, Mr Cheyney, the Moriers & Sir Wm. Gell. They were very witty. He [i.e. Henry Edward Fox] mimics Ly Haddington in an wonderful way, Mr Rogers, the duke of Devonshire. He envies me a gift from Ly Haddington. He looks so ill that without any poisoning his black cousin [i.e. Henry Stephen Fox] has a good chance.[354] Sir Wm told us Berkeley Craven's speech to his Mother.[355] K[eppel] Craven never comes out but for the pleasure of going home & never asks anyone but for the pleasure of getting rid of them.

A visit to Mrs Talbot. Mr T.'s apparition in a yellow & red dressing gown looking thro' the door at Sunset. Sir H. L[ushington]'s miseries about Mrs Kidd[356] whose school for scandal he is applied to to clear up. The Nobleman who took away her character so incensed Mr Kidd that he wrote the sillyest of Letters to Mr Hill.

Sunday, 1st Aug't [1830]. I have been two days in bed with I believe a bilious Fever with the window open & had just enough life from sleep & faintness to tell Georgina that my will was in the black book: I felt as if I was sinking out of life. I often think that this year is to be the last of my life, that I may die, & that is maybe a good thing for me & mine - perhaps.

Today I am better. Papa who is a little ill but can't doctor himself sent for 5 Napoleon's worth of Roskilly who found me well, but so weak &

---

[353] The 2nd Marquess of Downshire had died in 1801. In the 1820s, his widow had spent much time on the Continent with her younger daughter, Lady Mary Hill.

[354] To succeed Henry Edward Fox's father to become fourth Lord Holland. In fact, Henry Edward outlived his cousin by more than a decade.

[355] Henry Augustus Berkeley Craven (1776-1836) was the brother of Keppel Craven.

[356] M.T. could be referring to Mrs Kelly, see above, but there was a Mrs Kidd resident in Naples at this time.

bilious I can hardly turn in bed. A Ther. of 82, at Naples of 92, has made this complaint the fashion. Sir Wm Gell is going & takes Haji Baba with him. The King of Naples landed yes'y.[357] The people were ordered to rejoice but would not. The King is definitely[?] changed. The Queen fatter than ever & she desired nothing might be said of the Travels as the King attributed his present state to them. The duke of Calabria looked more cross than usual it was remarked. The bombast of the Gazette is excellent - it seems some one in the mob cried out it was not worth three millions to look so ill. Medici was disgraced before he died, for his dispatches from Pr'ce Metternich were opened & he writes to Medici: I pity you knowing to what a bigot & stupid man you have to say all this.

Papa saw the Dey of Algiers yesterday in a french ship in Harbor.[358] He has 59 women & suite & money. His vessel is surrounded with boats & when they go off, he appears. He is a fat Man with a sallow complexion, grey hair & wears a Turban. By this time, it is Dey & Martin, for he goes to the Vittoria.[359] When Lord Guildford went to the Dey, he asked to see the appartments & not the Ladies. The Dey said he was so ugly he might see them all if he liked.

William the 4th has taken the line of popularity. His kind & amiable letters, his reading for & promoting all his children, his keeping the D. of Wellington, his sending his french cooks away, his extraordinary affectation of cordiality & bonhomie have been hitherto his part. They say if there is etiquette, it will [be] the Queen's doing who as a German likes it. The King says that the only person he will dine with is the D. of Wellington, but Holland House not being in London, he will go there. How well I remember Ly Hollands impertinence to his daughter pretending when her son asked leave to marry not to know the existance of Miss Fitzclarence, & some one coming from the wedding to our Opera box & saying her present to Mrs Ch's Fox was a

---

[357] After his ten month absence in France and Spain.

[358] On 5 July 1830, Algiers had capitulated to the invading French. The Dey of Algiers was sent into exile and had arrived at Naples with his suite on 31 July.

[359] *Day and Martin* was the name of a well-known blacking warehouse in Holborn. One traveller of the time wrote: 'You will smile when I tell you that nothing English is to be seen about the Neapolitan shops but "*Day and Martin's Blacking*", a commodity which, I am told, is exposed for sale in every city, town and village in Italy.' (Malcolm, *Letters of an Invalid*, p.20). The *Vittoria* was one of the best hotels in Naples.

silver Papboat, saying she wished to give her some thing useful.[360] George the 4th's memory is vilified by one party & cried up by another. Be kind to poor Nell is echoed thro' all the papers.[361]

Sir Wm Gell has been very pleasant; his ideas of right & wrong are a little zig-zag & he & I had a warm argument for a Ther. at 82 on the fashion & *ton* of the Miss Berry's wh. I denied, & on the morality of gamblers wh. I afermed existed. He says that there is no distinction of morality amongst Gamblers - I say that there is & that the gentleman-like gambler who loses, pays & goes to Van Demans Land, [*c. 5 words crossed out*] or is ruined & leaves off play, is better than several others that may be named. I did not choose to bring forward two neighbourly examples - of the Man who dupes the dupe & the other of whom I heard it said: "You know he can't be trusted for they all know he wd sell his dispatches for a thousand pounds."[362] Sir Wm Gell thinks them all the same, once a Gambler, & their honor, that is their word, is nothing.

3rd [August 1830]. What a sunny person is Mrs L. Brook, gay & good humoured. Poor Mrs Talbot has made a bad job of her marriage - she is so happy & important about trifles, but she walks about the woods here alone & will meet with something disagreeable. How all people whose character is doubtful hold tenaciously to character. They are all in the high road to quarels at Naples. Mr Blue Fox told Mr Black Fox that I said he was a Rinoceros - untrue - but Mr Morier was asking me what he was like & I described him, adding & just now he is like Nebuchadnezar, for he has been grazing in the fields, & Mr Fox['s] Tiger Cheyney heard this & repeated it thus - where one gets with these London people - God help one! This little clever spirit of Mischief is the terror of all. He looks very ill & as if his cousin might be Ld Holland. All the little crooked women & tall young Men complain of him from Mr Dundas, 6 feet 2 - 2 feet 6. Mr D. is supposed to have left Rome like the lyon tiezed by the little dog. We never had all this nonsense at Naples, silly twaddle fit for fools or servants' hall &

---

[360] On 19 June 1824, Charles Richard Fox (1796-1873) had married Mary Fitzclarence (1798-1864), daughter of the Duke of Clarence (the future King William IV) and his mistress Dorothy Jordan. A 'pap-boat' is a boat-shaped vessel used for feeding infants.

[361] Presumably reflecting the words attributed to Charles II on his death-bed: 'Let not poor Nelly starve', asking his successor to care for his mistress, Nell Gwyn.

[362] Henry Stephen Fox - see above, entry for 19 January 1830.

house keeper's room. 'This filching from me my good name.'[363] Mr de Ros said, 'I know his opinion of me, for here is a letter sent back from Eng'd with it!'

What is a good education? Ly M. Deerhurst is not of a giving turn they say, nor cares that her Daughter sd be so. When Miss Coventry[364] is with Sir W. G[ell], she writes for Money for the beggars, but she said, "I can't get it but will put down the money as Pins & needles & threads & tapes to Mama."

4th [August 1830]. P'ce Dentice came to play at Whist here. He says 'Le roi vient demain peutetre pour mourir - c'est un balon avec un Chapeau sur la tête!'[365] Life is now a *Conte des Fées*. Here is the Dey of Algiers at the Vittoria with his 22 wives. The Ladies are veiled & put up blankets against the key holes to prevent Europeans peering into private life in Africa. They are said to be ugly. Their feast is rice, into wh. a sheep's head is cut off & they dip their fingers into its blood. Did one ever hear anything so disgusting! The Dey speaks Turkish & Arabic. His suite is 109 persons & we are told he is thinking of being our next neighbour for next winter - only Pr'ce Paterno's house has no Garden for his wives - we shall want another Haji Baba. Another *Conte des Fées* is that from France - Charles X at 73 proves himself a despot, & a Bourbon, & a fool. Noel Hill is making Frankenstein at the top of the Belvidere; he will not see thing or person. The Moon is glorious. I like Mr Morier, he is so even & quiet in this hot weather; Mrs's Morier, Parker & Shiffner[366] are too much of a boarding school. I finished my 24 hours & dispatched it to Charlotte. Ly Acton has a pleasing manner, a mixture half shy, half quiet, with that low & honey'd tone which is false & pretty. I see she is all for a *tête a tête* when she is neither shy or melancholy. When we talked to her about her youthful looks, she told us that when she first went to Eng'd, they used to call her & her son, Sir Rd & Ly Acton, thinking he has married an old woman, & Sir Rd looked with great anger on her. She said our society here is very stupid being wholly husbands & wives, wh. society, while without being immoral, stupid people make worse. Here some are afraid of each other, others sit looking at each other knowing

---

[363] Cf. *Othello*, Act III, Sc.3.

[364] The daughter of Lady Mary Deerhurst. (See note 196).

[365] 'Perhaps the King comes tomorrow to die - he's a balloon with a hat on his head.'

[366] Harriet Brooke had married Robert Townley Parker in 1816. Her sister Emily had married Captain Henry Shiffner R.N., in 1825.

all that the other can say, others stupified. Married people ought to go different way[s] I think & brighten up each others fireside by variety.

11th Aug't [1830]. Our newspapers are stopped & we are miserable for want of news. Report or rather courier says that the Tuilleries are one scene of bloodshed, that the King & his family are gone to London. Mr Hill has had no papers.

12th [August 1830]. Last night we heard wonders. Ch's 10 & the Duc d'Angouleme[367] have taken refuge at St Cloud. The Duc de Bordeaux under the Duc d'Orleans is on the throne, 17,000 are killed, the Swiss cut to pieces, P'ce Polignac's house sacked ... if Austria or Eng'd meddle, adieu to peace they say. Read yesterday Mr Fox's speech relative to La Fayette in 1796,[368] the same who is now forward in the cause of liberty. Wrote to & heard from Sir W. Gell. When the Dey heard of the proceedings in France, he said, in the Turkish style, God is just. The King of Naples fainted away on getting the accounts. Several persons, for merely whispering the news, have been sent to prison, & Papa meeting the Duc de Cajanello,[369] said in French that the donkey boys might not hear, that 17,000 had been killed. He looked round very uneasily, & said "Il faut avouer que ce chemin est changé pour le mieux,"[370] so terrified was he. I got up at 1/2 six to draw. At 7 it was too hot & I met the princes coming home on donkeys.

Aug. 14th [1830]. At last the newspapers are come & have made us sick & sorry at the numbers who have fallen a sacrifice for Ch's 10 who neither knows his own interest or glory or that of his subjects. It appears that the *Liberaux* have all behaved well. Amongst the distinguished Deputies are C'te de Laborde & B. Constant. It is thought that the D. of Orleans with his family will be satisfied. To P'ce Polignac, every crime past, present & to come is set down.

We rode to Posano. I dislike a woman having *le ton aigre* or speaking loud. How we shall scream next year what with Mrs L[angford] B[rooke] & Ly Isabella. What a life of toil & trouble is that vocation

---

[367] The Duc d'Angoulême, the son of Charles X.

[368] Speech 'on the conduct of the war with France', 10 May 1796. (See *The Speeches of the Right Honourable Charles James Fox*, London, 1815, Vol.VI, pp.191-2).

[369] Don Pasquale del Pezzo, 6th Duke of Caianello (1809-1884).

[370] 'One must admit, this road has been improved.'

of mother. Mrs Parker is an excellent good person & that little Ouisa oussy[371] is a beauty & knows it. Mr L[angford] B[rooke] is a silly Man & dont know it; she is bannale, too universal in manner to gratify me by being liked by her.

15th [August 1830]. The name of Polignac has twice made the misfortunes of France. They say that his only talent is obstinacy. This revolution is an exact copy of the English Revolution having the same interval of years between Charles 1st & King William, & the Orleans branch will triumph as the Orange branch did. The english women are like fools wearing the tri-coloured cockade, & it is to be feared Austria will intrigue to bring us into a war & we shall have it for our lives. The next great people will be the Americans, who like Scotchmen, each understands his affairs.

17th Aug't [1830]. I have been very ill in bed for 24 hours. Things are quiet at Paris. The promenades & shops opened. The last accounts are that Ch's 10 & his 150 carriages are at Rambou[i]llet. The Duc d'Orleans harranging the *chambres* & announcing the abdication of Ch's 10 in favor of the Duc de Bourdeaux, *déposé dans les archieves de l'empire* - Marmonts his'y is a most melancholy one.[372] The last Courier had great difficulty in making these events understood by the papal govern't & M. de La Passe wd. not understand it till M. de Beugnoit came to fetch M. de la Ferronaye[373] to his Ambassade.

18th [August 1830]. Last night we were all here crushed by the news. That the folly of one Man sd have lost France to the Bourbons, & in one week turned it into a republic & been the cause of the loss of life & ruin of fortune of thousands!!! Paris is like a Town after a seige. The Str[eet]s have hardly a stone left, as the people carried them up to

---

[371] The Parkers had a five year old daughter, Louisa Lucy.

[372] Auguste Marmont, Duc de Raguse, had been a marshal under Napoleon, but had not supported him during the Hundred Days. As a result he was taken into service by the Bourbons. In 1830, he had the misfortune to be Major General of the Royal Guard and forced, against his better judgement, to open fire against his fellow-citizens seeking to oust Charles X. The rest of his life was spent in exile.

[373] Auguste, Comte de la Ferronays (1777-1842), former French ambassador in St Petersburg and briefly Minister of Foreign Affairs in Paris, had been appointed ambassador to Rome in 1830. He and his family had moved to Naples for the summer at the beginning of July and thus found themselves there when Louis Philippe seized power in Paris. They subsequently settled in Naples, occupying a villa on the Chiaia. In 1802 he had married Comtesse Albertine de Sourches de Montsoreau (1782-1848).

the roofs of the houses to hurl down upon those under - we shall have a War & go to England where some will sheet up the wings of their houses & live in a corner over their solitary fire & expecting the Mob in the snow to arrive from the next county town while others will shiver in a Parlour at Brighton while the wind blows up the carpet, & thro' the blinds they will see the gay bonnets of those who have risen on the debries of their fortune, Mrs & Miss some one, who take their place in the world. I think it is La Bruyère who says "Comme un moment change la disposition de notre ame."

Good news, it is all calm & peace, le Duc d'Orleans is Philippe 7.[374] The poor old King who has united the folly of 12 years old & the twaddling of 80 is forced to leave France. The Angouleme Duke & D'chess & the D'chess de Berry are coming to Naples & so is Gl Boumond.[375]

20th [August 1830]. Our society is *borné* but unworldly, my boarding school, at the age of discretion - the women pert for wit & smart for elegance - I except from this bad character Mr Morier who has an eastern calm & placidity of mind, I was going to say, but who knows man's mind; it may be

"like the lava flood
That boils in yonder mountains breast of flame."[376]

A calm manner in all societies, & seasons, is desirable & gives an aplomb upon wh. the other qualities may be made. It is an advantage to a silly man, & a greater advantage to a clever man. For hours I have seen Mr Morier what people would call very dull & did call so from absence or indolence or something that wears off. His wife is an enigma I can't understand. She is not quite a fool, but caprice & irritation she has enough [of] to kill anyone tied to her for life.

I have two charming letters from Sir William [Gell] full of news & nonsense & my answers being about Mrs H[?] I have kept. I have a

---

[374] The previous King Philippe, Philippe VI, had reigned in France between 1328 and 1350.

[375] Comte Louis de Bourmont (1773-1846) had had a colourful military career. His anti-Republican stance had brought him back into favour during the Restoration and he had played an important part in the capture of Algiers.

[376] cf. Lord Byron, *The Giaour*: 'like a lava flood that boils in Aetna's breast of flame.'

Letter from Maria Lushington who is passing her E'gs with the diplomates at Naples. What with the heat & the French revolution, they are all as bilious as possible. They give out all the jacobinical reports & Philippe 7 kills them with his constitution. Gl Toledo looks as if Spain was already in revolt.

21st [August 1830]. Here Vesuvius has smoke & flame.

> Deep thro' the sky the hollow thunders roll'd
> The storm hath ceased, but still the lava tides
> Roll down the mountain-side in streams of fire
> Down to the sea, they roll, & yet roll on,
> All burning thro' the waters. (Southey)[377]

Sunday Augt 29 [1830]. I have not written. I have been dismally, dismally out of spirits. The present has kill'd me with vexation, a subject I can't write upon, & black prospects of the future hover round a diseased & distempered spirit - enough - Tomorrow we are going a grand party to the Camaldoli della Torre.

30th[31st] Aug't [1830]. Yesterday we went to the number of 14, a picnic from Castellamare to the Camaldoli below Vesuvius. We left our house at 1/2 2 in broiling heat & leaving the high road wound up a romantic lava stony Lane edged with Aloes to the wood of vines & stone Pine & oak, where we left the carriages & walked up boldly & rang at the Convent Gate. A Monk looked thro' the barrs of a little loup-hole & stormed at us as excommunicated persons for having dared pass the Convent Cross, & sent us down the hill. After walking about we settled ourselves at the edge of the woods & the Servants got Tables & chairs & laid the dinner there in sight of the Convent while the Sun was setting - & the Monks brought Wine out from the convent & assisted in spreading out the *recherché* french dinner; it was an odd scene altogether with the Monks, & the Chasseurs, & the Servants & the Lazzaroni bringing all the Ice from the plain. The dress of these Monks is particularly picturesque, long white flowing robes, with cowls, & long beards, & a black leathern belt. At dinner several of them came out to look at it & the more pious (*Padri chiusi*) peeped at us from over the Garden wall of the Convent. I was struck with their honest open expression of countenance. Mr Morier made some

[377] Southey, Robert, *Madoc in Aztlan*, 5, *War denounced*, Verse XXVII, ll.1-4, London, 1812 (3rd edition).

sketches of them while we were sitting at dinner, & the Moon rose & Vesuvius burned a bright flame, directly above our heads. The views of the bay of Naples are enchanting from this Monastery. I made many sketches for drawings while Sir Wm Gell was in high grace talking to the Monks & the donkey boys & doing the popular which he loves. The day must have been an event to the Monks of the 14 english eating the french dinner by moonlight close to the Convent cross. Their fine countenances struck me as extraordinary: are bigotry, & disappointment, calculated to give this fine open handsome expression?? - but it is the Monks in solitary spots only that have these good countenances. I don't think that the party was a particularly agreeable one, but I was low & out of spirits & ill calculated to enjoy a species of scenery while I saw no one but myself entered into or cared for - I believe I am growing very cross, very *mausade*, very reflective - but really my reflections lately on the present & future have soured me, I suppose, & I think the event of the day was the ice having been carried to the Custom house - wh. next day the Duke of Calabria was told of. Our drive home by Moon light was too enchanting & fresh.

3rd Sept. [1830]. Last night we had a pleasant evening. We rode up to Monte Coppola & met a large party of Italians & admired the scenery & returned by bright full moonlight to drink tea with Mrs Parker; saw the Eclipse from her Terrace at 1/2 9. It became total in about one hour, but never was what I call total, as the Eclipse was only like a black crape drawn over the Moon, & seen distinctly through it. Mr Morier was describing to us an eclipse of the Sun at Mexico & that the magnificence & splendour of it is beyond anything in Europe.

4th [Sept. 1830]. What a scrambling walk we had last night & what a fresh beautiful ride home: & how all the women screamed & roared, & how all the Men were astonished at us for enjoying these scrambling stoney ways in these hottest of times. Mr Morier says very funny things sometimes; one knows him to be clever from his books, & his character, his placid calm manner & smooth forehead make you suppose him steady & good-humoured, but I fancy it is all a mistake - & that he is *très leger*, *volage*, & *ennuyé*, & tho' he wd not do a bad action, he is by far the worst husband I know. Then he is bored to death, but I wd not be his wife for a good deal. He likes the book that he is now engaged in - it is full of Love & Murder, but he talks of the usual difficulty of getting the people off their knees. I wanted him to write on an English subject, but he is more at home in Persia. I think [378]an eastern love tale flat,

"A persian heaven is easyly made.
It's all black eyes & lemonade,[379]

dull to read of, & I am convinced that in romantic countries, romantic from beauty, climate & poverty, romance exists not. It certainly does not on the shores of the Mediteranean.

5th Sept.[1830]. Yesterday was the most tremendous Sirocco I ever felt, & last night was the most tremendous storm of Thunder & lightning I ever saw, or heard, or fancied. The blue lightning only ceased as the shutting of an eye lid that winks & a thunder bolt fell in the plain below.

We had a Party at Tea. I feel solemn - my moral not my phisical death takes place in 8 months, must & will. - "I cannot fly from fate, And fate will find me there."[380] I look to nothing for the rest of my days but breathing fresh air, reading, & writing - meantime, I dont much like people here except Haji Baba. The Miss Byrnes who are comical Ladies say Mrs Morier "lives in a beautiful cage with a Persian Bird to sing to her!" I suspect that she has but little of his singing. I have read much lately. Mr Talbot lent me his translation of *Wm Tell*. It has all the spirit of an original & makes one feel in Switzerland. I have read *Vivian Grey*[381] in 5 vols. - it is as clever as at the first reading; Hume's *Hist. of Eng'd since the reign of Henry 7*, Massillon, & Chalmers, the most eloquent & superb of Preachers - but to Politics, all gives way now - a revolutionary spirit creeps in every where, & one now begun in Belgium. Barbanera[382] has been curious this year. Everything he foretold has come to pass: Algiers & the F. Revolution, & he foretells an Earthquake & the death of a King in Oct.! The Hereditary Prince is said to be a Nero in disposition, a Coward, & a Tyrant tyranical to the Army, & governed by priests. His education has been a curious one; he hates women; he never heard of Benjamin Constant or La Fayette,

---

[378] *Zohrab, the hostage*, published in 1832.

[379] "A Persian's Heaven is easily made, 'Tis but black eyes and Lemonade." Thomas Moore, Letter VI in *Intercepted Letters*.

[380] Cf. Robert Southey, *The Curse of Kehama*, XIII, The Retreat, v.3, l.22.

[381] The first novel of Benjamim Disraeli, published in 1826.

[382] Long-running Italian almanac first produced in the 1760s.

& consequently had never read the French revolution; a grandson of Ferdinand who said Louis 16 was the only instance of a King who had been beheaded. The stories against the P'ce makes one wish his father to live - as it is reported that the P'ce proposed in council sending the suspicious to Ponza.[383] The King said that would not do. The Prisons are overflowing from those confined for giving political opinions.

9th Sept.[1830]. It seems that all the Elements are let loose & all ties, of blood, civil & religious, are to be broken. Today there was for one hour such a hurricane as I have seldom heard: the house rocked, the trees bent down, the waves rose, the rain descended, the thunder roared, the lightning played, the bells rang to Prayers.

Charles the 10th is in Eng'd. He says, were he to act again, he wd do the same he has, being determined to preserve the patrimony of his fathers as he received it. This is very obstinate or very heroic. He considers himself Saint & Martyr. M. de Montesquiou,[384] the Minister from *Le Roi Citoyen* is at Naples, but not yet received. Austria & Russia don't acknowledge him. Kiel & M de Menz[385] in a fuss.

17 Sept.[1830]. Today I passed a day to my liking. I wanted such a day. At nine o'clock we walked down to the Marina & went by water to Vico - the sea was smooth & beautiful & the day not too hot. The Marina there is very striking in its scenery. We clambered up to the Filangeri Villa situated upon a bold eminence that rises abruptly from the Sea. It is a strange sort of Italian house, half picturesque, half formal & fast going to ruin. P'ce Satriano's Father, Gaetano Filang[i]eri lived here as that uncommon character in Italy, a Philosopher. He was born in 1752 & at 30 year[s] old, he wrote his famous book *La Scienza delle Legislazione*.[386] He died in 1788. Ferdinand honoured him in his life time & regretted his death, & his children were educated at the expense of the King. They say that like his Son, he was so graceful & handsome that at the Court of Naples his philosophy was forgiven

---

[383] Island in the Mediterranean situated some 30 kilometres west of Naples.

[384] Anatole de Montesquiou (1788-1878), a veteran of the Napoleonic wars, had subsequently found favour with the family of Orleans. In 1830, he was sent by Louis Philippe to negotiate recognition of the new French government from Rome and from the court of Naples, a mission he successfully accomplished.

[385] Karl v. Menz, Austrian diplomat based in Naples from 1812.

[386] The work had been published volume by volume in the 1780s and subsequently translated into French and German.The villa in Vico belonged to his sister..

him, which was extraordinary as he acted up to the sentiments in his writings, & his abhorrence of spiritual abuses stopped short of irreligion. Vico reminded me of the scenes in the *Promessi sposi* as also in ajoining villages: graceful nooks in rocky scenery, narrow pathways & frequent openings to distant sea views. The Town was founded by Ch's 2, King of Naples in 1300, & there are several Martello Towers, formerly erected to give notice of the approach of Pirates who used to infest this coast; & latterly the French, when they occupied Vico & Sorrento in 1799, had Forts constructed to prevent any communication between the discontented & the English Fleet whose ships were ever hovering near these shores. We went upon Donkeys up to the suppressed Convent of Camaldoli, now called the Trinità which now belongs to a rich agriculturist. It is most picturesque & the vineyards are in good order, but in the olden time, when its gardens & cloysters were filled with Monks, it must have been one of the finest Camaldoli in Italy. I think it was suppressed by the French in 1799. Monks chuse glorious situations for their abodes, & this one of the most magnificent in this country, commanding extensive views both of the bays of Salerno & Naples. The great Gates of the Convent are left - but open. The bell is there, & opposite the entrance is the ruin'd Church, now a receptacle for straw & hay. All around are vineyards & a pretty garden neatly kept edged with roses & pinks. From this spot, looking back thro' the great gates, is a very uncommon & beautiful view of the Sea, Naples, Vico, & the whole vale of churches, convents & farmhouses. Over the Church door still remains the inscription on white Marble in a black Marble frame work. It is as follows[387]:

D. O. M.
CÆSARI ZAFFARANO
SICVLO V.I.D.
FUNDATORI
A.D. MDCIV

Behind the church is the Convent of pretty low architecture. There is before it a picturesque old well surrounded by very aged olive trees, & all the Cloysters have been converted into Pergola - & having now grapes in heavy massive bunches pendant from the interlaced canopy.

---

[387] On the left, M.T.'s transcription from the possibly foliage-covered church, subsequently demolished; on the right, the text as recently transcribed from the stone now in the office of the Villa Giusso, the current secular name of the former convent.

We staid some hours to make Sketches. I was thinking that, for a Philosopher, retirement from the world with books would not be so bad a thing for the little remnant of a not prosperous life. Here with agriculture & nature, one might be happy. We left it at 3 & we[nt] down to some old houses where my eye had been taken by seeing some girls & children at work at the silk. I regretted that I cd not draw figures, & then lower down, we stopped to draw San Giovanni, at Fornacello, a beautiful ruined Chapel surrounded by fine old Olive trees & backed by noble rocky mountains of grey, well wooded here & there. We rode & walked & scrambled thro' Mountain & rock home to Castellamare, stopping for the fourth time in my life at San Francesco. With how many different feelings have I walked in that silent solitary Avenue. The place is lonely & melancholy & as if murder had been committed near it. I liked this day. The fatigue of body wh. is extreame does me good & occupies me. The beautiful views of nature distract my thoughts from myself & from people: the bright Sun & the perfume of herbs & myrtles makes me pleased & good humoured & so I go to bed for the first time these ten days without a heart heavy as lead, & eyes sore with weeping.

Sunday Sept. 26 [1830]. How I like a journey *senza suggezzioni*, without carriage or servants to plague one, without the necessaries of life, no Townliness about one, without one's dressing box, or gold boxes, or bracelets, but with what you want carried on a mule's back, getting up, walking, drawing, riding, talking, eating & drinking, just as one pleases. This is the way to see country comfortably - so we three, taking only old cross Carlo to scold the people, went out on Donkeys at 8 o'clock on Friday Morn'g - we wound & wound up a horrid bad road into the woods to Agerola: it was very fatiguing & the only good part of it was the chestnut wood that kept the heat of the Sun from us, but it was very different from that *riante* succession of villages & vineyards that we had passed on the Nocera road two years ago. We arrived at the top of the mountain very completely tired - & there an extraordinary view surprised us. The height was so great over the Sea, it was painful to look down - all the bays & creeks, & the Tre Gali were like three pots.[388] The country was like that in the environs of Genoa: Carouby & Olive Trees & Oak woods; white villages & terrace gardens built in the boldest & most rugged situations; Convents & Old Towns, & Castles in ruins on every promontory. The Men seemed very expert as Guides or carrying the Portantina in wh. was

---

[388] Three small islands called *Li Galli*.

Georgina. They put the poles on their shoulders & step[ped] securely from rock to rock with a firm footing as if it was flat ground. I chose to walk & consequently arrived half dead at Amalfi & went to bed at 7 o'clock.

Seeing the Monastery of Conca to the right, on a promontory over the Mediteranean, the grandest species of scenery imaginable, we made a great detour to go there; but it looks better at a distance than nearer. It is a large white building built on a perpendicular rock rising abruptly from the Sea & all the rocky ground near is covered with enormous plants of the Indian Fig & others equally grand & magnificent. On the inland side of the Convent is a rocky mountain that seems lost in the Clouds. We scrambled up to the monastery divided from where we were stopping to draw by several ravines; it was two o'clock when we reached the Court Yard. All the nuns were asleep, as three old women, who were spinning like the Fates on the steps of the church, made us comprehend in the Italian way by putting their heads on their arms to show us how they slept. So we walked into the Chapel & out again & came away passing village after village & stone stair case & gardens & chapel, & stopping to draw a curious Greek Tower, as they call it there - & at four we got to Amalfi half dead with fatigue & heat.

The Cappuchin Convent is now an Inn & tho' a straggling place is clean & comfortable in fine weather. After dinner we looked over the convent & then went to bed. Two of the Cells were laid into one room which Georgina & I occupied. The ceiling was vaulted & the windows opened to a view of Amalfi & the sea & a distant one of Paestum & a nearer view of Saracenic Mosques & ruined Castles. The great fatigue I had gone thro' kept me awake but just when I was trying to sleep, groans disturbed me of one in violent pain & for some hours we were very anxious about Papa who was suffering from cramp. However, next day he was well, but not able to go thro' any more walking. Georgina & I went in Portantina attended by Carlo to the Torre di Minori, to draw it. It is one of the most beautiful of the Towers on the Coast, after which we returned back into the Town to the Cathedral where I saw the same beautiful woman with her black eyes & black veil saying her prayers that we saw there in 1828 & very little changed; Donna Maria de Ponza, I shall not forget. The Cathedral is very old. I sd say the architecture [is] of the date of that of St Marks at Venice, a guess only of mine. The view from the steps is a curious one thro' the arches & little Pillars of the entrance. It look[s] down the steps to an Old Fountain & a picturesque & busy population & beyond such odd strange houses & buildings & gardens, such convents with latticed tops, such saracenic remains of mosques, such terraces for oranges & lemons, that the whole looks to me more eastern than european, or moorish or spanish rather. A Town without a road to it or through it, is alone a curiosity in the 19th century, & most of the houses can be approached only by steps in the rocks. Amalfi has inspired several Poets, & Mr Rogers & Mr Sotherby's Lines tho' pretty do it not justice.[389] There sd have been a Ld Byron, as it demands the Language of passion, not of praise. We went into the Val d'Amalfi, where are the paper-mills. It was one varied scene of inchantment & we had but one day for drawing. I made 22 Sketches.

After dinner we amused ourselves with the architecture of the Cappuccini, our residence, & examined the construction of a fine Convent: first a long endless row of Steps to the grotto from wh. the figures of saints are removed & only the cross remains in its place - the entrance to a square Court of pillars & cloysters wh. I call Sarasenic pillars - the Chapel in ruins - the cells filled up for bed rooms for *le signori forestieri* - the Refectory - the dining room - the Garden having a fountain most beautiful & against the wall frescoes still remaining of the Madonna in large sleeves & a Hoop & a Man's figure opposite, almost worn away. I made a drawing of it. The garden is cut in the rock, & most beautiful are the views from it. We prowled about till dusk drawing & admiring & I could almost fancy I saw the Monks gliding thro' the long corridor with their cowls drawn over their faces counting their beads. They were Franciscans I saw by some old Pictures of them painted in the dresses of that order, to examine wh. I very near fell thro' the hole in the pavement of a cell, but the pictures were too far gone even for my love of trash to bring away with me. At night I read *Theodosius & Constanzia*, which I had brought with me.[390] We went to bed to rise to draw & this time I had a Portantina to carry me up the rugged mountain. As we wound up the hills, it being Sunday, we met a great many of the Peasants going to & coming from Mass; well clothed & gay & happy they seemed. There is [a] curious Grotto of San Chrystoffe with a fresco of the Saint bearing the *bambino* on his Shoulders & the Palm in his hand, & when we passed the Greek Tower we drew it again, & passing within half a mile of Conca,

---

[389] See Samuel Rogers, *Italy, a Poem*, London, 1830, and William Sotheby, *Italy and Other Poems*, London, 1828.

[390] *The Letters that passed between Theodosius and Constantia*, by John Langhorne, London, first published in 1763.

we distinctly saw a tall large Nun at one of the high windows of the Monastery in her white robes & black veil watching the progress of our Portantinas up the mountain. We got to Castellamare at 4 o'clock.

4th Oct. [1830] We waited for an uncloudy day to set out again upon another excursion with Mr & Mrs L. Brooke, & on Monday at 8 o'clock we left Castellamare for three days, first going to Sarno to see the source of the river which issues from the hills. It is pretty. The water is clear as crystal & looks fit for Nymph[s] to bathe in, with flowers growing in the bottom. Sarno is a curious & ancient town almost in ruins. On the hill above the Town are castles & convents of the time of the Normans & of the same style & date as Lettere & the castle of Castellamare. The buildings are in woods of Olive Trees & the ground is rocky & abounds in Aloes & Indian fig. The Town has remains of former grandeur & pieces of Saracenic buildings here & there. A little further on, on the Nola road, is the ruined Castle of Palma on the right which we did not scramble up to look at, & opposite to it, under the very smoke of Vesuvius, is the village of Ottajano, an obscure spot where M. de Medici & his family are buried. In him was talent & ambition to wh. he sacrificed his health & life & to an ungrateful King & country; & he might have said with Wolsey: "Had I but served my God, as I have served my King, &c."[391]

We stopped at Nola &, at the dirty little Inn, watched the unpacking of a family of neapolitans who arrived in a Caleche. First came out a bundle of dirty Clothes, tied in a sheet; under this lay a live Hen wh. I conclude[d] they were going to eat, for near it lay some Mushrooms that they had gathered. This class of persons at Naples know as little of comfort or cleanliness as the savages of America. At Nola we went to see the Excavations in the vineyards wh. was not worth the trouble & the Cathedral which is worth, having a curious & very ancient church under it where lights are kept burning. Nola, the first Town from Naples to the Southern provinces is a barbaric place. We got into a sad confusion about the convent on the hill, missed our way, & ended by dining on the grass under the trees in the wood by the roadside. After losing much time, we got into the road to Avellino. The pass of Monte Forte is one of the most magnificent in Italy. Monte Forte is a straggling Town bordering the high road under high Moun-

---

[391] Cardinal Thomas Wolsey had under King Henry VIII also met an untimely death, and is attributed with saying: 'Had I but served God as diligently as I have served the King, he would not have given me over in my gray hairs.'

tains. It bears the marks of war & fire, for here the Carbonari made a stand in 1820 & from hence made that triumphal march into Naples that we witnessed on their day of entrance. An old Church with a series of chapels up to it is on the very top of a pointed Mountain & is a striking object. We reached Avellino as it grew dark, with just light enough to see the dirty, yellow look of its inhabitants who were sitting at their doors or at the Caffes - the Inn furnished nothing & tho' the Master of the Caffe came to ask Mrs L. Brooke if he sd have the honour of serving her Eccelenza with Coffee as he had done two years ago, nothing ever came of all we asked for.

We got up at six o'clock & went two miles in a carriage to the foot of Monte Vergine, which is one of the highest of the chain of southern Appenines. Of the Convent I have written an account, wh. I intend one day or other for an Annual[392] - late that day we returned thro' Avellino & went the road made by Murat to Salerno - & such a road, & such scenery. We got to Salerno as the last rays of sun set were falling on it - & as a revolt was fully expected every day, we were not very much astonished at find[ing] the cannon & the troops drawn out on the Marina, so as to block up the approach to the *Sole*.[393] We were however agreeably surprised at finding it was only the birthday of Francesco 1mo & long may he live!

Oct. 6th [1830]. We left Salerno early, & have been so enchanted with our Tour that we meditate a second Tour on the same road. We came to Pompeii wh. I never thought so beautiful before, all the newly discovered Frescos being with bright colours of blue & yellow, & red, as vivid as if painted yesterday. The ground round Pompeii is covered with Aloes & flowers, the grapes hung in rich bunches & the festoons of vines all about the old ruins instead of walls of dust & wind with wh. Pompeii is surrounded in spring. Vesuvius is clear & brilliant. They have found a Table looking as fresh as if out of the statuary['s] hand. It is what I sd. call Egyptian, a consol Table, supported by Griffins. The most interest part of Pompeii are the Tombs. I went into three of them. One of them is solid in the centre holding an Urn of the ashes of the principal person. Some of them have remains of painting,

some are dismantled. One is thus:

392 It was published in *The Sketch Book of the South*, London (Edward Churton), 1835.

393 i.e. the inn *The Sun*.

I saw it on consulting Sir Wm. Gells book.[394] I find it is the Tomb of Naevolia Tyche. It is 6 feet 6 inches square, ill stuccoed & arched. There are niches for the urns, some of wh. are of coarse earth. There are Lamps & Urns of common earth in a corner. A small aperture was left for light & by the side of the Tomb are remains of the means of burning the dead & collecting their Ashes, deposited in the Urns. The custom of burning the dead fell into disuse in the fourth century.

Oct. 11th [1830]. Mr Craven & the L. Brookes & Shiffners dined with us. I thought the first dinner at six, by candle light, very comfortable. Mr C[raven] is very deaf & stiff & old fashioned, but he has knowledge & instruction & directs well.[395] The stories of Villiaume, the King's favorite are good & partake of the nature of the govern't here.[396] He gets something on every thing he does. Mr Dupont gives him a thousand ducats, & 100 a month, *buona mano,* for his army contract. The King thanked Mr Dupont saying "I'm much obliged to you for yr kindness to Villiaume. He's an old attached servant & I take all this kindness as done to myself." What a system of favorite-ism. Another story is still better. The King's Secretary had been ordered to raise the Pensions to the poor. He brought it to the King with a saving on one billet de banc, (I forget the Italian expression), for ten thousand Ducats. He said the expense was unnessessary & he had made this saving. The King, the Secretary fancied, did not receive it graciously, which he told Villiaume in going out & asked him to find out the reason of it, upon wh. Villiaume with a long melancholy face went into the King's room who asked the reason. He said, he had bought an Estate; & they had just come upon him for 10,000 Ducats. "Here," said the King "take this paper," holding out the savings from the Pensions of the poor. There is another equally good [story] about a French Clock, and another of the signature in council wh. Mr Craven told us still better. All matters for offices or places about court go before the council before the King signs them. The King was called out of Council by Villiaume sending him word "un affare de premura."[397] & so he came directly thinking it something about the Queen. Villiaume said

---

[394] Sir William Gell & John P. Gandy, *Pompeiana: the Topography, Edifices, and Ornaments of Pompeii*, London, 1817-1819.

[395] Presumably a reference to his interest in amateur dramatics.

[396] Francesco I's infamous servant, Michelangelo Viglia, enjoyed the full confidence of the King and, as a result, was able to engage unashamedly in acts of bribery and corruption.

[397] 'a matter of urgency'.

"Here's a place your just going to sign. I'm offered 20,000 ducats for it from a most deserving clever Man &c." The Man got the place.

The King can live but a little while; the Queen has found out her mistake in taking him to Spain, but her *avenir* is an unpromising one. Her Son hates her; he is said to be a cruel harebrained youth who fancies himself a Napoleon.

12th Oct. [1830]. Our second Tour of 12 hours & 42 Italian miles, that is to say 50 English with the same three horses to a Caleche & not as tired as we were when we got home. On a fine bright Autumn morning, we set out down of [a] winding hill at seven o'clock; about Nocerra we fell in with several Regiments going to the South which delayed us. After, we went the cross road to San Severino. The vintage is now at its height & the courts of the Farmhouses present busy scenes of wine making. About Baronesi we took a walk & drew while the horses were resting, & the kindness of manner & amiableness of the country people's manners struck us. They made us sit down & eat their grapes & only wanted the pleasure of asking us questions & looking over the drawing. The country is enchanting. We walked into the Church of the Franciscan Convent at Savo. It stands in a rich plain on a rising hill surrounded by Trees & its long line of arched Cells looked imposing at the other side of the road when we passed it. It was late in the E'g & as the bells were ringing for Ave Maria, the Grey-headed Friars, "with even pace & slow" were walking two & two up the hill to the Church. We admired the scene & scenery, but when we came today we found it like many other lovely things, best at a distance. It is a poor convent full of wooden images & trash for pictures. I made a sketch from the balcony that looks down on the plain & the poor Friar seemed enchanted at being put into the sketch & still more so at Papa giving him a little money for the Church. We came back by Salerno & I walked up to the Madonna degli Angelle, & in passing thro' La Cava, the Coachman pointed us out the abode of Donna Anna White[398] on the hill.

17th Oct. [1830]. I have a good deal of the *Ver qui ronge*:[399] we shall be gone from Naples by the 5th of May 1831. Papa talks of immediately sending his Plate home to England.

---

[398] Miss Anna Baptista White, a long-term English resident of La Cava.

[399] 'the worm which nibbles away'.

1830

One page of the manuscript journal conveying some of the energy and emotion of Marianne Talbot's writing and showing some of the difficulties of reading the resultant script.

The Hermitage where, on 29 April 1829, Sir Stratford Canning had organised a supper for the party descending from Vesuvius. For Marianne Talbot, it marked the end of the pleasantest day she had ever passed.

The Camaldoli della Torre, destination of a charming expedition undertaken on 30 August 1830. As well as Marianne Talbot, the group of 14 included Sir William Gell and James Justinian Morier.

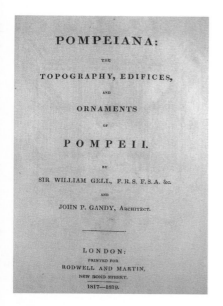

The two works by Sir William Gell entitled *Pompeiana* played an important part in introducing Pompeii to the British public.

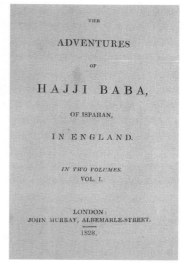

James Justinian Morier's two visits to Persia as a young man inspired two highly entertaining fictional accounts of the life of Hajji Baba, son of a barber in Ispahan.

(*Top left*) Sir Henry Lushington, British Consul in Naples 1815 - 1832.
(*Top right*) Sir Stratford Canning, ambassador in Constantinople and British negotiator on Greek independence.
(*Bottom left*) The Marquess of Hertford, regular visitor to Naples with Lady Strachan and her three daughters to whom he was guardian.
(*Bottom right*)   Sir Walter Scott who spent several weeks in Naples at the beginning of 1832.

22d. [Oct. 1830]. We have passed these beautiful bright autumn days in Excursions, & shivering by the fireside talking on these turbulent times. Ther. 60 in the drawing room. Sunday it was told us as a great secret that Genl Wm. Pepe[400] was to have made a descent upon the coast with 500 French, but that Govt. had information of the whole. Next day we heard from Naples that placards were put up calling on the people to revolt, wh. we[re] torn down. They had little effect & all is quiet. Tuesday we went to [Monte] Sant'Angelo. We were ten hours about it & were upon the Donkeys at 8 o'clock. The beginning of the clamber is tiresome but the day was perfect & we enjoyed it extremely. There is a pretty view from the Church at Piedimonte wh. I drew. When we got some way up the mountain, there commences a fine wild forest of beech Trees of g[rea]t size growing amongst Rocks. The scenery is very peculiar & quite in Salvator Rosa's style. Higher up a map of the whole surrounding country is seen. We seemed to look quite down upon Vesuvius so much higher were we, & the Sketches some of the party made were more like Maps than drawings. At the very top is a white Chapel where it is said the Devil took up St Michael, & the print of the Saint's foot is shown where he descended to escape from him. We staid an hour at the top; & again stopped half way down to sketch a very picturesque point where there was a Cross in the forest, & a Cacciatore with his dog were seated near in a most graceful manner - had there been but an Artist amongst us.

Thursday we passed at Lettere where the beggars swarm, & as we were riding back in a little narrow lane they called out the Buffolo was coming & so we seized our red shawls & in great terror scrambled up the tall banks on either side, but it was all Italian love of a scene, for the Animal passed quite quietly attended by Men with long Poles. To-day we took boat & went to the little Island of Rovigliano - & miniature Fortress. It is just like something described in one of Sir W. Scott's Novels. We all talked of it as a winter residence. Maria Lushington was sent for, her Father being come from Eng'd.

---

[400] Guglielmo Pepe (1783-1855) had been active in the Carbonari movement. Charles MacFarlane described him as 'that shallow coxcomb, that dull Neapolitan, that blundering conspirator and arrant traitor.' (*Reminiscences,* p.198). It is clear that Pepe, in London and Paris at this time, was being closely monitored by the Neapolitan ambassadors in those two cities who reported back to the Foreign Minister in Naples. (See Ruggero Moscati (ed.), *Guglielmo Pepe,* Rome, 1938, pp.322-326).

23 Oct. [1830] What a wonderful & extraordinary feel is destiny. Mine is settled & written down, my life, my death, my here & hereafter. My mind was occupied with these thoughts during the whole of the ride of yesterday. To me, bitter thoughts. The news wh. was accidentally told yes'y brought them to my mind in full force. There is so much to be liked in a proud imperious nature without vanity, that it has forced me to think. I remember once thinking that we were free agents, that our actions depended on ourselves, & that upon them we reaped here even our reward or punishment, or rather I wished to believe thus. Good Heavens, if anyone cd have fortold these feelings of mine, it must be for a reason.

I like these Lines of Grays so very much always, but today particularly

> "To each his sufferings; all are men
> Condemn'd alike to groan,
> The tender for another's pain
> The unfeeling for his own.
> Yet ah! Why sd they know their fate
> Since sorrow never comes too late,
> And happiness too swiftly flies:
> Thought would destroy their Paradise,
> No more - where ignorance is bliss -
> 'Tis folly to be wise." [401]

28th Oct. [1830]. Why do I keep this journal so full of trash: & how often I write to write only that I am unhappy; perhaps by my own fault - but all this is very dreadful - I pity her, full as much as myself. Today a terrible conversation did more harm than good. I must turn my mind from this hopeless business - if I can - from such a misfortune & turn it to England - really a change is for the best anyhow! - & yet - where is the spot to rest one's weary mind in - all is barren - a barren waste & a dreary desert - the next world there is - but then death & its horrors is between us & the grave, doubled horrors in England. Ld. Camelford was right! in his wish of being buried.[402] Let me leave this

---

[401] The final verse of Thomas Gray's *Ode on a Distant Prospect of Eton College.*

[402] Lord Camelford (1775-1804) designated £1000 in his will so that he might be buried on the Island of St Pierre (Rousseau's former residence) in the Lake of Bienne. His wish was never fulfilled - see Chapter XVI in G.R. De Beer, *Speaking of Switzerland*, London, 1952.

subject - & go to the morality of Gamblers. Story of Mr De Ros: if people will keep such company, they deserve anything. Feorina & his set say he cheats & hides his cards under the Table.[403] Ld Burghursh comes in May, & Mr Hill is considered ill used.[404] Mrs L. Brooke came & gossiped. I neither cared for the topics or the people. Sir Henry sent me Letters & a parcel of Political Carricatures from Eng'd.

1st of Nov. 1830. We came in to the Palazzo Serracapriola[405] where carpets & 7 additional degrees of warmth restored my circulation. The set is a vulgar one & consequently, like the society at Florence, is gossipping, quarelling, lying, which dont much interest me, as it is the story of a stupid novel thrown aside from ennui or disgust. Mr De Ros's character stands low. Mr Hill's debt[s] are talked of.

7th [Nov. 1830]. There is a great deal of gossip about the King's & Queen's two favorites. Here is a Femme de Chambre created Baronessa, & a Valet de Chambre *qui vole*[406] - the Queen quarels with her Son, & it is expected P'ce Metternich will soon be here to lay hold of the future King for Austria. Of French Gossip, there is of the tears & unhappiness of the Queen, of the sacrifice of the Ministers for wh. see Charles 1st & Strafford; & of the caricatures of Charles 10: Trait. with the Cow, & another counting the beads in full uniform by the roadside. The D'esse de Berry goes often in Mens clothes in Engd. & the old Housekeeper in Eng'd said she was the uglyest oldest looking boy she had ever seen, & the Duc & D'esse d'Angou'me are to walk with Peas in the shoes to Holyrood house. [*Comment added later* - 'this last a joke'].

9th [Nov. 1830]. Francesco 1mo died yesterday. He was sensible to the last & gave advice to his successor. He died surrounded by his family & Ministers; a six Months mourning ensues. It is said that etiquette obliges the Spanish Minister G[enera]l Toledo to call on the late

---

[403] In 1836, he was involved in a major cheating scandal (See Greville, 3, p.318-334.

[404] William Hill heard 'out of the blue' in the mid-October that he was to be replaced by Lord Burghersh, a move he considered would be disastrous for his finances. A change in the Foreign Ministry (Palmerston replaced Lord Aberdeen) and the ill-health of Burghersh were probably key factors in allowing him to retain his post.

[405] i.e. on their return to Naples from Castellamare.

[406] i.e. Caterina de Simone, the Queen's maid, and Michelangelo Viglia, the King's valet. *qui vole* - 'who steals'.

King every day until his burial & ask if his Majesty will drink some Chocolate. I dont know whether this is true!

13th [Nov. 1830]. I have quantities to write but am busy stitching black clothes. The Prince is an angel of a King. Monday night after the deathbed scene, the ministers said to the King that he wd certainly wish to retire for some days from Public business - he said No, a tear more or less would be of no avail for his Father & the business of the country sd be attended to. A Proclamation was published that gave g[rea]t satisfaction. The Queen is to have a new Court & all the old Courtiers swept off. He has sent Annunziata to Sicily to get the Viceroy on board Ship & then announce to him his dismission & Trial for various misdemenours & sins.[407] We had the St Johns & Men yesterday at dinner - Sir Wm Gell as usual & Mr de Ros, an insinuating & pleasing gentleman. He is very clever & persuades one without his taking the trouble to disbelieve *les bruits qui courent sur son compte.*[408] The St Johns I think repent their sad silly marriage; luckily there are no children, but he is weak, without any thing to make up for it. Her animal spirits are gone & now the Acton society say, "Ly Isabelle est si douce!"[409] Think of the change. Ly Isabella Fitzroy *si douce*!! That society I dont go to; both Ly Acton & Sir Richard are pleasing, but I dont like it & am afraid of them. M. Ch's de la Ferronaye is a *Demi-solde*, they say, an expression I dont understand but believe he has *le ton d'un employe imperiale.*

Mr Hill dined here yes'y. He seemed wretched but after drinking a good deal, he talked like a book wh. if one had here & there drawn a line across wd. have been clever, original & entertaining. He talked of Ly Dry & her dressing room & the pictures already there of Ly Burghersh & the D. of Wellington, of P'cess Christine clever & gay, of the King who was like a passionate old Squire, calling for Isabella & knocking his stick on the ground till she came, of the Queen's language of the eye, of the dishes of entrails of Quails, & of his sick Nephew, Noel Hill,[410] of the whitewashed room, of the Coffee & the

---

[407] General Nunziante was sent to Sicily to remove the Viceroy Marchese Ugo delle Favare. He was to be replaced by the King's brother, Prince Leopold (1813-60). For the early days of Ferdinand II's reign, see Acton, *The Last Bourbons*, p.48 et seq.

[408] 'the rumours doing the rounds about him.'

[409] 'Lady Isabella is so gentle'

[410] Richard Noel Hill (1800-61), the son of Rev. Richard Hill (1774-1848), William's younger brother.

Priests, of the *Chasses*, & of the cutting up next day of the Animals, the most disgusting thing in the world, he said, at wh. Christine & the Queen assisted. This conversation amused me, it was so descriptive. Poor Mr Hill, I pity him.

We have got a King not 21 till next Month, a hero & an angel in six days. It will be a just but severe Govt., they say. The *Chasses* are abolished, 180,000 ducats of the civil list given up to pay the Debts, a stable of 500 Horses given up & 70 kept, the Viceroy of Sicily banished to Florence & the third P'ce to be Viceroy, P'ce Charles to be Ld High Admiral.[411] The queen cries all day & regrets the Stick. She is to do the will & pleasure of this King & dare not go out without his leave.

16th [Nov. 1830]. We dined at the Vomero - crashing[?] from Eng'd - revolution - fires. I shall be glad when the State funeral is over - for the details everywhere are disgusting; the present King is *beau comme l'esperance*, his 8 days reign is a wonder; & if the story of Menz & the Liberals is true, greater changes still may be expected. The love of stealing is to such a degree that the spices for embalming were stolen, & the consequences are enough to bring the plague into the population that crowd into the Palace to see the King lie in state. Four Officers stand as Mutes at the four corners of the Coffin & they frequently faint away from the heat & smell. The Duc de Serracapriola as Ld of the Bedchamber was to put up the King['s] stockings &, they say, saw the Legs drop off the other night. I hate to see anyone who has been there - it is all so sickening.

19th Nov.[1830]. We yesterday went to the balconies of the Accademia to look at the funeral procession. It was a summer day, & the gayest Carnival I ever beheld, no mourning but in the bonnets & gowns, & thousands of spectators on every house top & at every window - 12,000 Troops in procession, a black & gilt state carriage, a car containing the body in a yellow velvet & silver Trunk. In the Car with the body were the Chaplain & the Confessor, seated at the top & bottom. Then came 16 of the King's carriages with 6 horses to each, & after, a procession on foot, in dresses, clothes without Hats, bearing each a Torch, the gentlemen of the bedchamber. All sorts of stories are in circulation of Ferdinandino as the King is called by the people: that he came disguised in green spectacles & a white hat to see that the lying

---

[411] Charles, Prince of Capua (1811-62), was the oldest brother of the new King. Leopold, Prince of Syracuse (1813-1860) was the 'third Prince'.

in state was properly managed, that he is Anti-Austria & is to be *en moyens* a 2d Napoleon.

20th [Nov. 1830]. There are several strange Etiquettes of Spanish origin - many have been left off since the death of the last King. However, when the body of the king reaches the Chamber, the Marquis Tommaso asked "Is this the real body of Francesco 1mo?" After three repetitions they opened the Coffin & the Duc de Sangro answered "Egli è desso."[412] The Horses of the King's coach become the perquisite of the coachman. He asks at the church door for the King's orders upon wh. the Master of the horse says: "His Maj'y has no further occasion for yr services." The cup of Chocolate is not true, but there is an old charter to the Convent of Sta Chiara of a dinner worthy of any thing written in Mr [Matthew] Lewis's Poems. The coffin is laid on the Table at this barbarous repast, there are 12 Courses they say, & each dish is offered to the coffin.

Sunday 28th [Nov. 1830]. There was near being a row at the King's Funeral between the Sicillians & Neapolitans. Ferdinandino, they say, was brusque to Statella who laid the batton at the Kings feet, who gave it to San Valentino.[413] He goes on with his economies resolved to pay his father's debts. They say he is a miser - perhaps he may be, as each generation is alternately spendthrift & miser. He went into the poultry yard at Portici & asked "Whose fowls are these" - Yours - "How many are there?" - 2000 - "What do they cost?" - three grains a day - "I cd. buy them cheaper at market." He desired them to be sent to the Poultry market, but the Man said 22 are mine - "Take yr Fowls, but remember they have been fed with my grain."

I have quantities to write, but am grown so lazy that I cannot prevail on myself to do so.

6 Dec. [1830] The pardon of Mathiais has given disgust - never was clemency so ill bestowed by a Sovereign.[414] The King goes on with

---

[412] 'It is he.'

[413] Don Ferdinando Capece Minotolo, Duke of Valentino (1762-1833).

[414] Francesco Nicola de Mattheis had been a brutal, over-zealous official, in the Province of Cosenza, engaging in intimidation and torture to repress both political and personal enemies. His seven year trial ended in 1830 with a 10 year prison term. The young King pardoned him, along with granting an amnesty to political offenders. (See Acton, *The Last Bourbons*, pp.44-5 & 50).

his economies, & used Lamps instead of Candles - Barbanera comes true in all particulars. The Pope is dead. The calculation of the duration of life of a Pope is most strange - it is thus:
Pius 6, Pius 7, and 10 make 23. He died 1823.
Pius 7 & Leo 12 and 10 make 29. He died 1829
Leo 12 & something the 8th & 10 make 30; The last pope died 1830.
Prophesied that the next will reign Eleven years.

The Duke of Wellington has resigned. Gl Sebastiani is made Minister of Marine.[415] They say "que le Roi l'avoit mariné afin qu'il ne se corrompte pas."[416] - upon the Oath in France being administered, a major said he had no objection to *preter serment* as others had done to Charles 10! "alors on le rend comme les Autres."

I have dined out 8 days running, the last at old Stacks, crowded.

7th [Dec. 1830]. We had yes'y a large dinner of Harrowby's[417] & Corps diplomatic. The change of Ministry occupies everyone. Ld Sandon[418] writes that all are to be swept out neat & clean. Ld. H[arrowby] is an agreeable Man, neither old or stiff. Milady is sumptuous & dignified, but not the real dignity for everydays wear. Ly Harriet[419] a good humoured great talker. They are come from Vienna. P'ce Metternich takes for his 3d wife Mme Molly Zichy's daughter.[420] Mrs Fitzherbert wears tweeds for George 4th - & goes to the Pavillion. The King has seen all the papers proving her marriage, both by an english & a protestant clergyman - & yet in the House, Mr Fox was authorized to contradict their perjury, a blot never to be washed out in the King's character. Poor Mr Hill. Georgina says this is his story. I dont think so, & I believe him unshackled, but a bankrupt in health & a pauper in

---

[415] Horace Sébastiani de La Porta (1772-1851), a Corsican by birth, had been a soldier under Napoleon. On the political Left, he had endorsed the assumption of power by Louis-Philippe, who appointed him first Naval Minister, then Minister of Foreign Affairs, and subsequently ambassador to Naples and then London.

[416] 'The King marinaded him so that he did not go bad.'

[417] Dudley Ryder, Baron Harrowby (1762-1847), had played an important part in British politics in the first decades of the 19th century. On at least one occasion (1827), he had declined the premiership. He had married (1795) Lady Susan Leveson Gower (1772-1838).

[418] Dudley Ryder, Lord Sandon (1798-1882), eldest son of the Earl of Harrowby.

[419] Daughter of Lord & Lady Harrowby, b.1811.

[420] Metternich married Countess Melanie Zichy on 31 January 1831.

circumstances - & all by his own fault - the saddest reflection a Man can make. He is so strange a mortal that nothing was ever heard like him. Ld Harrowby told us that at the taking of Copenhagen, George the 3d said to his Ministers "At least don't be shabby in yr iniquity."

18th Dec. [1830] I have been out of spirits, & I don't know why unless it is the caprice of my Sex, [4-5 words scratched out] or the heat of M. de Stackelbergs ultra party last monday. M de la Tour Maubourg, the new F[rench] Am[bassado]r,[421] was there; He looks quite english, with a fine Expression, a person to be trusted as if he wd scorn to tell a lie for his advantage, the best look a Man can have. I dare say he is a bad diplomate. I certainly do like the *grandioso* that lasts, & will bear both wear & tear through life. That little M. de Lebzeltern[422] is a sort of Asmodé,[423] the image of Mr Luttrell,[424] but smaller & wickeder. They say he is the cleverest diplomate of them all & places the very devil amongst them - as for Old Stack, he is intent to have the cholera pass like the Angel with the flaming sword through the revolutionary countries & sweep away all who think or act for themselves. Poor Mr Hill is very unhappy, so justly to be pitied &

---

[421] Marquis Florimond de Latour-Maubourg (1781-1847) had arrived on 6 December but departed almost immediately to be a special envoy at the Conclave in Rome. He returned in February 1831, but had a further leave of absence after the death of his father at the end of July. He returned again at the end of October 1831.

[422] Ludwig, Graf von Lebzeltern (1774-1854), career diplomat in the Austrian service, who had arrived in Naples in October 1830 with his wife (Zénaïde de Laval, the daughter of a French count who had become a naturalised Russian) and young daughter Alexandrine.

[423] A character in Lesage's novel *Le diable boiteux*. 'Although Asmodeus is not malignant, yet with all his wit, acuteness, and playful malice, we never forget the fiend even when he is most engaging.' (E.Cobham Brewer, *The Reader's Handbook*, London, 1887).

[424] Henry Luttrell (1768-1851) is described at length by Charles Greville in his memoirs (Vol.I, pp.63-5) as a person who 'has a lively imagination, a great deal of instruction, and a very retentive memory, a memory particularly happy for social purposes, for he recollects a thousand anecdotes, fine allusions, odd expressions, or happy remarks, applicable to the generality of topics which fall under discussion. .... towards the world in general he is rather misanthropical, and prides himself upon being free from the prejudices which he ridicules and despises more or less in everybody else.' Lady Theresa Lewis adds a note to the *Journals of Miss Berry* to the effect that Mr Luttrell 'was distinguished through life by his conversational powers; he had a fund of anecdote at command and a ready flow of epigrammatic wit; but his satire though pointed, was seldom calculated to wound, and he was a favoured guest in every society in which he lived' (II, p.148)

grown so amiable in his sorrows, & they tell me as Pity is akin to Love &c., but No, there is a defect in his understanding, a want of method & arrangement, a want of common sense, a want of Scotch blood, wh. by the by is worth 2000£ a year always. I do pity him altogether from my heart, not from my head. In fact he is mad, very amusing a humorist, but what care they for humour at the F[oreign] Office. His is a life *manqué*! & he had friends too, for Mr Canning said that he would rather do anything than plague or vex Mr Hill. We dined Tuesday at that Man of wood, Mr Craven. His new house is like him - cold, stiff, fine, frippery & *mesquin*. He is well informed, well bred, accomplished & *rangé* to a fault; if he had tried to spend money to spoil a room, he cd. not have succeeded better.

Xmas Eve [1830]. I wish I cd. keep up my old Custom of writing down things, but destiny seem[s] to me now so little worth while writing. Ly Isabella & Mrs L[angford] B[rooke] hate each other. Oh how much do they hate each other: one is a person of the world with no manner; the other is a person not of the world with a great deal of manner. De Ros is like Pelham[425] & has an affectation of doing nothing.

26th [Dec. 1830]. I amused myself yes'y in reckoning up 14 Xmas days & thinking how I had passed them - on the whole that of 1828 was the happiest; many have been brim full of strong & bitter feelings - but to that of yes'y - the day was a stormy & rainy Sirocco that threatened the blowing in of all the windows. Ther. 60. The dinner intended to be 14, by the Lushingtons absence, was 10. Sir Wm was out of spirits, Mr Hill too till the Madera had worked him into good spirits. Mr Seymour[426] was fresh from Constantinople on his way to Florence. He brought news from thence. He is a prim stiff-looking little Man. Sir Brook Taylor,[427] a nice gentle person quite deaf of one ear. De Ros, charming all ages & sexes. St John - a Gambler, & Ly Isabella - the wife of a gambler. Today we have been to Church & heard a young man, Mr St Quentin, preach a beautiful Sermon; I was quite overcome by it. It is so rare to hear anything good abroad. His Wife &

---

[425] The hero of an eponymous novel by Lord Lytton, first published in 1828.

[426] George Hamilton Seymour (1797-1880) had been posted to Constantinople in July 1830, and in November had been appointed Minister to Tuscany, to replace Lord Burghersh.

[427] Sir Brook Taylor (1776-1846) had been replaced as British minister in Berlin in October 1830.

Miss Wellesleys[428] sat near & I dare say felt proud of him. He seems far gone in a consumption.

3rd of Jan'y [1831]. Another, & another, & another year slips by, & I grow old & wrinkled. I don't know why these personal reflections, as I never cared much about it, but I have just finished *Sir Ch's Grandison* & that detailed his'y of marriages & Old Maids has set me a'thinking. It aint all over yet, & perhaps then I may regret youth, good looks & liberty. This year has begun with Revolutions, a likelihood of War, Roses & Violets, & a stupid Stackelberg day.

14th [Jan. 1831]. What a time since I have written!!! We have had 3 days colours, 3 days Triumph, 3 days of fatigue & 3 days of wonder at our young King. I never wished to be a King till 12 yesterday. He has kept his own secret well. We went to P'ce Dentice's to see all this out of the windows.

22nd [Jan. 1831]. A Ball at San Saturnino's.[429] The King there. Prince Charles danced with the English (ladies) - les Arroubi[430] are very popular.

The Hertford set[431] have dined here - Ly Strachan walked in this Morn'g - she began with "I am not come to tell you my story." However, she was & she told me: Sir Richard Strachan's Will, her prospects for her daughter & her wish to marry her to Ld Yarmouth - her birth, a mystery - & the Brussels story of Ld Elgin - & Ld Hertford having made the Father give her 50,000£ settled on her & that she has promised not to ruin the legitimacy of an Héritage, &c. - & then her present position - marriage, her marriage & the amiableness of Ld Hertford. This was an odd visit. Her *Ton* & manners are vulgar, but she is very handsome & good natured.

---

[428] George Darby St Quintin (1803-1872) had married in 1827 Georgina Wellesley, the second daughter of the Hon. and Rev. Gerald Valerian Wellesley. Emily and Mary Wellesley, the older and younger sister of the preacher's wife, were not yet married.

[429] Don Raimondo de Quesada, Marquis of San Saturnino (1761-1849), was the Sardinian ambassador at the court of Naples between 1815 and 1836.

[430] the Harrowbys pronounced *à la française*.

[431] i.e. Francis Seymour-Conway, third Marquis of Hertford, accompanied by Lady Louise Strachan, widow of Admiral Sir Richard Strachan, and her three daughters (Mathilda, b.1813, Charlotte b.1815, and Louise b.1819) to whom the Marquis was guardian.

30th. I have a good deal to write but I dont write. Ly Acton's Plays are very amusing - we had *La 2de année de marriage, Vatel,* & last night we had *Michel et Christine* with *le Sourd,* with new Calembourgs. *M. et C.* was very affecting, every woman in the room had the tears in her eyes. Ly Strachan looks handsome & vulgar & is beautifully dressed. Her daughter is gentle & lovely - the Ball on Thursday was fine. Most people wore black velvet & diamonds.

We have dined out five or six days *de suite* - yesterday at the Lush'tons. I sat next M. de Lebzeltern whom I like.

Feb. 8th [1831]. Mr Vesey FitzGerald[432] dined here. He is the only Irishman except Gl Church[433] that I ever saw that I cd bear - he put me in mind of Old times & my nerves & my shyness were not up to him for half an hour.

We had *La V[i]eille de 15 ans* at Ly Actons; at dinner Mr Hill surpassed himself in oddity & strangeness about Ly Dry & her Furniture & her ball. Ld Ponsonby is talked of for Constantinople.[434] Mr Craven a stick.

15th [Feb.1831]. This is Ash Wednesday & even the sky is dark & lowering & our sack cloth & ashes are like our prospects - bad - bad - bad - uncertain as the summer breeze, but stormy as the winter. To carry Home, to a No Home, years spent uselessly, wrinkles & old age, to have lived abroad until mild skies & soft air disgust you with your native Land & Fogs & *Frisson* - To have passed yr life in refinement until you are become as sensitive to vulgarity as the Mimosa plant & then to go & live with Dandies & Dow[age]rs & all you condemn & dislike - but to the present, & the present is all we can venture on, we

---

[432] William Vesey-Fitzgerald (c.1783-1843), politician and diplomat.

[433] General Sir Richard Church, a veteran of the Napoleonic War when he had fought in Greece, had, in 1817, been taken into the Neapolitan service and set the task of ending the lawlessness of the southern provinces. In this, he was successful, but appointed commander in Sicily, he found the insurrection too firmly established to control and was fortunate to escape to Naples where the King, under Carbonari influence, had him imprisoned. He subsequently returned to Greece and became an important figure in the fight for Greek independence.

[434] At the time Viscount (John) Ponsonby (c.1770-1855) was Joint Commissioner to the provisional government of Belgium. He was to take up his duties as British Ambassador in Constantinople in March 1833, but before that, in the autumn of 1832, he took over from William Hill as British Minister in Naples.

had a dinner of Hertfords on Tuesday - really the bonhomie & innocence of that connection makes one think it so. Ld Hertford seems a good natured & well bred man, but so shy. They are all so shy. Here is Ld De Ros shy too. As for Ly Stra[chan], she is vulgar but good natured, clever & *naturel*; it's impossible to dislike her for she says every thing to everyone that people generally say in confidence to their best friend. Miss Strachan is as beautiful as fair hair & blue eyes & lilies & roses can make a girl. Her mother says she is to marry Ld. Osulston & that it is all but settled. As for Ld De Ros, he is sick, quiet, gentlemanlike & slow, not the clever, wicked, ill-natured person his foes represent him. Mr V. Fitzg. is just what he was ten years ago - he has an eloquence which carries every thing before it, a sense & acuteness, wh. make his Irish tones & his appearance forgotten. Mr H[ill] & he hate each other, I believe by instinct, as holding each other cheap - wh. they do greatly, & wd willingly roar each other down on all occasions. Mr H. is enraging with his prose & his prejudice, but still he has such a sense of humour & so much originality that one forgives &c. When "Les ennuyeux qui ne veillient jamais"[435] got their cloaks & shawls, & were off, Mr FitzG. & Ld de Ros & Mr Hill sat down to have a good gossip. Mr Hill was soon distanced & Ld De Ros who makes the best listener in the world bent to Mr FG's eloquence. Ld Byron says that it is only the French & the Irish that are eloquent. They got upon the D. of Wellington & his candour & his greatness & sang a Hymn of eulogy over him - & then they went to French gossip & to St Simon & Mme de Genlis[436] & were very amusing indeed. I have found out after six months that now I begin to know Ld de Ros a little & that we hate the same people, a strong tie, Ld Clan. & Sir J. C.[437] I don't think he is a Man to be in Love with, but more to have a cool friendship with. He is a good intimate acquaintance but I doubt his powers of loving or liking much. On Friday we had a very pleasant dinner.

22d [Feb. 1831]. Ld Wallace, Mr FitzGerald, De Ros, Harrowby, Lebzelterns & Stackelberg.

---

[435] 'the bores who never stay up late'

[436] The Duc de Saint-Simon was famous for his *Memoirs* covering the period 1691-1723. Mme de Genlis (1746-1830) was a well-known writer on the education of children.

[437] Possibly Lord Clanwilliam and Sir Joseph Copley. The first name might read Lord Clare. Sir Joseph Copley appears to have been a friend of Sir George Talbot.

Another dinner. I would rather level with the vulgar english every day than have such a stalled ox of a dinner.[438] There are riots at Rome. The cry in the street is "Il Papa e Pellagio".[439] All the travellers are dispersed.

23d Feb'y [1831]. We dined at Mr Garniers. It was a curious day altogether with the gall stones, & the dress, C'te Byland[440] & the Magnetism, Ld Hertford & the Music, & the writing, economy & corked wine, Ly Strachan & Mr Hills quarels - she says I sd like to know who had had most success in life, him or me - Mrs L. Brooke in her rasberry-jam cap, as Mr Hill called it, & My earrings. I like Ld Hertford. I believe we both love money, delight at being at our ease with people, & have charity for Vulgarians. Sir Ch's Monck,[441] a great oddity, was near me at dinner. He is a mixture of a radical & an aristocrat, he seems an odd'on, has a lobster Pond in his park, & says that his Mother was a haberdasher's daughter. Mr Craven was there who puts me out of patience with his pedigree & pretentions, his dullness & deafness. I believe single life is better than yawning away an existence upon Ormulu & ennui on the Chiatamone at Naples.

28th [Feb. 1831]. I am better mind & body, better for not being harassed & plagued, better for 8 days dining out, better for talking & not thinking. Naples is pleasant now. Mr F. who has an insinuating address to Man, woman & child is here. He is vain, very vain, but makes his vulgar look forgotten & forgiven by his great powers of pleasing. Our stiff old Beau goes on as usual & our good old bear too. Lady Strachan might be wiser if she chose, Ly Isabella might be quieter[?], Ly Harrowby might be pleasanter, & so I would reform mankind & womankind, but we have company without end & forget Revolutions & hear of Brighton scandal & quarels. The Queen, people say, is anxious to have a moral court & tries to keep Ly Aldborough's conversa-

---

[438] See *Proverbs*, Ch.15, v.17: 'Better is a dinner of herbs where love is, than a stalled ox and hatred therewith.'

[439] Presumably an ironic linking of the reactionary new Pope Gregory XVI with the early Christian theologian Pelagius, i.e. 'The Pope and Liberty!'

[440] Possibly Lt-Gen. Count William Bylandt (1771-1855), a Dutchman who had served in the British army and had married the daughter of Admiral Sir Hugh Christian.

[441] Sir Charles Monck (1779-1867), a friend of Sir William Gell, had a long fascination with Greek architecture which fed into his building plans at his residence at Belsay Hall in Northumberland. The son of Sir William Middleton, he adopted the surname of his mother, Jane. She was the daughter of a prosperous merchant draper.

tion & Ly Lyndhurst's dress in order, but finds it too much for her. The King's Natural Son[442] preaches to them every Sunday.

1st of March [1831]. How many lies I heard last night, not one of wh. I contradicted. I was at Catalano's Concert[443] & a ball at Ld. Hertfords. Ld de Ros enchants all the old women. How he sd think it worth his while!! He has bewitched my father! He is good natured & amiable, but with so many skins & peelings that you feel you never know him & that he is that sort of character that never can be known, & yet one has no right to accuse him of Hypocrisy, because you see no motive for his being a Hypocrite - I don't think him a Man to like or dislike very strongly. People who would be much liked sd have faults - he is determined not to have any. What a contrast to the other who has no good looks & is fascinating without means.

4th [March 1831]. I am better - summer scenes today began - I have been reading the best Romance of Cooper's I have read for ages called *The water witch*.[444] It proves vulgarity & low life is much [more] amusing than the *tracassoni* of a London salon. Naples is crowded. Conynghams & the Hertford set wh. last do not make a very respectable figure on the Strada Nuova. Yes'y the King was riding & P'ce Ch.'s & his suite; following close behind was that Girl of 14 Charlotte Strachan with some Men, & the painted Ladies after, standing up in their Barouche. It has really a very bad appearance. Ld Harrowby is reckoned the cleverest Man here. Mr F[itz]G[erald] is a much more brilliant specimen of powers of speech I think: Irish more now than I ever thought him. I wonder how he will end - but I never [*one word scratched out - possibly* 'never'] see him but in public now.

On Valentine's day, I got these verses written, I conclude, by Sir Wm. Gell:

> Young Ladies who have wit themselves
> Look with disdain on those about them
> Plant their admirers on the shelves
> And only look upon, to flout them.
> But Marianne, You have a heart
> That sometimes beats response to mine

---

[442] Rev. Lord Augustus Fitz-Clarence (1805-1854), illegitimate son of William IV.

[443] Domenico Catalano, a wealthy lawyer who used to lay on concerts and balls.

[444] First published in 1830.

And you'll accept me - do not start -
Tis only as your Valentine.

The 10th of April was Sunday, a day to think on & ponder on. Good
Friday & Easter Sunday I pondered on too - I have had thinking
enough these two months to ruffle the smoothest flow, disturb the
coolest mind, but thinking in my case does no good, & so now Adieu,
the season is over, & balls & parties & agreeables & family torment,
all is finally settled for Months to come. The first laughing I had about
it was last night. Georgina was in spirits & made a joke of everyone,
of the Turccachio Maladetto, of the beau millieu, of the Mountain
spright.

Were I to write all that has passed this year, were I to sum up all the
gossip of this year, the hist'y of Ly Strachan, of the King, of P'ce
Charles, of Charlotte Strachan, of Mrs Wyndham, of Ld Albert, of Ly
Conyngham, of My lord & of My lady & Mrs, my journal wd be an
odd one - & so I don't. I keep no journal - I have left off writing &
thinking. The people are all going, all without exception. What is my
impression of them all? Milord & Milady Arroubi, he a little vulgar in
sentiment, & refined in expression, good worldly people, the girls well
brought up & immense talkers about nothing; Ly Conyngham talking
of George 4th, good natured & a praiser, vain of her rings, bracelets &
carriages; Ld Conyngham like one of the people in Miss Edgeworth's
Tales, low humour, & Irish wit; Mr Vesey F[itz]G[erald] very clever,
with a little bad taste, *un peu volage* in his feelings, not settled down
yet; can be what he pleases to whom he pleases, has immense pliabil-
ity of disposition, strong feelings - & is witty certainly, but whether
wise he himself knows best. Ld Hertford is wiser, better, & cleverer
than the world allows him to be; he is not a happy Man. Ly Strachan's
nature has done much for & want of education has ruined - she has the
notions of a Lady's Maid; her principles I doubt; her maxim is to be a
warm friend & a little enemy, but either a straw would turn; imprudence is her bane & will be the ruin of her graceful beautiful daughter.
Mrs Wyndham is a very odd person, *très commun* in her *maniere d'e-
tre* at first, but she rises gradually into something clever on investigation - "Cette femme ira loin."[445] The St Johns are meddlers & makers,
but they like us. Ly Acton is soft but her *caractere* & principles are too
yielding. Mme Riarno[?] is a Souffre douleur, a good creature, she
preaches - & they wont bring her again abroad. Mrs Langford

---

[445] 'This woman will go far.'

B[rooke] is gone - she is a pleasing woman of an ordinary cast of character - she is insipid & I'm tired of her. Ld de Ros - an inexplicable. The St Johns are off, and the Hertfords & Conynghams go tomorrow.

> My boat is on the shore,
> And my carriage at the door, &c."[446]

We stay another year. I am much entertained at the hatred of Ld De R[os] & Ly S[trachan], two of a trade never agree. He says she makes her daughters a cat's paw to go after the King & seems to think it interferes with his plans for his Lady. A pretty sort of corrupt discourse took place the other day wh. was repeated to me. She said to him why you'll never marry with that Lady, not that I admire your taste. He said I always found I did as I like. I'm a fortunate Man & if I had a mind to marry some one, no doubt wd take a fancy to my Lady & marry her, or perhaps, what would be better for her, make her a large settlement, & tho' you may not approve of my taste, others do. He never minces terms or expressions about Ly Strachan; he says she is the greatest liar in the world; he says she throws Notes or makes her daughter do so into P'ce Charles's carriage; he says she is vain of not looking like a lady but like something else - in short that her reign must come to an end & that shortly. Ly Strachan was here yes'y. Her discourse is silly & clever, frank & cunning. There is something *très peu distinguée* about her, yet she is out of the common way & I dont dislike her. The other night at Ly Actons she was telling me with fits of laughing of the two reasons she was found fault with - her not being sufficiently attentive to Ld Hertford & her not receiving his company. Mme Riarno[?] says that he is infatuated about her & seems to say that they wait for Lady Hertford's death to marry. Her hist'y is extraordinary. Lord Elgin, when at Brussels was called out of the room to a Lady in great distress who had a beautiful child with her. She said she was the widow of an officer & that her own name had been Dillon. Ld Elgin went the next day to see after her & he found she had made away with herself. They never could discover who she was. The child was sent to Old Ly Elgin who brought her up with P'cess Charlotte,[447] & when she grew up she was on the point of being sent out to

---

[446] Cf. Lord Byron: 'My boat is on the shore, And my bark is on the sea', Marchand, V, p.250.

[447] When she died in 1810, the Dowager Countess bequeathed Louise Dillon her best clothes and £4000.

India to Mr Bruce, Ly Elgins brother,[448] there to be married, when Sir Richard Strachan proposed for her, but repenting of his offer, offered her after 2000£ to let him off. In the mean time Mr Bruce died, & they wd not let off Sir Richard Strachan, & so he married her & she had Lovers in abundance. She used her influence with her husband to appoint Ld Hertford Guardian to the children. Ld Hertford has [had] been at Walkeren & had lived in Sir R. Strachan's Ship[449] & then became Lover to Ly Strachan. Sir Richard died & Ld Hertford tried to find out who her Father was, who they say was discovered & brought by the lawyers & Ld H. to settle 50,000£ one fine day on Ly Strachan on condition that she makes no claims to her birth & situation. Who this Father is, is the mystery, & Ly Strachan gives one to know he is a Peer with children. I have advised her to write her Memoirs tho' if she did I dare say one sd not be allowed to read them.

There is a Congress at Rome[450] - but Reform monopolizes all discourse. I have got Mr Hill to lend me Mr Canning's speech on reform & its magnificent forebodings of what would be the consequence of carrying Ld John Russell's ideas into practice. When I asked Ld Hertford if he sd return here next winter, he said Yes, England was no longer a fit place for a Gentleman. Sir B. Taylor was met by the Courier going to England, who brought dispatches to order him back South as mediator at Rome; he stamped & swore against little Men, like a Madman, the Courier says.[451]

April 25 [1831]. I don't know why I write for it does me no good scribling away all the folly that comes into my head, all the misery I feel & the hopelessness of matters at home. I have finished Ld Byron's Life, a curious story of uncontrouled passions - great vanity, great powers & a mobility of character that spoiled all. I have written out much. His likeness, both of looks & faults, to Ld Durham is strik-

---

[448] Hon. Charles Andrew Bruce (1768-1810).

[449] In 1809 the British had landed troops on the island of Walcheren in the Scheldt estuary. It was withdrawn a few months later. Sir Richard Strachan had commanded the naval force.

[450] A number of insurrections in Northern Italy early in 1831 gave rise to concerns that revolution might spread more widely within the Papal States and lead to serious conflict between France and Austria; hence this congress was convened to advise the new Pope on reform measures he should take.

[451] Britain had no diplomatic representation at the Vatican, so Sir Brook was drafted in as an 'unofficial' participant at the congress.

ing who has the Byron faults without the talent. I have also thought of that uncontroulable english character (wh. I have, along with others, & wh. a foreign residence has partly cured me of) of not giving way to circumstances, of that selfishness that feels so deeply, deeply indeed for itself, & that we call feeling & admire so in Engd. & that comes to no good with any of us English. This very selfishness has its charm with me. The Book leaves a strange impression & Lines to Ly Blessington express what I feel sadly now.[452] This Morn'g now the post has come in & has brought us a bundle of bad news. There is a sentiment in it very good "Cash is Virtue." 500£ loss by the house in Burlington Str.,[453] a long arrear of bills & expense in perspective for the Canal bill of the River Colne Company. I want to fall to economy with spirit. I dined yesterday in a new house or rather our old house of Torella at M de Lebzeltern. The house is *bien moulée*, the Servants wait in white Gloves, & Mr Hill was saying where is the Sour Crout & smoking of old times. He says M de Leb. is an old Necromancer. Both he & she are clever; they have a nice little Girl called Alexandrine, all spirit & gaiety, & she wishes to have another called Olga. She was a Russian; her name is Zenaïde. Bonhomie is M. de Lebzeltern's pretention. Mr Hill was passing strange at dinner, made me laugh. Cash is Virtue there. We talked of Mr Canning; he says all the Foreign Diplomates cried him down - now they have found out their mistake. Ld De Ros no favorite with Mr Hill.

26th [April 1831]. I sent to buy in my first 500£ into the Chile state stocks. I never saw but 6 things perfect in my life:
Ld Byrons beauty.
Mr Hill's Dog
Mlle Mars acting
Prince Metternich's manner
a sun set on the bay of Naples
Pope's Verses.

Ld Byron says amongst his perfect things:
a Lion at Veli Pasha's in the Morea & a Tiger at Tuppu in Creta Marese.

27th April [1831]. The Hertford set are off & really Milady has behaved more sillyly than her beauty or wit did before & very much like

---

[452] A five stanza poem *To the Countess of Blessington*. See Madden, I, p.86.

[453] The London property of Sir George Talbot was in Burlington Street.

the woman who when a child put Coals on the fire wh. Ld De Ros de-
clares she did. Ld H[ertford] is bewitched with her "et cependant avec
toute sa diablelesse, il l'appelle mon coeur et ma vie."[454] I told her it
would please the Neapolitan Ladies if she wd receive his company &
his friends, if she was more attentive to him - she died of laughter at
my advice. She is *vulgarisima*; all the time she amuses me & I like
meeting her better than Mrs Parker or any excellent good precise
woman, but as to conversation No Lady is on a par with her; a Man of
the world is more than a match for her, for she is not clever enough for
them. It is a vulgar but not a tedious Tale, the one of this year: Charlotte S[trachan] & P'ce Ch's & the King. Ld De Ros says there is
more in it than we know of. Her attack on him about his Mistress is
really wonderful, & he spareth her not, says her reign must soon end
& insinuates that she is no better than she sd be. The truth is she sees a
Lover[?] a mile off or is determined to have one. "Il l'est, il fut, ou il
doit l'être."[455] She is too unrefined & vulgar & frank for a Coquette,
but she is fresh & handsome in hair & complexion & teeth. I wish Ma-
tilda was well married; her Mother will be her ruin. They have pursued the King. She went to Court & spoke first which was against Etiquette, to wh. he answered - "Mme vous etes Courtisan-ne," an extraordinary answer but wh. was accident & not wit.

1st of June [1831]. The summer come at last and the season now is
past! All have flown & have left but faint traces of London gossip &
the odour of their good name - we have Flowers in abundance & the
strangest, maddest, oddest twaddle of a dear old Minister. In Eng'd we
have a law suit with a river God.

> "And when will it be over
> And the Demon answered - Never."

Mr Hill is the only person I know who can furnish you with a story the
365 days of the year. It seems Miss Pulteney[456] had talked to him at
her own house, so he said to Mrs Falconnet: "Now for God's sake
dont come talking to me. I've had enough of yr sister Fanny - she's
talked me dead at dinner." He said to Mr Garnier: "Now go to Castel-

---

[454] 'and yet, with all her devilry, he calls her my heart and my life.'

[455] 'He is one, was or will become one.'

[456] Frances Pulteney (b.1809), a sister of Mme Isabella Falconnet. Clarissa Trant met
'the beautiful Miss Pulteneys' in Rome during the Carnival of 1826. (*Journal*, p. 181).
Isabella and Frances had two other sisters.

lamare, dont come you know two years running to the Vomero plagu-
ing me."

We went to the Miracle at San Gennaro.[457] I had heard it much talked
of, still I was astonished at its heathenish workings & astonished too
at the treasure. The whole bust & head of the Bronze half Statue of
San Gennaro being covered with diamonds, emeralds, & sapphires,
the gifts of Kings & Queens. When the Liquifaction of the blood was
proceeding, the girls & Old women who scream & implore it to work
for the sake of our Saviour & the Mother of God & all the Saints went
on for an hour. By the by, it never liquefied, but that is nothing; the
blood is in a finely chased gold & glass bottle & mass was performing
at the adjoining chapels. The Chapel of San Gennaro is very fine &
very picturesque; 34 busts of saints in silver & 18 saints in bronze are
placed amidst a profusion of Catholic bigottry & ornaments.

What a state is poor England in!! the excitement of temper seems terrible: it seems that the wives are scolded, the children whipt &
screaming, the servants sworn at, the dogs kicked. This is life now.
Our old friend Sir Rd. Vivian[458] probably now thinks Ladies, educated
& talking Ladies, more troublesome than he ever did in his romantic
days of 1821. For us now, we think of nothing & do nothing, but walk
about this beautiful country in perfect security & bless ourselves. My
eyes are dreadfully bad. I have consulted a Dr Petrulli who gives me
nervous Medicines & an application of Laurel Water, & in time I shall
read Newspapers & small print, but never again pass whole nights
reading Ld Byron in bed by Lamplight. Such a walk as we took
yes'y!!!, *bella, bella*, on the terrace walk above Puzzuoli - Sea, islands, mountains, wood, towns, castles, lake, Vesuvius, aloes, Roses,
Festoons of Vines, all gloriously beautiful.

The River Colyne company have taken or intend taking a hole out of
our Kensington Farm to make a reservoir for Dogs & Cats or the peo-

---

[457] St Januarius, the patron saint of Naples. On three occasions a year, a phial of his
blood was central to a religious ceremony during which it was supposed to liquefy.
Marianne would have attended in early May.

[458] Sir Richard Hussey Vivian (1775-1842) served in the Peninsular War and led a cav-
alry brigade at Waterloo. He subsequently became an M.P.

ple of London to drink.[459] They will give 9000£ for this hole to my Father. Ld Hertford is a kind friendly man & a King of an adviser as to money affairs - I have got a little of his advice gratis too & have bought in here a thousand £ for wh. I have got 70£ a year & I have got 500£ in the Ohito[?] for wh. Viva my Ld Hertford!!!! say I for getting 106£ a year instead of 30£. I love money better every day. We have here an excellent King *l'esprit sage*, with order'd Economy & every thing hated by the upper ranks in this country.

We have dined once on the grass - the last time the dinner rolled down the hill. Mr Hill always says he will come; better a dinner of Herbs rolling down a Hill than a stalled Ox with the *Corps diplomatique*. Mr Canning in one of his finest speeches makes use of a simile "one perfect & entire Chrysolite", & so we were much puzzled to know whether it was to be found in the Bible or Shakespeare. We found it in *Othello* who says "Had Desdimona been true, If heaven wd make me such another world of one entire & perfect Chrysolite I'd not have sold her for it."[460] By the by, Ly Canning is like one perfect & entire Chrysolite.

The last week we had a rich formalised[?] dinner at the Duponts, Mme Dupont in such a set of Rubies as make ones mouth water; they are little stones set close in most beautiful ennamel. She is as fat as prosperity & pate de foie gras can make a woman. The *corps dip. d'aujourd-hui* are bores; however round the Tea Table I was amused at the Fr. Amb'r talking of the price of washing to the D'esse Fernandina - & how they tear his clothes to pieces on the stones here. He is very handsome & as if he scorned to tell a lie. The Duchesse is a good creature but not *La grande dame* one sd. expect belonging to every thing g[rea]t & grand & heroic in Spain - Palafox's Sister. Mme La Tour Maubourg did not come wh. I was glad of, as it was so very hot & she is so dark & fat, & I hate fat women. "Ses yeux nagent dans la grais-

---

[459] The Portobello Farm in Kensington had been bought in 1755 by Sir George's father. In the late 1820s the River Colne Water Company had plans to create a reservoir. These did not materialise. (See *The Times* of 7 August 1829, p.2, and *The Survey of London*, Vol. 37, London, 1973, p.298).

[460] *Othello*, Act V, Sc.2. The quotation was used by George Canning in a speech on 3 February 1824 (see *The Parliamentary Debates*, Vol. 10, p.77).

se"[461] as M. de Stackelberg says. Mme de Lottum is a Ninny.[462] Mme de Lebzeltern is the clever person, a sort of North of good humour[463] & very ugly.

June 19th [1831]. We have been leading a charming life lately enjoying *Les Diners sur l'herbe* in the open air, in this delightful season. The other day we dined at Cape Misenus - & yes'y at Astroni where was a regular *Fête Champêtre* got up by Sir Henry - people more tried to be pleasant than were. Mme de Lebzeltern looked like a plain Cook. Mr Hill was as black as possible until he had swallowed a bottle of Madeira when he looked up & said "Well, its very pretty."

There are two marriages going on in Eng'd now, very odd ones. Mr Warrender to Miss Arden after an infidelity of 20 years; then he was gay & good humoured & silly; he is now old, grey, *dévot*, with two children & a fortune.[464] Mr Seymour marries Gertrude Brand.[465] They say he was dying to break up his menage & she to leave duty, table cloths & dry toast. Ly Isabella writes to us, it was love at first sight. Ly Conyngham is gone to Eng'd, having taken the two old Cabinets in wh. she hopes to find treasure. Ly Warrender[466] has got a *Cavalier servente* instead of Mr F.G. who I think if he had common sense wd marry Ly L. Percy, but as he has not, will not, being uncommonly unreasonable & clever. The Ladies in Eng'd are said to be very troublesome & his F.S. & his P. Bradley[?] politically[?].

26th June [1831]. Yesterday we had a very nice day - much the pleasanter owing to the absence of many invited. They eat & drank like 11 famished persons in the vineyard above the Cardilo Villa & then we

---

[461] 'Her eyes swim in fat'

[462] Friedrich Hermann, Graf v. Lottum (1796-1849) had been appointed in 1830 as Prussian Minister at Naples. In 1828, he had married to Klotilde, Gräfin zu Putbus (1809-1894).

[463] Lord North (1732-92), former British Prime Minister, had the reputation of acting in an unruffled and good-humoured manner.

[464] John Warrender, brother of Sir George, married Hon. Frances Henrietta Arden, on 25 June 1831.

[465] George Hamilton Seymour married Gertrude Maud Brand, a daughter of Lord Dacre, on 31 July 1831.

[466] Hon. Anne Evelyn Boscawen had married Sir George Warrender on 3 October 1810. They had no children.

rode home by moonlight by the Terrace walk & the Ruffo Villa. Think of the priests having put a Linen gown on the Venus de Medici.

1st of July [1831]. We had last night the prettiest of E'gs; like many other pretty things, it was a bore, a great bore, but indeed I am just now so sleepy that I am not fit for anything. It was a Fête given by Moonlight to 40 or 50 people at the Schilla Villa[467] to keep the aniversary of Mrs L. Brook's 13th wedding day wh. for some reason or other, I sd have thought as well forgotten. The gardens lighted up with coloured Lanterns amongst the Trees like something in *Lalla Rooke* wh[ile] the Moon shone on the bay & Vesuvius. There was Punch & a long, long supper wh. lasted till 1/2 1 & I was extinct. They drunk toasts & happiness, past, present & future, & cheered & answered speeches, all very well in a *diner sur l'herbe* but *déplacé* in a mixture of people & nations. I begin to think Mrs L[angford] B[rooke] a silly noisy woman.

I had a Letter from dear Ly Belhaven, all kindness & gaity, tumult & jollities. She is keeping open house as the wife of the Ld High Commissioner of Scotland. They were received beautifully by their Tennants who would take the horses from the carriage & draw them home to the tune of "There is a luck about the house while the good man's away." There was something in the way it was done & the way Ly Bel. tells it that made me cry. Dear Scotland, I do love those people & that country. She tells me of dear little Ly Canning being prettier & nicer than ever. Sir Henry Lushington gave me a curious MS he has written for me, entertaining enough, of his brigand Adventures. Coloured lantern Fêtes are all the fashion now at Naples & beautiful they are. The summer is wonderfully cool & we enjoy these *Thés* much. I like summer & the only thing wanting is a commerce with those you love - *Senza Suggezione* - now I love no one here & dislike no one. *C'est la plus belle indifference et c'est mon unique bien.*[468] Dined at the Falconnet Villa.

Mme Dupont came to [a] broad summer day light dinner, a wonderful sight of wig & finery. The place is perfectly lovely. I like fair women in lilac or blue, dark in green or red, or Oiseau. There was a Ball. Pr'ss Centola lovely with her hair plain & *a feronnière*. Mr Hill said to Mme de Forli: do persuade P'cess Centola always to dress in that

---

[467] Presumably the villa of Prince Ruffo di Scilla.

[468] 'It's complete indifference and it's my one and only quality.'

manner. We did not stay for the Lantern festival & supper, but came away at 1/2 12.

Tonight we drove about Naples. The illuminations for the Queen's birth night seemed to light up a Town all peace & happiness. What a different scene it would be with a London Mob. Moonlight flourishes here. I see no Love & much indifference & the *Dolce far niente* predominating everywhere.

> The sky was flooded with moon light.
> Below were waters azure bright,
> Palazzi with their marble halls,
> Green gardens, silver waterfalls,
> And orange groves & citron shades,
> And Cavaliers & dark eyed maids.[469]

July 17 [1831]. Ther. 84. We dined at Sir Grenville Temples. News: The Cholora Morbus & the Comet foretold. Citizen Brougham, the writer of the poor Mans friend, driving them to kill King, Peers & priests. Mrs Jordans son Earl of Munster on condition he votes for reform.[470] The Emperor of Brazil singing songs at Concerts. The D'esse de Berry running thro' Europe *en Cavalier* & being cavalierly treated. Ch's 10th counting his beads at Holyrood.

How these english women do row their foreign husbands & how attentive & amiable & *aux petit soins* these husbands are, & yet I wd not for worlds marry a foreigner, not for worlds either Mr Fal[connet] or Mr Dupont, & yet Mme Dupont is a marvelously happy woman, knows it & says it. Ugly women are always the happiest I have remarked in life. Old Don Craven wd have done better to have married her. What has he got by not, growling & grumbling by his fireside, or boxed up in his house on the Chiatamone.

We went to a child's ball at the D'esse Serracapriola; again Chinese Lanterns. Naples is now moral, good menages & estimation[?] - & poor dear Eng'd grows wickeder & wickeder. Public matters are here incessantly discoursed of - repeal of the Union, Reform & Anti reform

---

[469] See Laetitia Elizabeth Landon (L.E.L.), *The Improvisatrice and other poems*, 6th ed., London,1825, p.83.

[470] George Fitzclarence (1794-1842), son of William IV and Mrs Dorothy Jordan, was created Earl of Munster on 4 June 1831.

- *Les Glorieuses*[471] in France. D'esse de Berry comes here tomorrow. Ld Ponsonby is on his road here. The Cholora at Triest - as for Eng'd, I lament its glory gone. Cromwell & the covenanters at work. The Comet coming, a Mountain fallen in, a volcano between Malta & Sicily has opened in the sea & the Fishermen were so terrified at the sight that they fled in a little boat & left their larger Vessel.

July 25 [1831]. The reform question is carried. Fumigation & fright has begun to seize people. Here we are stewing, night & day, but from 6 to 10 it is charming - & to sit drinking Tea in a long Spanish veil & with a Fan *a l'espagnolle*, by Moonlight amongst the flowers on the Terrace wd enchant all but an *habituée* to such scenes. The King has been received in Sicily as he deserved wh. is everything - he shed Tears of joy. He made that mad old Mrs Vanneck,[472] our english disgrace, dance with San Cesario, vis a vis the handsomest woman in Palermo. Cholora is all the conversation. Dr Quin[473] is gone to Warsaw to see about it. It is now a hundred miles from Vienna, in Prussia & at Petersburg. The Arch Duke Constantine has died of it,[474] & the well being & health of Naples is a wonder.

Naples July 1831. I have spent a fortune in Emeralds, many of wh. I bought in Piazza dei Orefice.
one Emerald with rose dia. 24 D[ucats].
Earrings finished 20£
Emeralds various 36D
some at 15 & some at 20D each.
In the Piazza they offered us a curious Toy of one Pearl & some Rubies 50 Piastres
a Crown of precious stones 250 D.
a pair of diamond Earrings 270 D.
Two large Diamonds 100D.

---

[471] The three days in 1831 (July 27-29) which had ushered in Louis Philippe and led to the exile of Charles X.

[472] Presumably Charlotte Vanneck (1782-1875), widow of Gerard Vanneck. She and her husband both died at Naples.

[473] Dr Frederick Quin (1799-1878) was a British pioneer of homoeopathic medicine. He had gone to Italy with the Duchess of Devonshire and had been with her at her death in Rome in 1824.

[474] Archduke Constantine of Russia had died of cholera on 27 June. He had been heir to the Imperial Crown, but, on the occasion of his divorce in 1820, had renounced it in favour of his brother Nicholas.

Villa Coreali (Sorrento), Aug't 5 1831. We came here on the 2nd, stopping to look in at our dirty Château at Castellamare by the way. Sorrento is the most innocent place I know & the most sequestered except Amalfi round Naples. It is a very oppressive air & ones strength is gone by one o'clock. The place & the very air are melancholy; neither one or the other have the enlivening powers of Castellamare. I went last night to see my old haunts of 1820. The Cocomella[475] where the ruin & the dirty Court & the ragged people, & the orange trees, & the Linen hanging to dry, & the old broken picturesque well, all seem as I left them then. Then we went to the Cappuccini[476] wh. looks as charming as ever: the long narrow passage with the Portraits of Monks, the old living Monks seated in high gossip by the doors & the black cross & the white walled Terrace at the end overlooking the sea. This Convent has been established 250 years. There are 7 convents in this plain of Sorrento. Many I see have the dates of 1710/20 on them. I went the other day to the Studio Library at Naples to find some book that would give an account of the Monasteries in this country wh. interest me much, but none exists. *Italia Sacra*[477] relates to the Bishopricks & not to the Convents. I have been reading over the Polish Letters. One day they will make a Novel. I spent yes'y in Tears, reading *Destiny* wh. is just come from Eng'd.[478] It is very affecting, an image of life - a swift life driven on by wind & tide. After, I dreamt all night, I was so agitated by the book.

Sorrento is magnificent in scenery, but I don't like it, an eternal sirocco, no view of sun sets until you clamber up a high high hill. Sir H[enry]L[ushington] came to us, a simple minded man, just the person to be happy in this low world. We all like him. His wife is a mass of affectation & twaddle, but she is [a] poor woman fast getting that curse of woman, old age, & so I cannot say any thing against her. We went some clambering walks & rides wh. Sir Henry enjoys like a person escaped from Cities to Liberty. Pollio's Villa, I always admired, &

---

[475] La Cocumella, an inn, formerly a Jesuit convent, situated on the coast between Sant' Agnello and Sorrento.

[476] The Church of the Frati Cappuccini in the commune of Sant'Agnello had been built at the end of the sixteenth century.

[477] Presumably the 10-volume work by Ferdinando Ughelli, published in Venice, 1717-22.

[478] *Destiny*, a three volume novel published anonymously in Edinburgh in 1831. The author was Susan Ferrier (1782-1854).

those fine rocky abrupt nitches of Capri - & the ruined Tower & the wild plants & we went to the *festa* at Massa[479] where we found Gingerbread & relicks & cotton night caps to be sold in Stalls, a church all hung with gold & silver finery, in silks, & tissues, & lighted up, the Organ playing & the population walking in & out, some saying their prayers on their knees & often staring about them. The whole *festa* was orderly & joyous & as we rode 5 miles home by Moon light, the country people were all good humour, talking & screaming & singing & dancing the Tarantella barefoot & playing the Tambourine dressed in Brocade silk jackets & their earrings like large frogs[480] of gold or pearls, but the days of fine costume are gone by as formerly, & the Jews Harp is now oftener heard here than the guitars. I thought of Eng'd - & what a scene all this wd have been of riot & disorder, of snarls of rudeness & drunkenness, & in a foreign country we heretics felt quite secure amongst priests, monks, & an ignorant peasantry.

19th Aug't [1831]. The air is charming & here we are established at Castellamare. The heat is not diminished yet we feel revived. I have seen only Dr Wellesley[481] who seems *déplacé* here & Mme Falconnet who if she would speak gently wd. be a very nice person but she does scream terribly, & looks so soft & pretty all the time, that I am sure that Katharine in the *T[aming] of the Shrew* was a blonde & had a blue eye; indeed I have made up my mind that the dark hair'd, dark eyed persons are the quiet & calm in life.

Fair:	Dark & yellow:
Mme Falconnet	Charles Greville
Sir St. Canning	Ly Ponsonby
Uncle Brodrick	Ly Mansfield
Ly Ruthvens eyes	
all the Percy's	
Lord Harrowby	
Mr Ponsonby	

One person here makes against my system, Mrs Garnier, who well bronzed with the summer & with a shabby straw bonnet thrown back, is Meg Merillies,[482] or an old Gipsey to the life. I suspect her a Shrew

---

[479] a festival was held annually on 15 August.

[480] frog - an ornamental fastening for a frock or gown.

[481] Hon. and Rev. Dr Gerald Valerian Wellesley (1770-1848).

[482] Meg Merrilies, a character in Sir Walter Scott's *Guy Mannering*.

if ever there were one & if I had a silver sixpence, I'd make her cross my hand. Her husband is a good old gossip with 365 stories at least & what is odd he is like a North.

I had two Letters - characteristic - one from Mrs L[angford] B[rooke], all twaddle & insipidity, & another from Charlotte, all life & spirit. She says Mrs Drummond de Melfort who is coming here is charming. I wonder if she is or if she is quite the reverse. Charlotte has had a providential escape & as she is my Heir in case of the Cholora sweeping us all off, I hope she is safe for every reason, but I speak thus lightly of what I feel strongly. Reform goes on. The Members worn to Ghosts. There is to be a procession at the Coronation that Ld. Munster's wife[483] might walk & a pretty walk she will make of it. Then there was to have been no banquet on acct of Expenses - the banquet *a manqué* only in Ch's the 1st reign, too ominous a precedent. The King don't find it so easy to be King, they say.

Aug't 27 [1831]. I have kept my room in days. Have been ill, very ill with - Fever - just as my nerves were beginning to mend with a purer air & a calm life.

2d Sept. [1831]. I have been very ill - & Papa too. The summer is fast disappearing in heat & long days - & now there are two Month[s] left to get strong & well & four months of ennui & representation come, & then a break up of life, habits, home & an entire change of existance to look to. I don't now regret it. I have been reading until my wits are puzzled, & writing too. Ld Byron I see was struck with all that has struck me in Italy. First with the lock of fair hair at Milan wh. long haunted me, then with the Tombs at Lido & the Armenian Convent at Venice, then with the Campo Santo: which I   persecute Georgina & Papa each time that we go near, to let me go to. I have a 2nd time read his letters - I have considered & rewritten my own scrawls, read, read & read, until my poor weak nerves are exhausted & I pine for a ride in the woods & mountains, & today it rains an Autumn rain & my wishes are not likely to be indulged. Till this year I have saved my money, but what with books from Eng'd, Emeralds, my gown at Constantinople, & a case of clothes from Paris, charged 160D & paid 19D, [*c. 5 words scratched out*] my finances will only cover my expences this year.

---

483   The coronation took place on 8 September.

Vesuvius is magnificent. Mme de Stael says: "Le phénomène du Vésuve cause un veritable battement de coeur."[484] She is right - it does - all the greatness & splendour of the world are not comprised in the powers of Man, & we feel its powers conducted by laws that we can't penetrate, mysteries that we can't penetrate; matters we know nothing of, protect or menace our existance. Vesuvius is the descent into Hell, certainly poetically so, & a little wd convince us of its being really so, as the Sailors & lower people think it. The new Volcano near to Sicily occupies people at Naples.[485] An english Captain first landed there & struck the Eng. flag, & one day Mr Hill said in joke that he believed P'ce Cassaro wd write to him to tell him of the deed, but when he came up after dinner, he found two Letters of 8 sides to complain!!! to his great delight. The erruption opposite to us is a great amusement, volumes of smoke & flame ascend every E'g.

Ld Hertford writes from London that Ly Clanricarde[486] has had the Cholora & several others. Here is the cure. 50 drops [of Cajeputta Oil][487] at a time & repeated at a few minutes interval - this agrees but little with the frightful accounts from Vienna & Hungary - & still more melancholy details which Mme de Fiquelmont writes from Petersburg[488] - [s]he gives also an account of the Revolutionists & this M'g (Sept. 11) comes an account of the Massacre of the Russians at Warsaw & of the burning of the Ambassadors houses at Constantino-

---

[484] *Corinne ou l'Italie*, Book XI, Ch.2, p.163 in Vol. 2 of 7th ed., Paris, 1818.

[485] Seismic activity began towards the end of June and the new island developed rapidly during the first weeks in July. Captain Humphrey Fleming Senhouse of the *St Vincent*, flagship of Vice-Admiral Sir Henry Hotham, landed on 2 August, raised the British flag, and took possession in the name of the King. Given the name Graham Island by the British, it was shortly afterwards designated as Isola Ferdinandea by Ferdinand II. By the beginning of 1832, rapid erosion had caused the island to disappear again below the surface of the sea, thus removing any cause for dispute over ownership.

[486] Lady Clanricarde (1804-76) was the only daughter of George Canning.

[487] Oil obtained from the Cajeput tree of the Moluccas believed to have been a remedy for cholera. In a diary entry for 16 August 1831, Philipp von Neumann described how his friend Lady Clanricarde had been at death's door with cholera, but had been given 180 drops of oil of Cajeput in a single dose and that 'this had saved her'. (Neumann, *Diary*, I, p.256).

[488] Dorothea von Ficquelmont (1804-1863), the wife of the Austrian ambassador to St Petersburg, Karl Ludwig von Ficquelmont. For most of the 1820s, he had been Austrian minister at Naples.

ple. In the papers are details of the most horrid of Shipwrecks, details that make one sad & sorry of the loss of the steam packet.[489]

I have finished Ld Byron's Life having read the greatest part twice over as well as the 2 R[eviews] upon it, & now I want the Edinbro' Review. This book has interested me beyond every book I have met with, for a long, long time. I remember my first impression of Ld Byron. It was at Ly Glenbervie's in the height of his beauty & popularity, or rather fashion. It comes before me as if it were yesterday.[490] Then the book is filled with remarks upon those I know. Then it is curious how all that strikes me in Italy struck him too. The Lido burial ground, the lock of Fair hair at Venice, the Campo Santo at Bologna, he dwells upon in a way that proves they touched his imagination as they did mine & I never found any traveller who cared for these objects except Ld Byron. To his Mother's weakness & want of education, to her passionate & wicked temper may be attributed his errors, joined to a nature in wh. hereditary insanity was already implanted. All amicable Men love their Mothers, or their Mother's memory, or are forced to execrate it. That fine passage in *Manfred* on Insanity comes fearfully forwards, & what will his daughter be!! a fearful future for her Mother. There is a strong paralel between him & S. Per.[?]! in two particulars. Insanity & shame for their Mother's conduct, to say nothing of looks & eccentricity. Fate also ushered him into life with theatrical effect, but how different has been the sequel. Then his loves. The beautiful graceful Mrs Spencer Smith dying of a lingering disorder at Vienna, was ever there a woman to be *epris* with,[491] but the only two

---

[489] On 19 July, the *Lady Sherbrooke* sailing from Londonderry to Quebec with 280 passengers had foundered on rocks. *The Times* (30 August 1831) reported only 32 lives saved.

[490] In her journal entry for 2 April 1812, Mary Berry records having spoken to Lord Byron at Lady Glenbervie's. (Berry, II, p.496). Could this be the occasion when M.T. first saw the poet?

[491] Byron had met Mrs Constance Spencer Smith in Malta in 1809. He described her to his mother on 15 September of that year: 'Her life has been from its commencement so fertile in remarkable incidents, that in a romance they would appear improbable ... since my arrival here I have had scarcely any other companion, I have found her very pretty, very accomplished, and extremely eccentric.' (Marchand, Vol.I, p.224).

he seems really to have liked are Mrs Chaworth[492] & Mme Guccioli[493] who both attached him by their amiableness & not their beauty. Mme Guccioli was soft & had a mild manner & spoke both English & Italian beautifully - as to beauty or grace or even that *je ne scai quoi* so talked of, or elegance, where was it - I never cd find it with all my trying - & yet she was in mourning for him & unprotected & under circumstances that created interest - but it was not possible to catch any enthusiasm as to her, as all the time she lamented him & said that after loving Ld Byron, one cd think only of God, she seemed much inclined to think of Ld Dudley Stuart,[494] & dispute his conquest with his present wife. Her reddish hair & large feet were not pretty, nor the italian style of dress, as bad as possible, wh. she indulged in. Ly Davy who thought every thing connected with Ld Byron charming, was charmed with her. The English were scandalized at finding her *en petit comité*[495] & Bertolei says "that Ld Byron has chosen her that he might have no rivals even after his death." I must own her manner was *très sucré* & pleasing.

I seldom write on home concerns. It is dangerous, unfair by one self & those belonging to you & painful. My Father & half the Men in the world at 70, I believe, are the same miserable beings, with fortune, the use of their faculties, their families not tormenting or troubling them - miserable beings from total want of occupation, interest or pursuit: excepting that of their health, their food or sleep - sad existance of a numerous class! I cannot, I feel, impart interest, occupation, interest or happiness to him, & yet without us, he wd be still more wretched, as the small interest he has is in the question & answer conversation he has - what an unhappy existence. As for me, I have thrown up what is called Happiness in this world, falling into the seer & yellow leaf; I have neither spirit, energy or health to struggle for society or amusement: constituted as Free him now - & Georgina now - & I must be

---

[492] Mary Chaworth was a childhood acquaintance of Byron. She lived at Annesley Hall, not far from Newstead Abbey, the Byron residence. When Byron fell in love with Mary in the early 1800s, she was in love with someone else and did not return his affection.

[493] Byron's love-affair with Teresa Guccioli had been the final serious and long-lasting relationship of his life. He had first met her in 1818, became in the early 1820s her *cavaliere servente*, and, after her divorce from Count Guccioli, lived with her and her family at Florence and Pisa..

[494] Lord Dudley Coutts Stuart (1802-54) had married Christina, a daughter of Lucien Bonaparte in 1824.

[495] 'in an intimate group.'

content the remainder of my days to vegetate, & live, *au jour, la journée* - & so, such a set of watergruel people as we are now, is rarely found & makes me often smile & sometimes miserable.

We received last night two very amusing Letters, one from Ld De Ros to Papa from London, very amusing - he says that the threatening tone about Politics is lowered a little - but that Sons have been against Fathers, Wives against Husbands, & even lovers against Mistresses - most often Ladies are Antireformists - & no wonder, for they must dread having a stupid husband sitting at home evening after evening. He describes the Cholora panic as ridiculously as possible - & that instead of Eau de Cologne, the Ladies carry little bottles of Cajeputta oil 200 drops of wh. wd completely cure you for life. He says that Ly d'Orsay is gone off from her husband, a mysterious business, upon wh. things are whispered of perfidious friends, &c.[496] He describes Paris as totally changed & all the brilliancy of it gone. He says that the women wear Ginghams & stuffs instead of silks & satins, & wear little mean bonnets & high laced boots! Ly Isabella St John's Letter is still more amusing - as it is a woman's Letter - showing things as they seem. She describes London as terrible, that it is the sublime & terrible of society mixed together, such size, such numbers, so much beauty, such running after one woman, & such running after many Men, such vying of ball & assembly givers, & such talking of only the event of the moment. What an unreasonable & awful life!! Of Herself she says that she shall follow the general rule, of every one for themselves, & God for us all, & she finishes by saying, she has finished a Novel & is writing another, & that Colburn has chosen to call it *Wedded Life*.[497] She says that the Political game is more amusing at Paris than in London, that in London the game is merely personnal.

La Cava. Sunday 18th of Sept. 1831. We came here on Thursday having been all ill & wanting change of air & change of scene. There is no Inn or Lodging house in this great straggling village. La Cava is composed of white houses & very pretty ones, churches & convent detached, & situated on a Valley & the surrounding Hills. Sir H. Lush-

---

[496] In 1828, Count d'Orsay, who, for some years, had been living on intimate terms in the household of the Earl and Countess of Blessington, married Harriet, the 15 year old daughter of the Earl. The marriage, arranged more to gratify the adults than to satisfy the needs and desires of the young bride, was a disaster. (cf. Note 70).

[497] Published in two volumes by H.Colburn in 1831 under the title *Wedded Life in the Upper Ranks*.

ington with his usual activity & good nature got us a Private House for a week wh. is a fine proportioned, gloomy & uncomfortable Palazzo - we came here in pouring rain & so it continued all Friday, but Saturday it cleared up & we went to La Dame du Paroisse, la dame blanche.[498] She lives in a charming old straggling looking house, all oddity & comfort, with a foreign wellbred look about it. Loggia's filled with flowers, & pictures of Abbots & Ancestors on its walls. What an odd existance is this Miss Whyte's whom no one knows the hist'y of but who knows everyone. She must be a benevolent minded good woman I think. We went a long ride with the Lushingtons, up a high mountain, on the topmost point of which, having a view of the Bay of Salerno, are remains of a ruined Chapel & Hermitage which, after looking over, we rode by winding paths down into Salerno, where a great Cattle Fair was going forwards. Herds of wild Horses & Buffaloes were kept well in order by Men on Horseback with long Poles in their hands. These Men wore the pointed Hats of the Southern Provinces with a Feather in them & a flower too often & looked as wild as the Animals they were guarding.

Today we started at ten o'clock to go to hear Mass performed in the Trinità Monastery. We joined Sir W. [Gell] & the Lushingtons. It amused us to see the groups of peasants; one little Girl with beautiful sentimental eyes like Ly Mansfield's charmed me. Poor child, I sd like to have given her a new Jacket, hers was so ragged, but I cd not manage it, & this group of children playing near during the Service pleased me more than the well gotten up Mass. The Music began with slow Organ music well enough, but shortly got into the Finale of *Tancredi*, & from that to the *Barbiere de Seviglia*[499] & "took the rapt soul," & lapt it in San Carlo![500] I do not like profane Music in sacred places, nor do I ever like gay music on the Organ sending your Soul upon a jig to heaven, but it suits the purposes of the Catholic Religion which evidently wishes its followers to have as few disagreeable moments as possible. The Church of this Monastery is newly done up & it has lost that look of great antiquity wh. it makes claim to. After the Service we went into a Room over the door of which was written "Donne Forrestiere" & there the priests brought Sir Wm Gell & Mr

---

[498] 'the white lady', i.e. Anna Baptista White/Whyte.

[499] *Tancredi* and the *Barbiere di Siviglia*, operas by Rossini first performed in 1813 and 1816 respectively.

[500] M.T. re-uses this expression in her essay on the convent in *The Sketch Book of the South*, p.84. The phrase 'rapt soul' occurs in Milton's *Il Penseroso* (1.40).

Strangways who are both learned, the curiosities of their convent: The Grant of Lands by Rugiero, King of Sicily, made 750 years back, & besides Lands, of peasants, Saracens as well as christians, it specifies. This grant is framed & glazed with the Seal & signature. Afterwards they showed us a thin volume containing the Lombard Code of Laws on parchment, with paintings & figures, much in design & colouring like those on Playing Cards. They have a Bible of which they are very proud of the 7th or 8th Century - the lettering on Vellum, & the Chapters are noted in silver upon lilac & blue vellums. The book is square & in collumns. Sir Wm. thought some parts of this Bible were of the 7th century, but that it was mostly much later. There was another Bible in Latin too, handsomely illuminated on Vellum of the 14th Century.

After leaving the Monastery, we rode down to the grottoes by the river in the Valley. There are pathways in these low grounds most beautiful, & looking above you see the Convent on the Rock above & the Mountains still higher above it. When the Chant was heard at Vespers, & the learned Monks walked in this low ground with book in hand or pondering over some old MS., one can imagine the charms of this retirement to learned Men wh. these Benedictines were. This Convent was founded by Adalferio,[501] a P'ce of Salerno, who was a pious Hermit here who inhabited the grottoes in the Valley. The Convent was built & rebuilt until the French suppressed it when they occupied Naples. Since, it has been restored, but not to its ancient splendour or to the Lands it formerly possessed. The Grottoes where there are still traces of an Hermit's residence & the remains of an Oratory are beautiful - the Stalactites with wild hanging plants, & the deep ravine with a rude one-arched bridge thrown across it, & the marks of waterfalls in tempests make it romantic beyond any of the neighbouring romantic spots, & it is still a Hermitage for Painters, Poets & Enthusiasts. We rode up the hills to the villages near. It was the fête of La Madonna de 7 Dolori[502] & some of the Churches were open & the figure of the Madonna within was dressed like the figure of night, darkly, with silver stars & seven swords emblamatical of the day stuck through her heart. The Views of the country from the platforms round the churches were generally lovely, the country looked gay & smiling & rural, & from these villages without even a road thro' them, we often looked down into the high road about Vietri or Salerno, leading to the Southern Provinces, now, owing to the fair, crowded with herds of Oxen &

---

[501] S. Alferius.

[502] Our Lady of the Seven Sorrows, a popular devotion within the Catholic Church.

Sheep & Goats, & with carriages & carts, Priests & Soldiers passing & re-passing.

19th Sept.[1831]. We are come home very tired, having been a scrambling ride over mountains, with the Lushingtons. Sir Henry owns to 18, but his conduct in these excurtions is still younger as a *no road* over a perpendicular precipace has charms for him. We crossed the Mountains as the crow flies, & found ourselves descending near to Baronesi, where we found the carriages & came home by Salerno & Vietri. The people in the villages in these wild parts came out in crowds to look at us, never having seen the like of Ladies on Donkeys.

20th [Sept. 1831]. Today we had a beautiful ride by the Rottola, & view of the bridge, the Town, the convents, the Sea & the Mountains, & which gave us the idea of La Cava having formerly been a great place. All this day we talked of eyes & Ly Adams eyes - she is an old beauty & the Neapolitans say of her "Lunghi, Lunghi, secca, secca."[503] I am sorry I have not seen the Tombs of the Abbots of La Cava - who are buried in the Rock, in the church of the Trinità. We went into the Cathedral & the Franciscan Church in La Cava. A great number of Tombs of Jesuits with curious & flourishing Inscriptions are in the first, & some very pretty Tombs are in the Franciscans. Raymundo di Monceva on the ground, leaning on his spear:

22d. [Sept. 1831]. We are going, & very sorry we are, for the country is enchanting. Our house is not uncomfortable. My Father is amused & gets good food (a great object) & Miss White has plenty of stories of Saints & old Legions [legends], & old Anecdotes, & is very kind & hospitable, & has books too. We went today to see the Pigeons Towers, & manner of catching the flight from Africa, called here "Giocchi de Palumbi!!" It seems that in the olden time when the world was rich or poor, for I never can make out which it was, people came from all parts to destroy the Pigeons that came from the South & they played at Cards until their arrival, until the Men on the Towers gave notice of the approach of the Birds. The Pigeons Towers are on elevated points

---

[503] Presumably 'Old, old, dry, dry'! Diamantina Palatino (c.1797-1844), the widow of Count Souffis, had married Sir Frederick Adam in 1820 in Corfu. Sir Frederick served as Lord High Commissioner of the British protectorate of the Ionian Islands from 1824 to 1832.

in glorious situations; one looks to Vesuvius, Nocera, with such a view! The Nets are fastened by long Poles behind the Towers; a Man stands on the top of the Tower, having a quantity of white stones the size of Pigeons & looking like them. He throws them at the Pigeons, who have approached the Towers & who disperse right & left towards the Nets which by a string are pulled over them & enclose them. When we were there, all was prepared for them & the Men were on the Watch for the arrival of the flight.

25th Sept.[1831]. Castellamare. Father Strangways[504] & the Lushingtons came to dinner. The Capt.[505] is a consequential would be Hero. There is much irritation between the Neap. & the English Govt. just now. Ld Palmerstone has sent orders for the Quarantine to be abolished for England. Orders with a Fleet like ours, & Mr Hill says, "Now I have orders, you will see how I shall act," & Sir Wm. Gell raps his fingers on the Table, & says "we shall see!" In truth, I have no wish to see the scenes of Lisbon acted at Naples.[506]

Sept. 29 1831. Castellamare. There are moments of one's life that are most serious, not bitter, that is not the word, but that give one a feeling of awe that is most painful, where the power of questioning your destiny lies heavily on you, & you know not why Providence thus sports with yours! probably for wise & good purposes, & because you are made to bear it: such a moment have I had tonight.

2nd Oct. [1831] There are moments in one's life that one does feel so serious that the weight of the world is on one. I try & occupy myself & not think of this same black destiny of mine, that pursues me all thro' life, pursues me in happiness. People talk to me as if I was so good, so prosperous, so indifferent; if they knew the truth! but they don't guess (thank God) at this miserable mind of mine. This day 13 years I remember well & indeed I remember all days, miserable & un-

---

[504] According to Sir William Gell, William Hill had always called him 'Old father Strangways with his icicle nose & mother Shipton hat, looking for daisies & daffodils under a hedge.' *Sir William Gell in Italy*, p.111.

[505] Captain Stephen Lushington, R.N., second son of Sir Henry.

[506] In the course of 1830 and the first months of 1831, Portuguese officials, clearly with the acquiescence of Don Miguel, had carried out a series of acts of aggressive harassment against British residents and vessels. Only when the Consul General's demand for reparations along with the dismissal of the offending officials was backed up by British warships off the mouth of the Tagus, was the conflict resolved. (See *The Annual Register ...of the Year 1831*, London, 1832, pp.442-4).

happy ones; however now the scene is closed for ever & ever of youth & even of affection. I thank God & my Grand Mother's example for my love of books; it is my only true & real consolation & wipes of[f] stains, & dries tears, & is the real happiness of life. What an extraordinary history when one comes to think of it: Pride, & Prejudice, conquered - !

I went a long ride on Friday with the Lushingtons when much talk of public news took place & Yes'y we went into Naples. It was very hot - & I was glad to come back to the calm & quiet of this place which agrees with me. I think I have now but one distinct wish left, a wish not to be buried in that horrid vault at Dorking, but to be buried in the Sun. I dare say I shall go to Eng'd, die of the cold, & *faute de mieux* be buried there. Sir Henry, who is a good calm, simple, quiet, goodnatured man, had a conversation with me on our actual situation, his surprise that we had not married, & his quick perception of all the troubles & pains *vis a vis* of my Father wd have amused had I been that day in a mood to be amused.

14th [Oct. 1831]. How I have written this summer (Monte Vergine. The Cardinal Lover. 24 Hours Journal. La Cava),[507] & this week in Letters 26 sides. The times are curious & give *de quoi faire la conversation* even with the Neapolitans besides Ronzi de Be[g]nis[508]& "Avez vous profitez de la journée."[509] There is a volcano Island started up near Sicily, by them called Ferdinando, by us Graham's Island. We have now from the windows a superb erruption of Vesuvius. The fall of Fyers; it is in the shape of a Waterfall threatening Bosco Reale every night, & every day showing a quantity of black lava hourly increasing.

---

[507] Most of these pieces are to be found in *The Sketch Book of the South* published by Edward Churton in 1835.

[508] Giuseppina Ronzi De Begnis (1800-53), a lead soprano at San Carlo opera house. After a long absence from the stage she had returned to San Carlo at the beginning of June 1831 and was much acclaimed in the title role of Rossini's *Elisabetta d'Inghilterra*. The King, who had never been known to applaud a singer, led the applause, and in the final scene, 'she was generally allowed to have surpassed any singer, of what eminence so ever, who had preceded her'. (*Morning Post*, 24 June 1831). In January 1834, Hans Christian Andersen heard her in the title role of *Norma* and wrote of her divine voice, how she was overwhelmed with applause throughout, and, at the end, made five curtain calls. (*Romerske Dagbøger*, Copenhagen, 1947, pp.59-60).

[509] 'Have you had a good day?'

Far thro' the shadowy sky the ascending flames
Stream'd their fierce torrents by the gales of night
Now curl'd, now flashing their long lightnings up
That make the Stars seem pale; less frequent now
Thro the red volumes briefer splendours shot
And blacker waves roll'd o'er the darken'd heaven.

Deep thro' the sky the hollow thunders roll'd
And flaming horrors of consuming fires.[510]

25th [Oct. 1831]. There is much gossip about her majesty of Naples whose conduct with a Swiss Officer much annoys the King, & her Ladies have left her to the Swiss Officer & to the Villa Gallo.[511]

Reform & Anti-reform occupy the world of books, reviews & newspapers. Mr Hill has sent us Mr Croker & Lord Dudley's Reviews. Mr Crokers Epigram is

Jack & Will brought in a Bill
To make a Revolution.
And Will fell down
And broke his crown
And Jack his constitution.

Sir William Gell & Sir H.L[ushington] have been passing two days with us. We went & explored the ruins of the Castle of Sarno yesterday & of a pretty little Convent called Santa Cosimata near; they are surrounded by Olive Trees, Aloes & Indian fig, & command a vast extent of Valley in which are the windings of the Sarno & Pompeii. What is extraordinary is that the ground rises to the Sea which supposes a former erruption or different shaped country.

We have Letters from Engd. of the 3d. Ld Hertford [who] says if his body is not at Naples, his wishes will be there this winter. There was a Majority of 43 that night in the H. of Lords & they had nicely calculated the majority near 40. Charlotte says that the *On dits* are that Ld

---

[510] Apparently a compilation: for the first six lines, see Robert Southey, *Joan of Arc*, Book IX, ll.1-6, for line seven, see Book VI of the same poem, and for the final line see John Ford's *'Tis Pity She's a Whore*, Act III, Sc. 6.

[511] The Dowager Queen Maria Isabella (1789-1848) had purchased the Villa Gallo in 1831.

Brougham is making a Cats paw of Lord John Russell & brings in a bill of his own on this hated subject. There was a scene in the Drawing room about Ly Ferrers - the King turned his back, Ld Howe tore the Card, & the Queen cried, when Ly Ferrers came to be presented.[512] With regard to the D'ess of K[ent] & P'cess V[ictoria], the D'ess did not wish her to be mixed up with the FitzClarences & finding that she was to be placed in the box with them, staid away. Sir J. Copley's Son marries Miss Pelham. Sir J. seems as much pleased as if it was a daughter.[513]

We went to say Adieu to Pompeii. The last thing found is a Car, a roman Car. No one ever read or wrote more than I have done this Summer. *Destiny*, a crying & miserable Novel - *Hist. of Enthusiasm*, a clever book[514] - *Letters on Poland*,[515] interesting now - Bishop of Chester's Lectures on the Gospels,[516] Milk & water lectures. "Take no thought for the morrow" was always a stumbling block in my way. The Bishop has no disdain of monastic life, wh. increases the difficulties of the world to Protestants. The Historical plays of Shakespeare. Henry 6th is Charles 10 to the life. Lodge's Historical Characters[517] - Ly Jane Gray is a most truly pious life, that of an Angel on Earth. Pole & Cranmer excellent as the Papist & the Reformer. If any one wishes to write a Romance, let him look out "philosopher's Stone."

Nov'r. 2d [1831]. *Paris Observer* 1830
Hallams *Middle Ages*[518] - tiresome.

---

[512] The Duchesse de Dino gives a fuller, eye-witness account of this incident in *Chronique de 1831 à 1862*, ed. la Princesse Radziwill, Paris, 1909, Vol.I, p.5.

[513] Joseph William Copley married Lady Charlotte Pelham, daughter of the Earl of Yarborough, on 19 November 1831.

[514] Isaac Taylor, *Natural History of Enthusiam* had first been published in 1829 and had reached a fifth edition by 1831.

[515] Probably *Letters, literary and political, on Poland*, by Krystyn Lach-Szyrma, Edinburgh, 1823.

[516] John Bird Sumner, *A practical exposition of the Gospels of St Matthew and St Mark, in the form of lectures*, London, 1831.

[517] Edmund Lodge, *Portraits of Illustrious Personages of Great Britain &c.*, 12 vols., London, 1823.

[518] Henry Hallam, *View of the State of Europe during the Middle Ages*, 3 vols., London, 1829.

Bourrien[n]es *Memoirs* - not as good as Segur.[519]
Quarterly & Edinbro' Reviews.
Botta's *History of Italy*,
Daru's *His'y of the Republic of Venice*[520] [both] very very amusing.

Daru is like Sismondi filled with romantic histories. If anyone chose to write a romantic story, see Daru & the Bibl[iothèque] du Roi No 10090 is an act of Adoption of the V. Republic - The romantic adventures of Zeno, Ad[mira]l, an Otello in his'y & bravery. He died 1418. Catharine Cornaro Q[ueen] of Cyprus who abdicated 1488, & retired to the Chateau fort d'Asolo in the province of Trevise where she was "environné d'honneurs et de gardiens." The story of Bianca Capello 1577. The plague carried off 40,000, Titian amongst them. Archbishop Carlo Borromeo showed his charity & made his memory blessed. 1684 Cara Mustapha during a revolt in Hungary marched with 200,000 Turks to beseige Vienna, defended by Ferd. Degli Obizzi, a Gen'l who had fled from Padua, having revenged his mother's honor upon a Man who had been 15 years in prison. The Mother is the Lady of the Statue in the Hotel de Ville at Padua. Vienna was reliev'd by Jean Sobieski, K. of Poland who dispersed the Ottoman Army.
1472. Romantic story of Eliz. Barbo, sister of a Pope.

Nov. 12th [1831]. Naples. The times are a prey to Cholera thinking. In English [England] they are afraid of its coming from Hamburgh. The Gazette is the most awful I ever read. What they propose doing being the same as would be done in the Plague. I have not been living with the human race since I came back,[521] but Thursday we dined at a great stiff cold representing dinner in Moscovia as the servants call Stackelberg's House. Dull, heavy, flat & fine with 16 quarterings on all sides & with people having rights to wear hats before Kings. The world *est bon a voir* sometimes. I apprehend that the only clever couple are the Austrian Minister & his better half, quick as lightning, all instruction, energy & spirit. In the E'g there was an Assembly. Yes'y we had an-

---

[519] Louis Antoine Fauvelet de Bourrienne, *Mémoires de M. de Bourrienne*, 10 vols., Paris, 1829-30, and Louis-Philippe, Comte de Ségur, *Mémoires et souvenirs et anecdotes*, 3 vols., Paris, 1825-6. The Duchesse de Maillé stated that those who knew Napoleon considered the Bourrienne *Mémoires* to be 'very true to life'. *Souvenirs*, p. 269.

[520] See Carlo Botta, *History of Italy*, 2 vols., London, 1828, & Pierre Daru, *Histoire de la République de Venise*, ed. Alessandro Fontana & Xavier Tabet, 2 vols., Paris, 2004. The index in this modern edition helps to locate the particular incidents referred to.

[521] From their summer villa in Castellamare.

other sort of day at home - a little vulgar with M. & Mme Dupont, Maria Lushington & Mr Craven, a happy Poker, being with a woman who had been in love with him & with another who is dying to be so if he would give her the least little bit of encouragement, Father Strangways & the gay Sir William.

29th Nov'r. [1831]. We are *toute a fait retiree du monde* since we came here. Papa always ailing, tho' not ill, & myself lazy, & too indifferent to be bored by going to look for a world that don't interest me. Once to C'tesse Stacks, & once to the Lushingtons have been all my goings out. I thought the people bores. We think & talk but Cholora.

30th [Nov. 1831]. Last night Ly Actons Play, *La jeunesse d'Henri 5* was flat & stupid, but *Le Diplomate* was perfection. The stiff old fashioned Saxon Minister *qui parle franchement*, M de Redern[522] - the hairbrained Frenchman, the Chargé d'affaire here - Aug's Craven,[523] the young Prince - & his Father a Fanatic *per la diplomacie* - his daughter, Mlle Eugenie de la Ferronaye - Mme Nugent,[524] the Baroness, & the young La Greca,[525] "noir comme un Secretaire d'Ambassade, & long comme un Protocol."[526]

Dec. 5th. [1831]. Went to the Ball at the Austrian Minister. I was struck with the bad footing the english are on at Naples. Who is to keep them up with a Minister living[?] in an Inn or Mrs Laing

---

[522] Heinrich Alexander, Graf von Redern (1804-88) had recently been appointed as Counsellor of Legation.

[523] Augustus Craven, the illegitimate son of Keppel Craven, was an attaché under Mr Hill. In 1834, he was to marry Pauline, the sister of Eugénie de la Ferronays.

[524] Giovanna, Duchessa di Riario-Sforza (1797-1855), wife of Laval Nugent von Westmeath.

[525] Presumably Luigi, son of Luigi La Greca, a friend of the Actons, who resided at the Palazzo Pizzofalcone.

[526] 'as black as an embassy secretary and as long as a protocol'

Mason.[527] The[re] were many pretty women - Mme Volconsky,[528] D'esse de San Teodore, looking very handsome, Mme Falconnet in a blue velvet Hat from Herbaults, Ly Drummond was dressed in a pink *velours épinglé* made to the shape with a polish cap with jewels. Long live the old women!!!

15 Dec. [1831]. A long silence. Colds & coughs & Roskilly. Sir Stratford [Canning] is come & gone to Constantinople;[529] he dined with us & was very charming & looked clever, & well, & determined. Poor Eng'd seems in a piteous state, & Ly Canning's & Ly Isabella's Letters are curious - we were quiet & learned for Sir Stratford's dinner & not diplomatic.

I cd not go last night, 18th, to C'te Stacks Sunday night's ball, tho' all my wise & pious country people did so, setting aside the religious & civil institutions of their country out of respect to a russian Minister. The Corps diplomatique, called corps because they have no souls, dined here yes'y. Mme de Lebzeltern is by far the pleasantest of that stupid set from the fat french Ambassadress to the tody Mollerus.[530] Mme de Lebzeltern is a gay good humoured creature. Mr Hill was in a curious mood next to me & said she's a good creature & so clever too & old German sour crout is the true german. He is a creature that comes in smoke, lives in a bottle & goes to the Devil. Mme de Lottum, he asked her age; she said 28, Her Husband 42 & her child 9 years old, & Mr Hill said, you're too old to have such infantine manners. If ever there was a curiosity of a Man, its him. So we're reduced to you, he says to Ly Drummond. He is mad & merry & mischievous, but never deaf, blind or dumb like the others.

---

[527] Mary Whitelaw Wemyss (1792-1858) had married Gilbert Laing Meason (1769-1832) in 1811. The Laing Measons were acquaintances of Sir Walter Scott. After her husband's death in 1832, she married in 1834 Count Gustave-Adolphe Beugnot, secretary at the French embassy in Rome. (See note 6).

[528] Princess Zenaide Wolkonsky (1789-1862) spent much of the latter part of her life in Rome where, with fine singing, acting and conversational skills, she became a popular hostess. Mary Berry was charmed by her in January 1821 (see *Journal,* III, p.274-6). The house built by the Princess became subsequently the residence of the British Ambassador.

[529] Sir Stratford had left England on 16 November 1831.

[530] Nicolaas W. Mollerus (1787-1865), the chargé d'affaires of the Netherlands. He and his wife were described by Ramage as 'two Dutch beings, as heavily built and as dull in intellect as that nation generally is'. (*Ramage in South Italy*, ed. Clay, p.214).

23 Dec. [1831]. I have left off the habit of writing, consequently it is grown tiresome to me. We lead a dull, stupid life now & a solitary one; now & then the oddities of Mr Hill or the jokes of Sir Wm. rouse me, but we are all fallen into the sear & yellow leaf. The Hertford set come to represent *la bonne societé de Londres* on the 1st, otherwise no London people are here. Sir W. Scott comes out of Quarentine Xmas Day. Reports say he is in a state of imbecility; I trust not to the extent said. We dined with the Lebzelterns the other day; she is the only nice person here. Mme de Lottum is here a spoiled child. I sat with Mrs Garnier who gave us a ridiculous account of her Count & her magnetism. Her Father left her her fortune in her power which she had made over to Mr Garnier for 400£ a year. What more? - we took a country walk with Sir William & the Lush. & Old Father Strangways. The climate was charming & I went to that courageous woman Mme Dupont whose character rises in adversity wonderfully; to be ruined, & not break yr heart is heroic. "To bear, is to conquer our fate!!"[531] Society at Naples is bad & of non effect to our *eccelezzis*. Ly Acton's people all meet at the hour of ten & sit up till day. Many of the Corps Diplomatique are *sans ame*, having sold theirs to the Devil!! We had a curious visit from Malheureux complaining of his being thought a *jettatore*[532] & of people avoiding him. He does not know the truth that he is so extremely tiresome that they like the excuse of it.

Xmas Eve. We went into Churches. Both shops & churches are dressed so prettily with ribbons & flowers & *presepios*[533] & lights. In the Cathedral is the Minutolo Chapel; the frescoes are mostly done in 1300 - a row of Saints, & a row of Minutolos alternately. La Sanità has nothing in it worthy of notice. The Capuchin was dressing the Altars with figures & lighting the Candles. Monte Olivetto has court & cloisters without end & must have been the largest Monastery in existance. It served as a retreat for Tasso twice during his visits to Naples. Now the building is 'Intendenze de Napoli.' The church has some beautiful Tombs in it, but otherwise has nothing worthy of notice as Sta Chiara & the Cathedral have.

---

[531] The last line of Thomas Campbell's poem *On visiting a scene in Argyleshire.*

[532] *jettatore* - a person who brings misfortune. It seems likely that 'Malheureux' refers to the Dutchman Mollerus who had the reputation of being a *jettatore* - see *Sir William Gell in Italy,* ed. Edith Clay, pp.122-3.

[533] *presepio* - a nativity scene. The Naples area was renowned for the production and display of such scenes.

Xmas Day [1831]. I had a note from Miss Scott at 7 o'clock last night asking me to come to her. She is at the Gran Bretagna having landed from Malta with poor Sir Walter. As soon as I cd get the carriage I went. Think of saying poor Sir Walter! He could hardly rise from his chair to welcome me, & his speech was so defective that I could hardly hear him. His Son is a great tall oppressive person but good looking, like Ld Stormont in looks; & Ch's Scott was there, his daughter a good natured Girl, just a little vulgar, & this arrival wh. I looked to with such pleasure is turned alas into a no pleasure. Today I took Miss Scott to Church, & she fainted & I had to go with her out of church into Ly Lushington's Rooms, & afterwards she asked me again to see Sir Walter who seemed but poorly & was sitting at a Table with writings. We then went to see the *Presepios* at Sta Chiara which were decking out behind the Altar in the Nuns Chapel. The Nuns, I am sorry to own, were old & ugly, but they were getting it ready for *Mezza Notte*[534] & had fruit & flowers & a *presepio* & candles in abundance. We came home & C'te de Putbus called on us.[535] We asked him about the book published on Eng'd by P'ce Puckler, wh. is said to be clever & eccentric.[536] He says that he ran[?] to Eng'd to seek an Heiress, but took extraordinary means for his matrimonial plans - talking incessantly of his wife, a sort of Josephine from whom he had divorced & to whom he was much attached, & thinking that by putting forward his friendship for her, he sd induce some young Lady to marry him.

We had a most dismal Xmas day dinner at the Vittoria at Mr Hills, ourselves & the Scott party & Mr Strangways. How sad to see genius & imagination brought so low - for a man in the state Sir Walter is in throws a chill over a whole society; it is impossible not to watch him & to attend to him. His eldest son is handsome, oppressive, & dictatorial, his daughter not very [?], Charles Scott stupid. It is most melancholy to see the glory of England & Scotland sent to visit Strangers, & appear thus. It seemed a relief when they were all gone and Mr Hill sat down to prose & gossip in his strange way with us & old F[ather]

---

534 'Midnight Mass'

535 Wilhelm Malte Fürst von Putbus (1783-1854), father of the Prussian minister's wife.

536 Prince Hermann v. Pückler-Muskau's 4 vol. work was published in German under the title *Briefe eines Verstorbenen*, Stuttgart, 1831. An English translation by Sarah Austin appeared the following year. To revive his finances, he hit upon the scheme of divorcing his wife, with her consent, visiting England to find and marry a rich heiress, and of returning to Germany to live in a *ménage à trois*. The scheme did not work out.

Strangways. He was so odd & original, so strange, so puzzled & diffuse, that it kept one in a state of excitement to know what would come next.

27th [December 1831]. Called on Miss Scott & thought Sir W. more himself than he has been. He is evidently oppressed by that tall handsome Son, a very vulgar Man, the Major entirely. What an extraordinary thing it is that such a Man as Sir Walter is should have children so little like him. We went to Mme Cardons & did all the commissions for dress for Malta. Came home & was beautifully *coiffée* by that tiresome Ferdinand with Emeralds & went in a yellow silk to dine with Queen Golconda[537] who had a dinner of 25 beasts, male & female, packed like the animals in Noah's Ark; luckily I got by an open hearted Englishman Mr Garnier & we talked away at all rates of Nuns & Convents, Spain & Adventures, of *La jeune femme Colère* & of Sir W. Scott, of Mr Lockyer & of Gl. Monck, wh. last Anecdote shows Sir Walter's memory to be as good as ever. Abbotsford would afford a pretty *Voyage Autour de ma Chambre*.[538] Sir Walter gets 60,000£ for his new Ed. of his novels, 11,000£ for his *Life of Napoleon*, (wh. when the D. of Wellington was asked if he liked it, he answered "It is written by the author of *Waverley*,") & 9000£ for something that same year. Miss Ferrier is blind!!![539] Mr Garnier told me a romantic story of a Capt. Stuart who stole his wife when a Nun out of a Spanish Convent[540] & who afterwards sat next a Man at dinner who left him 8000£ a year. Ad[miral] Fleming also married a Spa[nish] Nun.[541]

Mr Hill was last night in his raving mood. He called Mrs Vanneck & asked if it were true that she had put part of her fortune out of her

---

[537] Golconda - an ancient city in India renowned for its diamond mines, the name therefore implying great wealth. Here M.T. may be applying the sobriquet of Queen Golconda to Lady Drummond.

[538] In the work of this title by the French writer Xavier de Maistre, the narrator describes his examination of successive objects within a room as if he were writing a travelogue.

[539] Miss Ferrier (1782-1854), author of *Destiny* which M.T. had been reading in August, was indeed losing her sight. It seems likely that M.T. received this sad information from the Scotts. Sir Walter was a warm admirer of her works.

[540] This must be the same story as that told by Madden (Vol.2, p.109). A second nun who was to flee with the ship's surgeon fell off the rope ladder, broke her leg, screamed, and was hauled back into the convent.

[541] Admiral Charles Fleming (1774-1840) had married Donna Catalina Paulina Alessandro in June 1816.

power, & then asked her Son; they said 'Yes' & he said, 'It is better than I expected from you.'

This is our last Xmas at Naples. Oh, I was so bored, so tired & made so melancholy on Tuesday. It was so Londonny. I was ill & low all yesterday - low as the ground in consequence. It was such a night of Rain without & such squeezing & crowd within. Very good acting - *Philippe* - how the two Cravens cd make themselves so ridiculous!! *Du sublime au ridicule il n'y a qu'un pas.*[542] *Le Diplomate* with Luigi La Greca, "Noir comme un Secretaire d'Ambassade et long comme un Protocol," & *l'Heritière* very pretty indeed.

31st. Pity Mme Fal[connet] has such a voice - she is so soft & pretty & well dressed. She & her husband are a curious His'y of *ménages*. I never saw a very lively woman who married a stupid Man that it answered but once & that is with instance of Ld & Ly Ruthven. They are ruined, people say, but it was all light & Or-mulu, all albums & *recherché*[?], the Baby all lace & pink &c. The acc'ts from England make us unhappy - prospects of revolution & the Bishops forced for security to take the Mitre off their carriages when travelling.

Miss Scott called yes'y. She is what is called Ordinary in all ways. Mme de Lebzeltern is getting up a *Bal de* heaven knows what. The women are occupied with it. Mme de Leb. abounds in Stories. She told me a curious one of a woman who had led a wicked life & repented voluntarily taking a Cure of a Mad Man, as a penance; she was a Catholic. Of all the women I dislike I think the species I dislike the most is that of a cringing character with honied speech. I sat between C'te de Monte Sant'Angelo with whom I got on an argument *sur la franchise*, well chosen!, & Mr Stewart who looks & talks more like a Shoemaker than his brother the Monk.

Last day of 1831, people at dinner. Mr Craven played & sang. Mr Hill not quite as bad as yes'y taken he told Miss Pulteney, who went to speak to him: "Now go away & don't come & teize me, I'm just come for a little quiet & you come like a Night Mare to torment me." Mr Craven I dislike tho' such pains have been taken to make me like him. He is pleasanter to another woman whom he holds cheap & who likes him.

---

[542] 'From the sublime to the ridiculous, there is only one step.'

1st of Jan'y 1832, Sir W[alter] S[cott], Miss Scott & Mr Laing Mason were run away with down the S[tra]da Nuova on the Puzzuoli side on Friday. Major Scott, a great tall courier looking Man, dined with us & made very light of it at dinner. I don't think he cares much about Sir Walter. Yes'y I went there & found Miss Scott very ill in Bed. They had a great escape of being kill'd, she says, & that if Mr L[aing] M[eason] had not been a stupid body the horses might have been stopped. Miss S[cott] has a silver ring taken from the hand of a dead Man wh. she is putting to a silver chain. I went to the ball & was very well dressed in some old Paris Clothes & got praised like a good child for being well dressed. The ball was very pretty & the women beautiful & so occupied with their dresses of the Novels of Waverley that one only heard in the crowd "Berangère, tocque, Ravenna, Voile, Rebecca, 'velours rouge', 'superbe', 'laide a faire peur'." I sat quietly with the St Quentins, Sir Wm Gell & Mr Hill. Ly Adam looked as if she never had been pretty; the horse shoe in her face is hideous. The old Gentlemen amused me & we got home at 12 & got thro' [the] 1st day of 1832 in time for Church! May it please heaven to bring me safely to its close. Mr St Quentin preached a most beautiful Sermon on our being born in Sin & dying in Sin, the subject Death; himself being the picture of frail life, pale & consumptive, it therefore came with additional force. This first day of the year being a solemn one, I cried as I dare say every one did. Mr St Q. is a most excellent person, pleasing, as is his wife, &, the circle forsaken, I went to the Lushingtons & we all agreed we sd be the better if he staid at Naples, & now I am going to bed with a mind resigned & calm, & have began the year at peace.

3d Jan'y. Yes'y I talked & thought all day of Sir Walter, beginning in the Morn'g with Roskilly whom I laboured hard to get to his confidence & to Miss Scott's as the means under heaven of restoring this fine intellect to what it was. I think he will either die in a fit of Apoplexy, or mind & recover with the Spring as it advances. After having been used to drink like a rich Scotchman, two bottles, he is reduced to two glasses of wine, or ought to be they say. His memory is as accurate as ever for distant events connected with Scotland or Litterature but faulty for every day events. They tell you that the Organs of imagination, superstition & religious veneration are said to be strong in his projecting forehead. Roskilly told me he went to see how he was after he was in bed last night & he quoted Scripture & said "the grasshopper is a burthen to me."[543] Now I think in that same verse in Ecclesiasticus is "& making of books is weariness of the spirit." I quote from memory.[544] Roskilly asked him what struck him at Naples & his answer implied his being worn out, but directly he rallied, & told stories in his own style with all his wonted spirit. What seems to give him most pleasure at Naples are some vile little prints of the scotch lakes hung up in his bed room in the Caramanico. I went to him at 7 & was to have taken Mr Mathias to him & Miss Scott, but I dare say that at 80 years old he was ashamed of having a cold & so would not come with me. Sir Walter was very agreeable, but his speech struggled with his imagination. He is slow & indistinct. Miss Scott is fond of her Father to raise[?] anxiety. She is nervous & in bad health. The tall Son was there & we all did very well & talked of the Ardens,[545] of Sir Pulteney Malcolm & his Greek Villa,[546] of the gossip of Malta, of Mr Frere,[547] for whom Sir Walter has a strong affection & who is settled on the rock of Malta for life, doing acts of kindness & charity to everyone near him, but having given up all the common habits of society, never sitting down to dinner, but like Ld Wm. Seymour[548] eating out of a Cupboard when he is hungry. Then we talked of the Spaniards & Mme Toledo[549] who says to her little girl: "Never tell a lie, except in the praise of your country." Miss Scott has beautiful Albums with drawings done by friends & some Verses, the prettiest of wh. are those of Wordworths on Sir Walter leaving Abbotsford.

5th [Jan. 1832]. I went to call for Miss Scott. She met me at the door with an "Oh indeed I'm sorry to keep you, but we've got a tiresome

---

[543] See *Ecclesiastes*, Chap. 12, v. 5.

[544] In *Ecclesiastes*, Chap. 12, v. 12, the relevant text reads: 'of making many books there is no end; and much study is a weariness of the flesh.'

[545] Frances and Catherine Arden, daughters of Richard Pepper Arden, first Baron Alvanley (1755-1804). Scott had been a friend of their widowed mother, Anne, and had made the funeral arrangements when she died in 1825.

[546] Sir Pulteney Malcolm had built 'a magnificent house, about two miles from the town [Athens], at the enormous cost of 3000*l*.' See John Auldjo, *Journal of a Visit to Contantinople*, London, 1835, p.28.

[547] John Hookham Frere (1769-1846) had played an active part in diplomatic life in the early years of the century. On account of his wife's health, he settled on Malta in 1820 and spent his time principally in literary pursuits until his death.

[548] Lord William Seymour (1759-1837).

[549] Dona María Joaquina de Silva, daughter of the Marquis of Santa Cruz had married Pedro de Alvares de Toledo in 1822.

little Prince, & Papa would not let me away." This tiresome little Prince turned out to be that *gran Seccatore* of Litterature Carlo Mele[550] who had called to take Sir Walter to the Archbishop of Tarrento[551] & so Miss Scott & I went shopping. What is very odd is she can't say a Yes or No in French which she says was owing to Ly Scott having been a foreigner & that she did not chuse she sd learn French.[552] She says that her Father dont take the interest he did in his writings & stories, that he liked his drive to Baia & that he is irritable & fretful, poor Man! We dined with Mr Hill. It was dull to extinction, an english dinner of strangers & I fell into a fit of musing on english society & young Ladies & Gentlemen after dinner.

6th [Jan. 1832]. Mrs Laing Mason is insufferable in vulgar pressing impudence. She is as great an adept in assurance as I am in decision. We shall see wh. gets the better. I won't know her. I was in hopes last night of passing a pleasant E'g with Sir Walter when in she came with her airs & graces & put all conversation to a flight with that horrid Scotch drawl. I could have borne Mrs Ashley & Augustus Craven & Mr Bailey.[553] Sir Walter had received the Arch'p's picture; he had liked his Cats. (He likes Dogs & Cats both). He & Miss Scott were delighted with Sir Wm Gell. Mr Aug. Craven talked Costume & Mrs L[aing] M[eason] prosed & told innumerable lies. She went away & Charles Scott said to his sister. "I'll tell ye what Anne, Shut your doors against her & don't let her in. She only writes to all her cousins in Edinbro' of how she protects you & introduces you to people, to every one."

Ly Strachan has brought us 3 Annuals. She reasoned ill on the subject of marriage, & went into a Rhapsody on the daughters' beauty & prospects. She told me that Ld Shaftesbury has always been severe on Mrs Fox Lane & her & so when she saw him last she said, "Well, Ld Sh., nothing has ever been said of us equal to what is said of your

---

[550] Carlo Mele (1792-1841), liberal writer, poet and publisher.

[551] Giuseppe Capecelatro (1774-1836), Archbishop of Taranto, had played an important part in Neapolitan life - political, ecclesiastical and literary.

[552] Lady Scott (1770-1826) had been born Charlotte Charpentier of French parents. She had arrived in England in her teens and had received an English education, thanks to the guardianship of the Marquis of Downshire, a long-standing friend of the family.

[553] Maria Anne Ashley, née Baillie, (1804-1891) had married William Ashley, a brother of the Earl of Shrewsbury, in March 1831. She had been accompanied to Naples by her brother Henry Baillie (1803-85).

daughter," & she made him turn green & yellow alternately, she says. On Saturday we had a dinner. I was horridly dull from the state of nerves I am fallen into. I went to the Ball with Mme Fal[connet]. That menage can't last, she is so violent all the time; I like her with her candour & imprudence. I am reasonable enough for myself & others too. I pity that poor husband who is growing very savage from being ill managed. He was once a kind hearted Man. The ball was fine, not fancy, & we moralized. Ly Strachan told me a story of ingratitude that gave me *de quoi penser*. As you reap you sow. Ly Acton & the St Johns. The St Johns & Ld Hertford.

10th Jan'y & what have I to say? - little. My memory is bad, my brain puzzled & my nerves bring floating images to view. I sd like to drink something that may revive this poor wretched decayed head of mine - worn out, but go it must soon. I spend the E'g with Miss Scott & Sir Walter, Mr Craven & Sir W.Gell. They talked Ghosts, a subject that don't interest me as I don't believe in it. Sir Walter said that both Col. Stanhope & Ld Castlereagh told him Ghost stories the last time they met wh. struck him awfully - they had destroyed themselves.[554] Miss Scott tells me that Mrs Chaworth is gone out of her mind owing to fright the night of the Fire.[555] Sir W. talked much of Ld Byron & told me of the Letter having been stolen out of the Greek Vase he sent him to Abbotsford.

11th [Jan. 1832]. Dined at old stiff Stacks, who looks as sour as vin-juice. I had rather an agreeable day of it, sitting at dinner between C'te Ludolf[556] & some Russian. C'te Ludolf is a regular Charlatan & was the Man paid off by Ly Sligo to let her off of marrying him. Ly Strachan is amusing - she abounds in stories true or false, but she is vulgar & plays off all the S[trad]da Toledo beaux most vulgarly. She is now setting her Cap at Spaccaforno to spite Mrs L. Maison [Meason].

---

554 Castlereagh's ghost story is set out in J.G.Lockhart's *Life of Sir Walter Scott*, popu-lar Ed., London 1893, pp. 486-7. Col. James Hamilton Stanhope had hung himself on 5 March 1825 (see *Gentleman's Magazine*, Vol.XCV, p.465); Castlereagh had cut his throat with a penknife in August 1822.

555 In 1805, Mary Chaworth had married John Musters of Colwick Hall. She was resid-ing there in October 1831 when the house was attacked by rioters protesting at the rejec-tion of the Reform Bill in the House of Lords. She died in February 1832.

556 Giuseppe Costantino Ludolf (1787-1875), career Neapolitan diplomat had recently returned from St Petersburg where he had served as ambassador. In 1816 he had married Tecla Weissenhof who, according to Neumann (II, p.243), had been brought up by the Polish Princess Isabela Czartoryska.

C'tess Ludolf, Técla, is a very ugly, very agreeable woman. I went last night to Sir Walter's where there is a cruel deal of gossip after he goes to Bed, & where they threaten to set up a good natured Club & making Sir Wm Gell President.

[*Note added at top of page*] Sir Walter Scott dined one day with the Archbishop[557] - they carried on the conversation in Latin - the cats were about on the Table wh. did not displease Sir Walter.

15 [Jan. 1832]. Dined at Ld Hertfords, dull & ill understood. I like a scarlet velvet gown. All the Men in Uniform & all the women in diamonds for the dress ball at M. de La T[our] Maubourg, the Fr. Ambassador. It was crowded - tiresome, & to sum up all - like London.

17 [Jan. 1832]. Yesterday a formal dinner at the Prussian Minister's. I sat between M. de K[iel] who prosed & Tartuffie'd & P'ce Dentice who praised our Cuisine exceedingly as he said one feels so well after eating *chez vous*, but forgot to add "a dinner for six people." Sir Wm Gell grows vain I think. Mr Craven is a stiff bore of a learned Gentle[man], not the Willow or the Osier - a pretty lover, & a worse Husband. A letter from Ly Belhaven.

18 [Jan. 1832]. A brilliant Ball at M. de Stacks. Such dress! Mme Branccacio all brown velvet & diamonds. Ly Strachan blue velvet & diamonds. Mme Vielenstein Emeralds & diamonds. Mme Ludolf in such a necklace of Turquoises & diamonds. The D'esse de Montemar in a blonde gown & Rubies & diamonds, beautiful dress generally. My countrywomen I am ashamed of - Mrs Garnier & Ly D[rummond] from their affectation of Youth & love of dress, particularly. Ferdinand dressing Mrs Garniers head as if she was 17 with flowers & her husband like a fond lover buying all the trinkets to be found to deck Anne & a neck of black grizzle. Ly D[rummond] having a lover of 25 who tiezes her, she says, to marry him. Mrs L. Maison [Meason] & the Strachans!

Last night I had a pleasant E'g at Sir Walters. He was very well telling stories, repeating Verses & a long Spanish Legend of Queen Arruc-

---

[557] Sir Walter met the Archbishop of Taranto on 5 and 11 January. On the latter occasion he was accompanied by Sir William Gell who remarked that the 'difficulties of language were opposed to any very agreeable conversation.' See Gell, *Sir Walter Scott in Italy*, p.7.

ca[558] which he offers to write for me in my Album. These are the E'gs I like the best, tho' I dont like his children. Miss Scott has a little uneasy Gossip about her quite unworthy of her; the Major is the Major & Charles Scott disagreeable.

Miss Strachan's Invitation to the ball. Oh, how Silly!

22d [Jan. 1832] Sunday. If I had sense I ought to keep a minute journal of all said & done but I dont. Of Ly Strachan & her loose Conversation & of Ly Drummond & her young Lover. Capt. Macarthy must be a Scotch man, I never saw any thing so well got up as the scene last night, the white pocket handkerchief & the tears & airs of a victym. No Irish fortune hunter with Mustachios cd have been half so seducing or have done it so well - indeed it was enough to melt the heart of weak woman. Ly S[trachan] is foolish not in her weakness but in her strength. She domineers over Lord Hertford. Her daughter being 17 & too old made an odd speech to me "Miss Talbot, pray dont flirt so with my husband, Sir Wm Gell," to wh. I answered it was a right I had had many years. "Oh, but you must not," she said, "for we've got a little boy, he's very pretty & the image of his Father," she said. "Dear me" said Sir Wm, "you've made Miss Talbot blush." What a style for a girl of 17! The girl is beautiful & ought to be married immediately. I had a talk with that learned Theban Mme de Lebzeltern on the subject of the Neapolitan women. It seems poor innocent I is wrong & that all the young & old except two or three have Lovers, & talk, not of the crime of having them, but of the folly of chusing them wrong - a bad lover is looked upon as a bad business & a woman pitied or blamed accordingly. P'cess Paterno, a *vieille* coquette, said the other night with great pride that Thank God she had chosen all her Lovers well thro' life, that they had loved their God & their King. Last night Mme de Lebzeltern & I were talking of the Butera ménage - she condemns her. I cannot, as I believe she had *une ame toute Royale* as Bourdaloue or Massillon would have said of her. As to the morals of the Italian women, if they all have Lovers, the priest who governs them [must] allow of it! or it could not be, a proof that the catholic religion encourages or permits attachments of this nature.

---

[558] M.T. must be referring to Queen Urraca (1079-1126). Sir Walter Scott's acquaintance with the story of the Queen can be deduced from his review of Robert Southey's *Chronicle of the Cid* in the *Quarterly Review* of February 1809.

[*Note added at top of page*] I heard today that Sir Walter Scott has been to the Library at the Studio, where all the learned were in great array to do him honor, but the only thing he took much interest in was a neapolitan version of Mother Goose of great antiquity.

Mr St Quentin - there is a good person - so young, so ill, so little methodistical; he preaches like Chalmers; he talks like an amiable well-informed man. He has made an intimacy with the Monks of the Camaldoli who ask him to dinner.

Thursday e'g. Sir Walter discoursed of Queens, & Courtiers, of Olive gardens & Cavaliers, & amused Mrs Ashley & myself much. Today he dined at Ld Hertfords & he seemed tired with heat & light & foreigners. Yes'y he dined here & seemed pleased with a little party at dinner, & Mme de Leb[zeltern?] came in & played National airs - to him. Her playing was enchantment. From grave to gay, her own compositions mostly. Sir Walter seemed happy, but Miss Scott carried him off, poor Man. Mme de Ludolf came in; she is a true pole, ugly & pleasing. He is a very gentleman-like Charlatan. Mme Ludolf puts me in mind of my friend A. Morcoska[?]. I showed her my ring & we talked of Poland & she was beginning to cry & said the unfortunate were never liked in England & I saw it was a sad subject.

Today I have been to Church & to the Lushingtons & Miss Scott with me. She is neither clever or good, a little cross, & says every thing possible against people. I was amused. M[ari]a L[ushington] said, we are going to have three plays. She said, I think Old Craven had better not make himself so ridiculous at going on in this way.

The only gay hours I pass are at Sir W. Scott's & where London news is rehearsed - & sad it is now: Cholera & Insurrection. Scandal reigns in that Palazzo Caramanico & lies innumerable are circulated. Still, it is life, & at home is death now.

24th [Jan. 1832]. We took a long walk in the hills above the Lago d'Agnano. It was a lovely warm day, all sun & brightness. We had the Lush[ington]s, old Father Strangways, & Sir Wm. [Gell] who fell from his Mule but was not the worst. I did not go to the Noja ball. The savings of our penny wise & pound foolish Ministry &c. Dined at Mr Garniers; she was decked out like a bride, jewels to wear &c. given by a misguided & much too loving husband. Ld Hertford & I talked of Ld

Fitzgerald.[559] I said he is too clever to have a grain of common sense. Ld. H. says I was right. When Ld Hertford was in Eng'd he met Mr Cholmondeley[560] & asked after Mrs Cholmondeley. She's dead, he said, but don't be annoyed for there will soon be another Mrs Cholmondeley. I sat next Mr Hill who laughed at his other night over Mrs Garnier, drank Madeira with the Tears in his eyes, spit out his dinner & raved. Ld Hertford was telling us that Wm the 4th is occasionally quite mad which present events show. When he was in the Admiralty, the Queen thought him so far gone she sent to the Minister to beg to have him removed at any time. The Play on Sunday at Ly Actons is said to be too bad. The Court are invited. C'tess Nugent is to play the improper Ladies. Ld Hertford's account of the Nojà Ball - Not a drop of wine, or water to be had, a servant ran away frightened at its being asked for.

No one is frightened at any Ghost except a modern Ghost; when your G'Father comes, it's serious, but who cares now for Julius Cesar? We went to try & find the Ghosts with Sir W. Scott. He went in the boat with Sir Wm Gell & seemed pleased & he proposed to me that the spot by the Well where the light fell strongly sd have a female figure with disshevelled hair! I think all the party were pleased. The walk was delightful.[561]

Friday [27 Jan. 1832]. Miss Strachans ball. The King danced with her & afterwards played at Riversi.[562] Ld Hertford received him in the English style of Etiquette & waited on him, wh. surprised the King. Mme Dupont & Mr Stewart criticised the Champagne. Came home tired & sat making gloomy reflections over the fire for an hour or two before going to bed.

Saturday [28 Jan. 1832]. A dinner; Sir Wm Gell dull; P'ce Butera, old & grey. I went to the Rehearsal at Ly Acton. *La haine d'une femme*, pretty. Pauline de La Ferronaye: acting quite perfect as the widow; her brother made but a cold lover, & the other girls, Demoiselles, good. C'te de Redern perfect, quite.

---

[559] Vesey FitzGerald had succeeded to the baronetcy on the death of his mother on 3 January 1832.

[560] Not identified, but possibly George James Cholmondeley (1752-1830), whose second wife had died in September 1825 and who married again in October 1827.

[561] For Sir William Gell's account on this excursion, see Gell, *Reminiscences*, pp.7-8.

[562] Reversis - a card game.

The second is the improper play *Le Mari et l'Amant*. Mme Nugent is [the] picture of an impudent Soubrette - the Man kisses the back of her neck - they say she is *bonne personne* (wh. dont mean a good person), but she has a *Ton de Garnison*. The audience to the Rehersal night were the Anti-Sunday nights,[563] & Children innumerable. The Swiss songs enchanting.

1st [February 1832]. Dining out & dining out. 27 persons at Stacks. Ly Strachan's golden chains, 140 Napoleons, weigh 90. The Italian Men more tiresome than any thing ever was. C'te Esterhazy a little horrid Animal. Mme Ludolf a true Polish woman, laments her sensibility that prevents her enjoying herself. My Ennui was great: & I dined well *par distraction*, had a bad fevrish night, awoke thinking of England & being buried in a Vault, & tears ran down my Cheeks!! Sunday would not go to the play, finished my Essays ready for publications; like the Trinità the best; both are natural wh. is the only good they can boast.

2d [Feb. 1832]. Dined at Ld Hertfords. It was pleasant enough. Ly Strachan's Magnificence, such Pearls, such diamonds, such clothes - she made great play & great fun with my Father. A hot crowded ball at Lady D[rummond]s. I sent my picture of Grand Master of Malta, an old bore, to Sir Walter, & he wrote me a pretty note of thanks.[564]

Worried to death last 4 Feb'y night having dined with old deaf Craven & met "the hospital",[565] Sir Wm & Sir Walter, I came home & got into such a state of agitation that I could not prononce my words. The veins swelled frightfully on my forehead & I had relief from tears, but I had a wretched night & today a nervous fever.

Poor Sir Walter was sadly slow & puzzled, his daughter not nice. One son says "My Father's better certainly, but you know he'll have an Apoplexy & die some day!" .... the other Son says of Ch's Scott: "I am glad Mr Hill finds him of use, but I can't guess how, for he is the d-est dull hound that ever was!" These are the Sons of the finest imagination we have & the Father's head even now full of old Legends & Knights & Ladies & of the good old time. It was as cold as it is usually at Mr Craven's wh. is saying every thing & in the E'g, at 1/2

---

[563] i.e. those who thought it inappropriate to attend a theatre performance on a Sunday.

[564] Sir Walter's manuscript letter is now in the Pierpont Morgan Library (MA1860/3).

[565] Term coined by Sir William Gell to describe himself and Sir Walter.

8, he plays on the organ a Dirge or Halleluah at our going away. Miss Scott asked me if Mr Craven was not a man of indifferent Character. I said I had never heard it. Next day, we dined at Papa Hills: I like that Original. He is going away & so we are all & to the Devil too, that is to Eng'd - to get into the Revolution & the Cholera. Ld Hertford says that the Crash will come this time next year. He told me a curious his'y of the Garter being changed in its fastening: Queen Anne wore it as a Girdle, Queen Elizabeth on her Arms. Buckingham & the Garter. See Arnesty's[?] His'y of the Garter.

Last night sat with Sir W. Scott. He is inclined to make a Novel out of Maltese His'y & I have translated him part of Caravaggio's Life, the Malta part - & he has borrowed all my books. I have lent him *Les Ordres Militaires et Religieuses*.[566] He says *Le Manteau a Bec* are Coats of Arms. Miss Scott has had advantages no other girl ever had: she has had besides her Father's society, intimacy with many distinguished in England; everything worth hearing she has heard. She was telling me of the life Charles 10 led in Scotland. He went incog. to Abbotsford;[567] they were away & he dined to see the Loc[k]hart children, & the little girl offered him the Chicken bone she had just sucked, & shocked the French Maid who guessed who it was. It seems that the D'esse de Berri left Scotland in a state of disgust at the bigotted Education that they were giving Mademoiselle.[568] The Confessor is the same who has followed the fortunes of the family thro' a long course of years & perhaps is the cause of all their misfortunes. He made Mademoiselle pass two days & nights without sleep as penance at Lord Hopetouns. They asked what she had done for such rigour & she said she had sent Ly Susan Hamilton into the Greenhouse for a pot of Lilies of the Valley & she had caught a cough. What Sir Walter likes most talking of is the King's Visit to Scotland;[569] & he takes great credit to himself for the management of Lords & Ladies, Highlanders, Taylors & persons of all

---

[566] Possibly either Pierre Hélyot, *Histoire des ordres religieux et militaires*, published early in the 18th century but republished in 8 vols. in 1792, or Jacques Bar, *Recueil de tous les costumes des ordres religieux et militaires*, published in 6 vols in 1778-9.

[567] The home built by Sir Walter Scott where he lived with his family including his son-in-law and biographer-to-be, John Gibson Lockhart, who was married to his elder daughter, Sophia.

[568] i.e. her daughter Mademoiselle Louise (1819-1864), later to marry Ferdinand Charles, Duke of Parma..

[569] For George IV's visit to Scotland in 1822, see J.G. Lockhart, *The Life of Sir Walter Scott*, pp.480-8 and John Prebble, *The King's Jaunt*, London, 1988.

tempers & all degrees whose obstinacy would have spoiled the Show. The King went to the D. of Buccleugh's & one E'g he sent the Duke across the room to ask the name of a tune Gows Band were playing. "Cameron has got his wife again" the Duke said; "The Devil, he has," said the King "it's time to be off." Now Queen Caroline was just dead.[570]

13th [Feb. 1832]. Time goes by - & I see nothing & do nothing; dine out with Crowds, dine at home with Crowds, & all is wearyness & vexation of spirit. What is the matter! Why this dreadful awful future. This Home to come - with no Home, this country with no country, this plague, this worry with vexation of every thing! Oh, I shall go mad, but to be rationnal & reasonable & say all I should, do as a Lady *tiré a 4 epingles* shd, (the pins striking in her like the 7 swords in La Madonna de dolore). We had a dinner where Mr Hill was madder than ever; he told the Garniers & us that Mme Falconnet with that voice will, after he is dead, raise him from his dread abode - I suppose like the Angel that appeared to Clarence - he is mad, mad, & to be pitied - the latter like him & emulate him.

The American Minister here is a bore, a man of bales of Cotton.[571] He can't speak French or Italian & he says to the Ministers: I dont want to understand you. I come for my four Millions!

Account of the intellectual Party to Pompeii,[572] Eating & Lovers, Mrs Ashley. I wrote out for Sir W. Scott the story of Sir Gilbert Talbot with wh. he seemed much pleased.

I went last night to Sir Walters. Sir Walter talked to me as Mme De La Ferronaye cannot speak english or understand his indistinct speech. He is full of his Maltese book which is begun, of La Valette's story.[573] He is going round by the Tyrol to see Hofers Tomb - & the Chapel at

---

[570] On 21 August 1822, the band of Nathaniel Gow played at a dinner attended by the King at Dalkeith House; his host, the Duke of Buccleugh, sat on his right. (See Prebble, ibid., pp.282-3). Queen Caroline had died in August 1821.

[571] Presumably John Nelson (1791-1860), appointed American *chargé d'affaires* in 1831. Alexander Hammett of Maryland had been American Consul in Naples since 1809.

[572] Sir Walter had visited Pompeii on 9 February in company with Sir William Gell and others.

[573] For details of this proposed publication, see Donald Sultana, pp.122 et seq.

Inspruck of which he is always talking of the Statues of the knights.[574] He talked learnedly, repeated Lochhaber & some ballads, but grew puzzled about the present time. He goes to Paestum on Monday. The Ladies are going to quarel about their lovers & their flirting - two sad silly women these are, Miss Scott & Mrs Ashley - heartless & a flirt, at the end of nine months, one tired of her husband & ready for any one else. The moral of my Tale will come, & shortly I think.[575]

22d [Feb. 1832]. A large dinner & pretty music at Ld Hertford. He will live here, or else why these mutual royal courtesies. It delights me to see the Corps Diabolique obliged to swallow him & it because they have set up vulgar english Fools of their own which they are forced to let fall. Ld Stuart & Ld Heytesbury's conduct is different as to Fools!!!!

Visited Miss Scott. Ladies Quarels. Had a visit from Sir Walter.

March 7th [1832]. Ash Wednesday. If I was not an idle & irregular writer, I sd have an amusing journal. I have not been out since Sunday fort't when I dined at Ld Hertfords - a chest & throat illness - & kept either to my bed or drawing room. Yes'y company at dinner: Naples is now grown a Florence in low vulgar company & gossip, petty quarels & amiable[?] love of fault finding. I really regret nothing but the climate & Sir W. Gell. There have been Duels & will be more. Mrs Ashley, whom no Man careth for, seems to have stirred up this by petty coquetry. The Acton set too, & Men who are Fools, & Women whose head dont stand anything, not even Branccacio. Think what a whirling head it must be!!!

No one is a Hero to his *Valet de Chambre* & why should not they, if the character's in keeping. Dr Hogg[576] lives with the Scott Family. He says to Sir William "The[y']re quite an ordinary Scotch family in their interior. They storm & scold & swear!" Alas poor dear Sir Walter. Miss Scott said to me "Think of Mrs Ashley coming home at 2 in the M'g with a Man of my brother's character!" Sir W[alter] takes little

---

[574] M.T. believed that Scott had borrowed from her a print depicting the statues at Innsbruck (see Gell, *Sir Walter Scott in Italy*, Plate 10 and p.49).

[575] Mrs Ashley was the sole executrix of her husband when he died in April 1877.

[576] Edward Hogg (1783-1848), Glaswegian doctor, who left Naples on 27 April bound for Messina. He subsequently produced a two-volume account of his travels entitled *Visit to Alexandria, Damascus, and Jerusalem*, London,1835.

interest in any thing; Malta interests him more. He is very good to me. Went to a hot party at that good persons, Mme de Stackelbergs. Took leave Tuesday of Mme Falconnet in her bed. Wednesday, dined at Ld. Hertfords & what do you think of me, Love, & what do you think of me, a Puppy!! Everything for us draws to a close. A large dinner at home & the Yellow Satin Room lighted & filled with company for the last time. Hertford set: Ld Hertford & his Men of go - an extraordinary specculation - Redern, sweet as Sugar candy - Stack & Tartuffe - Aug's Craven would be great - & is little - "unstable as Water thou shalt not excell,"[577] - Rothschild - C'te de Lebzeltern - Mr Hill calls him that old Necromancer - his philosophy in life: never to sift[?] people too much. It shows a bad experience of human nature. Story of Ly Strachan: Baron Valter who asked her, "Milady, Comment trouvez-vous les dames Napolitaines?" "Elle sont jolies, mais elle n'ont pas de quoi s'asseoir"[578] was her answer! - and his astonishment. Tone of Naples - changed.

20th [March 1832]. We had a large dinner, my spirits & powers are gone. Now I feel no regrets at going - all is business, weariness & affairs. Sir Wm. Gell I do regret. My adventures today concluded with Sir Walter, his misapprehension frightened me, his long Letter to me.[579] Dined at Sir Henry L[ushington]'s. C'te Ludolf is a sort of Gil Blas, I sd think. Ly Sligo gave him 10,000£ to be off of marrying him. I am growing rich in consequence of Ld Hertford's advice (by placing money in the Neapolitan Funds).

30th of March [1832]. Went today a charming walk to the Cappuchin Con[ven]t of San Gennaro at Puzzuoli. We knock'd & a good Monk opened the door of the long white passage hung with Portraits of Cappuchins & signified to us to be contented with the Church, for Convent we sd have none of. To the Church we went. On each side of the Altar of the side Chapel are let into the Wall ornamented Doors; in one of these is the stone marked with the blood of the Saint, in the other is the bust of the Saint & the affixed Rose according to the old Legend believed by the people. We then saw the place where the drawing had been made for me, & walked on to the Ruffo & descended thro' the

---

[577] *Genesis* xlix, 4.

[578] 'What do you think of the Neapolitan ladies?' 'They are pretty, but they lack the means of sitting down.' - Presumably, her way of translating into French: 'They lack bottom.'

[579] Original in the Morgan Library, cat. ref.. MA 1860(5).

Iron gates by a Cottage where a graceful child was standing *sotto la pergola* with its Dog in its arms. We found our carriages in the high road under.

31st [March 1832]. Went to Ld Hertford. Charlotte Strachan is like Spencer Perceval: her pretty countenance will create a passion; a Sister is a beauty & only a beauty, a good girl now & will be ruined soon. Mme Falconnet lent me Brock[e]den's *Passes of the Alpes*. It [is] the prettiest of books.[580] There are 12 passes: Simplon, Mont Cenis, Tyrol, Grand St Bernard, Stelvio, Little St Bernard, St Gothard, Mont Genèvre, Corniche, Grimsel & Gries, Splugen & Bernardin, Tende & Argentiere.

L'Incoronata where Joanna 1st was crowned; in the Chapel of the Crucifix is her Portrait by Giotto. Petrarch says the Chapel was painted by Giotto. It is a curious underground Chapel made one in 1331 having been a Hall of Justice.[581]

Sta Maria la Nuova, built 1268. Mass was going on & I tumbled over the people's feet who were very good humoured about it. There is an *adoration of the Magi* by Giordano much esteemed, & two Monuments in the Chapel of the Great Gonsalvo, a Monument to Marshall Latrec,[582] I think the translation is "from Gonsalvo his ennemy who would not let his bones lie unburied," & another to Pierre di Navarro, his nephew, I believe.

San Domenico Maggiore. I went there twice: once with Sir Walter Scott, who seemed much pleased & we sent Muller[583] to draw it next day. Many confessionals were full & the Nun in her black Veil drawn close round her white serge dress was being confessed by the silly fat Monk whose repulsive countenance I never shall forget - & is another

---

[580] William Brockedon, *Illustrations of the Passes of the Alps*, 2 vols. London 1828-9. Each section, originally published separately, is devoted to a particular mountain pass and illustrated by eight engravings and a map.

[581] The Church of l'Incoronato was built by Joanna I to commemorate her marriage to Louis of Taranto in 1352. The frescoes by Roberto Oderisi were wrongly attributed to Giotto.

[582] Odet de Foix, Vicomte de Lautrec (1485-1528) died of the plague while laying siege to Naples.

[583] Rudolph Müller (1802-85), Swiss painter who had been resident in Naples since the early 1820s.

argument against Confession. At the same time a Coffin lay in the body of the Church - & a Mass for the dead was going on. In the Sacristy is a glory of Solimenos, & some very curious Coffres, really the coffins of the Royal family, hung in the air. They are coloured velvet mostly & of the same form as the Kings are now buried in, with their Pictures hung over the Coffin. They are very old; many of them begin before the Kings were buried at Sta Chiara. The most interesting Tomb of tattered & discouloured Velvet is that of Ferdinand Francis d'Avalos, Marquis de Pescara who served under Ch's 5th. & the husband of Vittoria Collona. He died at Milan in 1535 [1525] aged 35 & was brought to be buried here. They say he has no Monument; his Picture hangs over the Coffin; near is a red velvet Coffin containing the bones of Giachina Napoleone, a niece of Murats, married to the Minister of Finance.[584] Royal blood. This is a fine Church, full of curious Tombs & Pictures & of true Catholic Sanctity & superstition.

The Cathedral called San Gennaro. It is very old. The Confessional called at Naples *Soccorpo* is the best part to see, being a little underground Chapel, beautiful in form having been the remains of a Temple of Apollo. A kneeling Statue of the Cardinal Olivier is beautiful & said to be by Michel Angelo.[585]

The Chapel of the Minutolo's where the walls are painted in fresco with figures of Knights, having horns on the Casques, said to be symbolique of Strength, strong as an Ox.

Il Tesoro, or chapel of San Gennaro, is the finest part of the Cathedral built in consequence of a vow made by the Town of Naples during the plague of 1526. There are busts of the Saints to the number of 36 in silver & in brass containing their relics: it is fine to look on, & the Chapel, when filled with the superstititous Multitude, & when the Treasure is displayed, of diamonds & Emeralds with wh. the image of the Saint is decorated, is really a curious sight.

---

[584] M.T. did not read the inscription carefully. It related to the death of Alexandrine Andrieu, Comtesse de Mosburg (1791-1811) and her three children, the last of whom was named Joachin Napoleon. She was indeed the niece of Murat.

[585] The statue is that of Cardinal Oliviero Caraffa who commissioned the chapel. It was executed not by Michaelangelo but by Tommaso Malvito who was responsible for designing the *Succorpo* area around 1500.

Today we went to the Scuola de Vergilio & roamed about with the L[ushingtons] in & out of the Fishermans boats, drawing, & thought Murder was committing in a house near. The place is covered with Indian Fig. The Fort on the Promontory was the Duke of Guise's point of attacking Naples. Where the Hermit lives was once the Temple of Fortune. A bust was found of the Son of Pollio. Pollio & Lucullus had houses here.

Studio. Here they copy Canaletti's Pictures very well at 15 piastres - *au naturel* at 40 piastres.

Domenichino. *An Angel shielding a child from Satan*; the attitude of the child looking up is lovely. It is

> "Lisping the eternal name of God
> From purity's own cherub mouth," [586]

The Angel looks down, & is guarding the child from Satan who is trying to lay hold of it, & how beautifully is represented the mental purity of the child over the bodily strength of the Devil. It is a picture that wd do more good than all the saints & Madonnas in the world. There is something in *Lalla Rhooke* like it:

> "There was a time, those blessed
> When young & hapily [haply] pure as thou
> I looked & pray'd like thee." [587]

La Bella di Parmigiano - a Squirel on her hand, a jewel on a braid of hair - the expression - Ly Dudley Stuart. I am sure she was awry.
A head of Antoniello, P'ce of Salerno by Giorgione of wh. no history remains. It is superb. I have had it copied.
Cardinal Bembo. Paolo Veronese (not his but a copy from Titian)
John of Austria Tintoretto.
Columbus - effeminate looking by Parmegiano (like the Red Rover as described by Cooper).
Americo Vespucci by the same.

---

[586] Thomas Moore, *Paradise and the Peri* (Part 4 of *Lalla Rookh*).
[587] Ibid., but an adapted quotation.

St Francis by Guercino, a head. "And tears that wash out Sin may wash out shame."[588] True affliction indeed!!

Leo 10 between two Cardinals, like that in the Pitti, the Cardinals have the eagerness of Italian menials. A rich Missal is on the Table & a Bell, and the Pope holds a finely mounted magnifying glass. One of the Cardinals was Clement 7 afterwards. Vasari says this picture was painted by Andrea del Sarto.

The picture of the *M. of Pescara* is in the Kings Palace.

Portrait of Massaniello with a white drapery & a Feather in his Hat.

2 fine Salvator Rosa's, one *Christ preaching to the Doctors* at twelve years old.

Spadara. *The Cloysters of the Grande Chartreuse*, the Monks prostrate to San Martino, who appears with St Bruno in the skies interceding for his Brethren with the Virgin during the plague at Naples when the painter took shelter there, & one of the figures in the crowd represents Salvator Rosa.

We went to hear the Nun[s] sing at the Church of the Sacrementista.[589] The people were very dirty & very devout, & the Garlic & the spitting disgusted me. As evening came on, the lights were gradually lighted & fell in lights & shadows on the statues in the Church. The moving figures of the cloistered Nuns cd just be traced above & then the singing takes effect, & your soul is poured out before God!!! The Catholic religion is one to work the imagination cruelly - & humble the spirit before God. We came home & found that by staying at this Church listening to the singing, we had just missed a *Poisson d'Avril*[590] as it is called in French - some people had come to dine & gone away. Camposuele & Sass had lost their dinner & some others & we had gained ours in peace & quiet by being out.

2d of April [1832]. Sold all my *garniture de table* in trays, Thermometer, & ornaments, to Rothschild at breakfast. Ther'r 67 degrees.

---

[588] cf. Matthew Prior, *Henry and Emma*: "Nor tears, that wash out sin, can wash out shame."

[589] Now called the Church of S. Giuseppe dei Ruffi.

[590] an April Fool.

The April Fool proved to be the work of Pr'cesse de Baufremont's daughter[591] who had sent out invitations for a dinner in Papa's name - we had luckily stayed at the Sacrementista Mass to hear the music. The people in the body of the Church, an immense multitude, for the Church is large & crowded, give the responses to the Nuns above. It makes a solemn & awful impression as the voices, increase[d] by the form of the building, give the idea of the Waves in a storm rolling along. What theatrical effect there is in the R.C. Religion.

2d [April 1832]. I am not sorry to leave a foreign life; my mind has been tempest tost, beat on rocks & shoals, & barren sands for two years since Nov'r 1829. I have had little happiness & some amusement. I am now a poor weak silly woman; I was not always that & the physique is as worn as the morale. Enough tho' of self! self is one of the joys of a journal; it is a pleasure ground to the *amie de coeur* or the Loon. I am leaving this view of beauty & splendour for ever! This superb nature, & these country walks so lovely that they restore the mind, & calm & please it. I am leaving a tiresome society of foreigners of whom I can only say that total & entire indifference is the only good; dislike perhaps! One person I am very very sorry for, an amusing & delightful companion whom I shall never see more - another, was he not insane, I should regret still more. Mr Mathias at 82 spends all his time & money in printing his poems & distributing them to his friends.   30 Latin Lines to Sir W. Scott on his visiting Naples came yes'y. Mr Mathias is not a pleasant man, eager & irritable, but a wonderful person at 82.

> "Learned he is, & can take note
> Transcribe, collect, translate & quote."[592]

7th [April 1832]. Passed a pleasant e'g at Sir W. Scotts where we left peoples characters - as we found them. Miss Scott, a wild girl. She was full of a Fête that she & Ly Temple want to have in the Casa de' Spiriti[593] where they were all last night by Moonlight. Mats are proposed for hiding the holes, Torches & Fires to light it, boats to convey

---

591 This would suggest that the perpetrator was the 11 year old Elisabeth, daughter of Anne, princesse de Bauffremont. Anne's sister-in-law Isabelle was a daughter of Prince Paterno.

592 Samuel Butler, *Hudibras*, Canto 2, ll.434-5.

593 The Villa of Pollio was called the *Casa degli spiriti* by the Talbots who apparently had a painting of the spectre and the place. (See *Sir William Gell in Italy*, pp.94 & 155).

people - & a Supper. It is feared that people will fall thro' the holes & be drowned.

8th [April 1832]. Intense heat. Party to Baia off.

10th [April 1832]. I was last night at Ly Acton's play. I was with Miss Scott who goes to Greece & Constantinople with her Father, Mr Baillie who goes with Dr Hogg to Jerusalem, & Ly Temple & Miss Baring who are going to Egypt & Barbary.[594] The play was pretty & *Sir Ch. Greville* is one of her silly extasies. I cried my eyes out at *Michel & Christine* wh. was acted incomparably. I cried because Christine is a fool like all women, & Michel (Aug. Craven) is an effeminate coward. Old Papa Hill was there. I am very angry with him & meant to abuse him but shall not & so after eight years intimacy we shall part friends. I am going to dine with him on Saturday. I envy these people going off out of Europe. It is rather enviable to get clear off in this way. It is said Sir R. Acton is refused by Mlle Dalberg.[595]

April 12 [1832]. A series of farewells! "Ce qu'on dit et ce qu'on pense."[596] Yes'y I dined a great dinner at M. de Lottums. I sat between the *Sçavant*, Santangelo, & a German Baron. The *Sçavant* made me remark that he being a Catholic eat only Meat & Fish for his *Maigre*, the money for the *indulgenza* goes to an *Hopital*. He raved of the King['s] virtues - whilst the German from Munick raved of Ld Erskine & his family.[597] We abused Michel; the German & I agreed that Christine was a fool. Alas, poor Women! we are all fools one way or other - too wise or too silly. Mme de Lebzeltern told me that Mme de Lottum was foolish in her choice. I hesitated not knowing whether she aluded to M. de Lottums dull german phizionomy - but she added "Aug. Craven has no feeling; I thought when I knew him first, he had, but now I see he has not." I said, "he is a little coquette, & thats all, a mere Coquette." The little Coquette thought we were talking of him & admiring him & came & discoursed with me; he is a very trifler, affected &

---

[594] They left Naples on 12 June along with Sir Grenville (see Sir Grenville Temple, *Excursions in the Mediterranean*, Vol.1., London, 1835, pp.1-2). Miss Baring was Lady Temple's sister.

[595] She did not refuse him, but did ask for breathing space. Sir Richard continued to press his suit through Joseph St John and was ultimately accepted. (See Acton Papers, Cambridge University Library, esp. Adds MS 8121(2), 1-2).

[596] 'What one says and what one thinks!'

[597] Lord Erskine had been appointed British Minister in Munich in 1828.

effeminate, probably has studied 'Les ruses de la Coquetry' & so succeeds with silly women. They are all in love with him - he can act, but I am too old not to see thro' all these ways. *Louis 11* by Delavigne,[598] he says, is very clever. He talked of Miss Kemble, but not as a man talks who is really in love. All the Italian women shake hands now! What a change in manners. M. de Sant'angelo has been very civil in the trouble he has taken for me about Werner. He is not to be traced in a Convent & probably took a name for the time he passed here.

Next day Sir Wm Gell & Mr Earldly Wilmot[599] dined with us. Sir W. Gell says nothing but he feels our going & our eternal Adieu, our lame, clever & agreeable friend; I am very sorry. We were glad to be quiet. We have had so many ordinary dinners as Sir William calls Ld Hertford's feasts. All my beautiful Drawings will be my last recollection of Naples. Mme Dupont has lent me the *Musée Francais*.[600] In it is a Print of a Statue of Fortune, holding 'la Corne d'abondance'[601] & accompanied by a winged Cupid to signify that in love, fortune has the preference over beauty.

Friday, we dined at C'te Stackelbergs, Saturday at Mr Hills, Sunday at Ly Drummonds, Monday at Lord Hertfords, & finished. The Cholera is in all its horrors at Paris & Hearses in the Streets instead of carriages. 800 persons died in one day. Regina is a Beau, who steals, not a good name, but a Cane. Spaccaforno is another beau silly enough whom Ly Strachan is making great play with to tieze Mrs Laing M[e]ason. Miss A. Scott & Mr Baillie ought to marry.[602] That great Gen'l, as Mr Hill told Sir Ch's Greville he was, is a great goose.[603]

---

[598] Casimir Delavigne's five-act tragedy had had its first performance earlier in 1832.

[599] Probably John Eardley Wilmot (1810-1892).

[600] A four-volume work, published in Paris 1829-30, containing images of statues in the Louvre before 1815.

[601] 'The Horn of Plenty.'

[602] 'The generous public have been so good as to give me *two husbands*, which is *contrary to law* - Captain Pigot and Mr. Baillie. Now I would sooner marry all the ship's company than the said captain; and as for Mr. Baillie, he happens to be the brother of an intimate friend of mine, Mrs Ashley, who was.... the fashionable London beauty for two seasons; and because [s]he lived for six months in the same palazzo at Naples, I do not see *why* I should marry her brother.' Letter from Anne Scott to Susan Ferrier, see *Memoir and correspondence of Susan Ferrier*, London, 1898, p.256.

[603] Maj.-Gen. Sir Charles John Greville (1780-1836) had served in the Peninsular War and subsequently as M.P. for Warwick.

P'ce Cassaro has married two of his daughters, one 14, the other 18, to two Sicilian princes. They dined at Ly Drummond. P'ce Giardiniera [Giardinelli] has received the last polish at Cheltenham at the Clarence Boarding house, a very feshoneble place as he informed me & with a very feshioneble Lady, Lady Ventry - what a vulgar thing, a vulgar englishfied Foreigner is! His bride, just fourteen, was so proud or very duped as a woman. Her sister Pr'esse Tre Case is very pleasing.

22d. [April 1832] We went up to San Martino.[604] The *Prophets* of Spagnoletto are reckoned its fine Pictures. I prefer the *denial of Peter*, a picture of M-A. di Caravaggio, to any picture there. In the 2d Chapel on the left are Massimo's pictures of parts of the story of St Bruno. The Sacristy contains the famous picture of *the dead Christ* by Spagnoletto, the Madonna, St John & Mary Magdalene wiping the feet of our Saviour. The Ceiling most beauty [beautiful] in shape, & paving is by Giordano. The Carved wood is beautiful. One of the Stalls in the Choir or numerous Tables belonging to the Church wd have made such a Cabinet, & the old damask Curtains, yellow with red lines; such Furniture! & such inlaid woods too with Marchitry. As to the View, it is allowed to be the finest in Italy, but the Convent is an Hospital for the blind Soldiers & where the glare & brilliancy must be hurtful I sd suppose. From the windows & from the garden you see Naples as a Map, & its beautiful Campagna & bay spread out before you!! The Cloysters are fine & the Statues round it, & within is a garden & the Campo Santo in former times of the Gde Chartreuse which was suppressed in [1806].

22d [April 1832]. Ld Hertford had his ball.

27 [April 1832]. Yesterday we left Naples, Sir H. L[ushington] & us three, to go to Mte Cassino. The four horses took us at a great rate; ther. 54; we stopped to bate a[t] one of the very worst Taverna's I ever was in by a road side wh. we sat in with the door open for the Cock & Hens to walk in & out, tho' it rained because the only window was without glass. There was a ladder to a loft, three dirty chairs for Furniture. Papa eat some poached eggs upon the Chairs while we made a sketch of the Room. Before arriving at San Germano, we passed an old Sarascenic Tower & also a Castle with Cells gradually round it on

---

[604] The Carthusian convent had, during the period of French rule, been converted into a military hospital. It was restored to the monks in the 1830s, but they were finally expelled in 1866.

a hill; both looked curious places. The last was probably a Hermitage. The first sight of San Germano is fine - an old town with two white Convents, & upon a very very high Mountain overtopping it is the Monastery of Monte Cassino wh. looks like an enormous Palace. The Marchese Imperiale[605] not having come to see his Son, our message had never been given at the best Taverna, which was occupied, & we with difficulty got two or three rooms elsewhere, full of fleas & very uncomfortable. By the help of a Pie wh. the Cook had sent with us - they we dined, with the door open to let out the smoke - & with the help of our own Clothes, we got some covering to sleep, as we were well tired. I had hardly lain down when such screams & moans near the Inn wakened me. The doors were all locked & I was too tired to move, but next Morn'g I found that Sir Henry Lushington with his usual activity had been to the place where the groans & screams came from, & where he had found the Gipsey Father of his tribe dying in a barn, & the howling & distress of the Tribe had been a strange scene he said.

Next Morn'g we got Donkeys to go up to the Convent. The ascent is in a zig-zag direction & has a view of the town of San Germano in the bottom, an old Moorish Castle half way up the mountains, a rich plain, & an Amphitheatre of hills some of which were still white with Winter snows. The first Chapel we got to is ruined; it is called "La Ginocchio", & contains nothing but the mark in stone of the knee of St Benedict's Mule, whom we are told knelt to the stone image of the Madonna which still remains over it!! a heathenish Legend! We turned many a zig-zag path. The day was beautifully clear & sunny, & we admired the view & thought of the scene that took place here in 1821 or 22, of Fathers coming down from the Convent to buy Provisions & being taken by the Brigands, & then the lay brothers rushing out to their assistance & being also overcome & carried off, & only ransomed at the price of yards of velvet & all the money & goods required by the brigands; a great year that 1821 was for those gentry, as the Frascati Massacre of the Monks & the murder of the Terracina Children took place also then. There is a cross & some fine Ilex Trees further up, & the Convent has the air of a Fortified Castle rather than that of a Monastic building. It is surrounded by ancient walls of enormous stones covered with ivy, & after passing another turning &

---

[605] A son of the Marchese Imperiali was being educated at the Monastery.

Crosses, we saw the entrance to the Convent before us which is an arched hollow way thus:

The windows are square, but here & there interupted by one or two of irregular form having balconies to them. There is every symtom of approaching decay & of the ancient splendour of this enormous pile passing gently away. Passing thro' the arched way, we arrived at Cloysters & then up a flight of steps to the more celebrated Cloysters called "Il Paradiso." It is strikingly magnificent. There are 16 statues, one by Le Gros of Pope Gregory 2d & reckoned very fine. Over the Cloysters is a Gallery which commands a view which is, as the Priest said it was, really "Il Paradiso". It extends 40 miles to Mola di Gaeta & the Sea. A staircase of Marble leads up to the Church which actual building was begun in 1649. This view is very fine of the Church. It has more the air of a Theatre than of a Church. Sir Henry Lushington has a Letter to a Priest, a friend of Mr Spencer's,[606] who was a lively looking person, not the least mortified or Tartuffe-like[607] & who showed us every thing. The pavement is of magnificent coloured Marbles. Luca Giordano's Paintings of the *Miracles of St Benedict*. Portraits of 20 of the Popes who were Benedictines all surrounded by gilding. Behind the high Altar is the Tomb of St Benedict & Sta Scolastica, his Sister, designed by M.A. Buonarotti. Here is a picture of the Saints thus:

St Benedict represented wearing a white Mitre & yellow drapery over his black dress & Sta Scolastica in black in a Nuns Dress. 13 Lamps burn here day & night. Behind the Altar are also Monuments: one to Pietro di Medici, a brother [nephew] of Leo 10th, who was drowned in the Garigliano while pursuing the french Army & another to Vido Ferramosca [Guidone Fieramosca] who left estates to the Monastery & I believe had a romantic his'y attached to him. He was the Lord of a ruined Castle we passed on the road. On the Monument is a female genius appearing to a Warrior with the name of Isabella Castriolla [Castriota] under it, whom I supposed was his wife, but was informed that no woman could be buried there. The Choir is the finest thing in the Church. It is 52 feet long & the[re] are 86 Stalls, & all the wainscoats of the finest Carving of bas-reliefs of Benedictine saints, each having a carved picture different & the Stalls of carved Cherubims in differ-

[606] In 1830, George Spencer (1799-1864), the youngest son of Earl Spencer of Althorp, had given up his Anglican living and converted to Catholicism.

[607] The main character in Molière's play of the same name. He hypocritically used religion as a means of making money.

ent attitudes. The reading desk is the finest of all these carvings in bas-reliefs, & upon it was a magnificent Missal of the Psalms grandly illuminated & grandly placed upon this reading desk. The Sacristy is fine - Oak Carving, gilding, relics, & painting by the Cavalera Cousa. The Curtain on entering it struck me - it was of scarlet & coloured Velvets - a magnificence in stuff of past days never now to be seen in modern Churches. It would take Days to see in detail the beauty of this Sacristy, the work of wh. was 260 years back. It is of *radice di noce* rich in *intagli* in wood. Under the Choir is the *Tugurio* or Confessional which was dug out in 1544 & consists of three Chapelles decorated with Arabesques like those of Raphaels in the Vatican & with painting representing the *Miracles of St Benedict* on these. Choir below is the Coro delle Notte.

Returning to the Church we went thro' the eight side Chapels. In the third Chapel is the history painted by Luca Giordano of Radelchi di Couso who having assassinated a P'ce of Beneventum, did penance at M. Cassino & became a Monk. The story being a very romantic one, I wanted to see the Picture, but the French had taken it away formerly. All the chapels are full of paintings of miracles, prophets & saints. The body of the Church is a mass of ornament. Luca Giordano has painted his Mistress over one of the Pillars as the figure of plenty giving milk from her breast to two dogs who are looking up to her. While we were looking at the Church, the Beggars were most troublesome & more loathsome than I ever saw them. Mass was begun & the stalls had each a Benedictine Monk or a young disciple. One of these was young Colle & another one of those *Diables* that I heard Mme Imperiale last week describe her children as. This poor child is 8 years old & the Marchese intends him for a Priest & says that his Son is very happy here, & thinks neither of the pleasures of San Carlo or the Capital. How Neapolitan of a child of 8 years old. We then passed to the Stanze di S. Benedetto, a set of small Appartments commanding a fine view, & filled with bad pictures. The Hospice is now deserted & falling into decay, & also the house where strangers were received on which is written 'Foresteria de' Nobili,' & the Refectory, all of wh. were modern.

We now took leave of our complaisant Priest & took a long walk on the outside, where the Monastery looked really warlike as its fortifications we[re] backed by the white distant Appenines. We went in search of the Albaneta, a convent built in the 10th Cent'y by a Monk returned from the Holy Land, but it has long been a country house, & Sta. Scolastica who came to visit her brother here has still a Convent 10 miles off at Piombarola [Piumarola] in the Plain. We walked down the hill & went to the Con[ven]t of Capuchins, a romantic spot where we stopped to draw, & the Monks came out to gossip with Sir Henry. These Capuchins are great gossips, but so picturesque that one is charmed to see them.

We went to see the Antiquities of San Germano where are great remains of the times of the Romans. The most remarkable is a Chapel & the Amphitheatre. The Chapel is called *Il Crucifisso*. It is an ancient Temple in the form of a Greek Cross formed of enormous stones that have resisted Earthquakes & built without cement. You can see this pagan Temple, the Amphitheatre & the Monastery all in one view. We are but four leagues from the Roman States. The Monastery was begun by Tottila King of the Goths in 529, burnt by the Lombards 589, ravaged by the Saracens 884, after which time it was fortified & given the finest priviledges & donations. It was a seminary for Popes, & a retreat for Kings, & became the most famous Monastery in Italy, still more distinguished for its learning than its greatness & power. Here ends my His'y of M[onte] C[assino] & our last excursion with our dear excursion friend Sir H. Lushington. In retiring we saw the Castle of the Lord of Minaco,[608] the beautiful ruins of wh. we had admired. His Sepolcro at M. Cassino, his wife raised to his Memory.

3d of May [1832]. No one would know the Palazzo Serracapriola. It is all dismantled & its comforts one by one have disappeared & left a range of stiff Italian Chairs & bare floor. Tragedy in the Lushington Family of a Suicide, Mrs Kidd - horrible passions of Servants.[609] The Garniers think that Ld H[ertford] wd not marry Ly Strachan - I said to her you had better write yr Memoirs, they will be very amusing. You had better bring them out Volume by Volume. She said 'No. I wait for the end! What bring them out like Harriet Wilson!'[610]

---

[608] i.e. Guido Fieramosca.

[609] Again M.T. introduces Mrs Kidd, (see note 356). A memorial in Naples cemetery erected by Sir Henry Lushington records the name of Eliza Brooks who died in May 1832 having lived in the Lushington family for 46 years.

[610] Harriet Wilson, the most celebrated courtesan of the early nineteenth century who, falling on hard times late in life, published her memoirs in instalments, but gave her previous intimate acquaintances the opportunity to buy themselves out of the text. Her communication with the Duke of Wellington produced the famous retort 'Publish and be damned.'

We think, dream & talk but of Cholera. It will be horrible at Naples - & all sorts of reports are afloat of the measures intended to be taken by G[overnmen]t like those of 50 years back in the Plague! Physicians to be in yellow liveries, baskets of provision put in at windows, well to be talked of by we who are going away, but dreadful to those shut in here. Cuvier the Naturalist says it will never come to Naples or to Sweden, a Theory he makes at Naples from the flux & re-flux of winds & waves from the Atlantic & Mediterranean across the different Bays in the neighbourhood.[611]

The King has behaved with the sense & spirit I expected from him in the late affair of the Camp at Sessa: The Neap'n & Sicilian Reg'ts quarrelled in his presence. He sent for the Swiss Colonel & ordered him to attack both parties. The Swiss said he would, but that it wd encrease the dislike here for the Foreign Troops. The King said he was right, & ordered his Lancers to disperse the Regiments. 25 men were wounded. The King held a Ct Marshal & shot two of each party. All here is quiet.

Monday we dined for the last time with Mr Hill - & for the last time I shook Pero's Ear, poor dog. His Master was as strange as usual, & said "It was not my fault nor at dinner either," wh. puzzled the wits of the Lushingtons much, wh. amused me as I saw they were in the wrong box. Mr Craven, Stran[g]ways, & Sir Ch's Goore[612] dined there. I had been harrassed all day, & my Father scolded me all the way up the hill, & my reflections were sadly melancholy, & I cried, & so ended my last day at Naples with all my friends!!!

On Saturday we went to Portici to the Garniers who have a lovely villa there & we went to see with them two remains of former splendours: The Monteleone & Bisignano Villas at Portici, where were Aviaries like houses for Birds, & gardens on a great scale & plants of great rarity. The Nosegays were tied up so beautifully I sent them off to Ly L[ushington] on my coming home.

---

611 Ironically, Baron Georges Cuvier (b.1769) died in Paris of cholera on 13 May 1832.
612 Presumably, Sir Charles Stephen Gore (1793-1869).

Sunday [6 May 1832]. Church & Visits, & dined. He & she are both pleasant people.[613] He knows everyone, [every]thing, all the news & gossip, all the books & old people & is a North much more than she is which is odd. She is a scare crow in looks & thinks herself a beauty & has the pretentions of 25, but pass that & she is very good & clever. He says he was at Langollen with Ly E. Butler & Miss Ponsonby[614] & was giving me an account of their coming in Habits to dine at Ld Dungannon's. Their Maid Mary, who ran away with them, is buried between their graves!!

Monday [7 May 1832]. Everything sold or packed up. I am tired & worn out, but went to pass the day, a last day, with the Lushingtons at the Camaldoli.[615] They have had a real Tragedy at home & their spirits are quite worn: so we are fit companions. We took Food & spread our dinner on the Grass in the Woods, after going to the Cento Camerelle, where is the best view of Islands & Ocean. Oh, such a view! The Camaldoli was founded in 1585. The lands belonged to Giovanni d'Avalos, a relation of my Hero Pescara, & given to them by him. Since then, Revolutions have dispersed the Fathers, but in 1820 they were again united here. They have now but the *Orto*[616] that joins the Convent, the C[oun]t Camaldoli having the Estates. We were much amused with the reception we met with from the Monks. Having begged Sir H.L. to ask admittance an old head appeared at the grating & called to a Monk to come down & open the door, but we appearing near, the monk seemed in a perfect agony. He was a handsome & very picturesque figure in his white robes, having a black girdle, a dark wood Rosary & a shaved head, black eyes & a long beard. I never shall forget his agony; he hid himself in the corner like a naughty child with a determination not to look at us or to let us peep in at the Cloyster door. Whether he was under a vow, or that he incured a pennance, heaven knows! but it was an extraordinary fright he felt. In going home we met three of the Brethren in large white Hats returning from Naples who did not seem to have any of this Monk's terror. The

---

[613] M.T. omits the name, presumably from distraction rather than intention. She must be referring back to the Garniers.

[614] The famous 'Ladies of Llangollen', Lady Eleanor Butler (1745-1829) and Sara Ponsonby (1755-1831). Their maidservant was Mary Carryl who had died in 1809.

[615] This Camaldoli monastery lay on the highest point of a ridge to the west of Naples, north of the Phlegraean Fields. Its principal attraction was its view. (See *Murray's Handbook for Travellers in Southern Italy*, p.415).

[616] 'kitchen garden'.

Superior has three Carlins a day, the Monks one each. When we were at dinner in the wood, they sent us out Liqueurs & a bad sort of sugar cakes. This was a last view of the Bay today, of the Islands, &, as it says in the description, of the *aspra ma cara isoletto di Nisida*.[617] We returned by the long lane.

8th [May 1832]. Mr Hill came to wish me Good by!!! half comic, half melancholy on his part. Beneventura & the Pigs, civility & the Nunzio asleep with Nits in his hair & such a rich turn of raving, & as mad & amusing as possible. And so Ld Dudley is gone mad![618] He was very strange they say for a very long time, & sitting next the Queen at dinner one day & having asked her 3 times if she would not have some Fish, she said, "Ld Dudley, you have asked me three times to have some Fish," upon wh. the Queen says she heard him say: "Yes & be d-d to you." & the day after the Duke of Sussex dined with him & he neither waited for him or got up to receive him.

Wednesd'y [9 May 1832]. The day past in packing & leave taking. Mme Dupont is a most sensible woman with a head for affairs quite extraordinary. I bought in yes'y 400£ into the funds here at 83 1/2. I have now 1100£ in the Funds at Naples. Lord Hertford has lost 550£ by selling out & buying in again. It only answers when the Money is to be sent to Eng'd.

I heard a good Story of Mr Lewes, Lady Lushingtons brother.[619] He asked Mr Sheridan to bet with him the receipts of the Play that was to be acted of his that night. He said, No my d[ea]r Friend, I never bet so high. I'll bet its value.

May the 10, 1832 - left Naples ---
My regrets are few as to persons, many as to place & climate, & dreadful are my feelings as to the future of my existance. Covered with dust we met all the world near the Camp at St Agata - all the beauty & fashion of Naples in an Omnibus & *centro piano*, all the Eligans at the Post House. This Gentleman is going to favor us with his Company in Eng'd, a bad specimen of a Foreigner. The Camp

---

[617] 'severe yet beloved little island of Nisida' - the 'severe' presumably referring to its use as a prison location.

[618] For further details about the sad decline of John William Ward, Lord Dudley (1781-1833), see S.H.Romilly, *Letters to 'Ivy'*, London, 1905, pp.383-6.

[619] i.e. Matthew Gregory Lewis ('Monk Lewis').

looked picturesque & Theatrical in the extreme at a short distance from the high road in the Forrest. The soldiers were busy & the sight gay, the bands playing & colors flying, the Tents were close together. This dusty day we followed a long line of Lancers & Artilery for Miles, to the opening of the new bridge over the Garigliano.[620] As we got leave to pass, the Soldiers cried 'Che Carozza' at the sight of the Coach loaded. What it was hit their fancy or was not like their notions of a Coach I can't guess. The shores of the Garigliano were crowded with Peasants in red dresses & white flat headdresses, & persons of all classes from far & near - the sight was pretty.

Friday was very cold. We reached Velettri & found Fires & winter Cloathing necessary, but lovely, lovely flowers never more to be seen by me edged the roadside: Lemon & orange flowers, roses & pome-granates, & quantities of all sorts known & not known.

12 May [1832]. Albano, having gone in the rain at Genzano to look at the Lake of Nemi.

13th [May 1832]. We lost the whole of yesterday at Albano. It was a cold bleak rainy day, & I sat by the Fire in the Inn from time to time watching the heavy black clouds that hung over the Campagna: the hill & the sea, & the Town of Pratica which is on the shore under Albano. I got to Rome woefully low, but having had a good bed & a good sleep in a good hotel (Baldi's), I took courage & wrote a long Letter to Lady Canning & told her all the news of these parts. Papa came in from Sir William Gell & says that the D'esse de Berry wanted to land at Fregus, poor misguided soul. What a Goddess is Fortune, &

---

[620] This highly sophisticated suspension bridge, designed by Luigi Giura and the first such structure in Italy, was opened by King Ferdinando on this very day, 10 May 1832.

so she is taken!!! Mr Dodwell[621] is dying & has confessed to please his wife; he cannot live the day out. Is he an Atheist, I asked? Not quite, they say.

I went out to walk about the Bath of Dioclesian, but this Pope has shut it against women on account of the neighbourhood of the Monastery of Chartreux. He shuts us out everywhere he can. Sta Maria degli Angeli is fine from space, & celebrated for its Meridian.[622] There is a beautiful Colorful Statue of St Bruno in his Robes, & the attitude & the countenance are both very sublime. On the tomb of Salvator Rosa his figure is represented painting, & opposite to his is that of Carlo Maratta. The Church of San Bernardo near, is more beautiful in its architecture in the style of the Pantheon. A priest was [teaching] a crowd of children their Cathechism which they seemed to hear very unwillingly.

14th [May 1832]. Called at the Boschetto Gellio[623] - & found him in all sorts of curious waistcoats & dressing gowns of various colours having the Gout & sitting with his dog in a very odd Room, half Pompean & half I dont know what. His account of the Scott party I hardly like putting down, as it seems terrible to have Sir Walter Scott thus exhibited to strangers so enclined to admire him. He is fast losing his intellect; he did not see the Vatican nor St Peters, Sir William believes. The Man who receives his MSS in London begged that they would not let him write more, but, what is worse, he provokes the ridicule of strangers, & they said he went to Bracciano to eat & drink & that he is

---

[621] Edward Dodwell (c.1776-1832) had travelled extensively in Greece, sometimes with Sir William Gell, in the first decade of the century. Aged about 60, he had married Theresa, daughter of Count Giraud, much younger than he; Henry Edward Fox considered her 'very clever' (Journal, p.341). Harris described her in his *Memoirs* as: The most beautiful Italian at Rome was a Mrs Dodwell, so famed for her charms, that a stranger, being asked why he came to Rome, answered, 'Sono venuto a Roma per veder tre bellissime cose: San Pietro, il Vaticano, e la Signora Dodwell.' (I, p.25). In her journal, Lady Blessington wrote of the couple: 'It is a strange sight to behold this lovely Italian sylph, all youth and sprightliness, hovering round a grave, sober English antiquary, who seems wholly occupied by his collection; and more disposed to descant on the perfection of his mummy, than to dwell on the fine qualities of his wife.' (*Idler*, II, p.277). He did indeed die on 13 May.

[622] 'On the pavement is the meridian traced by Bianchini in 1701 .... it was traced with exceeding care, and is said to be one of the most accurate in Europe.' (*Murray's Handbook for Travellers in Central Italy*, London, 1843, p.372).

[623] The residence in Rome of Sir William Gell.

gone off to see 16 Bronze Statues (I know them at Inspruck). It seems that Sir Wm Gell had said to Mr Cheyne[y] who had expressed a wish to know Sir Walter Scott, "He turns every thing to Prince Charles, & sees nothing but the Pretender anywhere" - & when Mr Cheyne[y] was introduced, [*4 lines crossed out*] - so after puzzling their brains for a long time at his meaning, they found that Albano & Albany he had puzzled together. Sir Wm has quantities of stories, but I dislike writing them. It is so sad, so cruel, to outlive g[rea]t reputation.

The Doria Palace. Fine old Genoa velvet in curtains over the Doors, yellow embossed with red. *Machiavelli* by Andrea del Sarto who looks like a Fool.
Andrea Doria. Cav're d'Arpino
Rubens first wife, look[s] cross, painted by himself.
Alfonso d'Este, Duke of Ferrara, Tintoretto
Innocent 10 by Velasquez
3 Musicians, a copy by Titian from Giorgione's Picture in the Pitti at Florence.
Prodigal Son by Guercino. I think one in London is the same.
Portrait of a woman by Murillio.
But the glory of the gallery is *Joan of Arragon* by Leonardo da Vinci.[624] Her Costume is rich & striking. It is a crimson velvet plain body & full skirt, muslin full sleeves & over the velvet sleeves buttoned with gold & lined with yellow velvet. The neck has a drawn Tucker over it & a regular boa thrown as drapery.

Palazzo Sciarra. *Modesty & Vanity* & da Vinci. I dont like either. A most beautiful picture of Titian with his 2 brothers & his Nephew, alive perfectly!! Caravaggio's famous Capo d'Opera.[625] The figures are perfect. I dont like the light & shade.
The Georgione there indifferent.[626]

Today began with the Borghese Palace, the finest thing at Rome in Pictures, old silks & velvets, Tables & gilding.
Julius 2d by Giulio Romano. The same as at Florence.
Raphael's fine *Portrait of Cesar Borgia*; he looks a bad Man; there is cruelty & disdain of opinion wonderfully expressed in the countenance. No passion but egotism, no feeling but self; it is an extraordi-

---

[624] The painting was by Raphael, and this version was a copy, not the original.

[625] Caravaggio's masterpiece (*capo d'opera*) - his picture of *The Cheating Gamblers*.

[626] The *Head of St John the Baptist*.

nary Picture, the eyes & eyebrows are dark, the hair is golden; he is very handsome, yet revolting & effeminate. The dress is beautiful: a black velvet Cap with a brown feather, a dress of close black velvet, one sleeve is displayed from the under dress with white in it which catches the light. I should think the sight of this Picture worth a journey to Rome to a painter.

a Cardinal by Raphael

Titian's *Sacred & prophane Love*, a duplicate of my Bassano, in the first Room - *Saul & Goliath* by Georgione - a *San Dominico* thought to be Georgione; a whole room of Venus's.

The Ceilings & gilding of the Palace are perfection.

St Peters, we then went to. Pius 7th['s] tomb is a disgrace to St Peters & to Thorwaldson; it is poor & meagre. The Stuarts are all buried together. Jacobo 3 & 4 & Henry, Cardinal de York; & opposite is a Tomb of the Pretender's wife, I think a P'cess of Poland. Sir W. Scott must have been here for they say it interested him much.

Corsini Palace. *A Spanish Woman with a dog under her arm*

Innocent 10 by Velasquez

Visitazione by Georgione. The contrast of expression very fine.

A fine Portrait by Albano in the style of Vandyck.

Emp. Charles 5th - Children by Titian dressed in grey.

Portrait of a C'te Gonfalioneri of the Ch[i]esa Cattolica.

Guido *Herodias*!!!

Woman taken in Adultery, colouring beautiful.

We went to Sta Maria sopra Minerva, to look after some Tombs. Clement 7 & Leo 10 have Monuments behind the Altar & on the Stones are many worn Inscriptions, one Philip Howard of Arundel & Norfolk, Cardinal who died 1694, who I take to be the famous Cardinal Howard who was Almoner to Charles the 2d's Queen - & Pietro Bembo, Cardinal whose Monument is at Padua.

Chiesa Nuova. The little Chapel of S. Filippo & Nero was all lighted up, & the devout, mostly aged & infirm persons, were all on their knees. What is that of the Gout & Clement three? It was too dark to see the Rubens or the Caravaggio.

Mr Spenser is in bad health, I hear, owing to his exertions in making proselites to the Catholic faith. His preaching today was a failure.

Never was such a year as this is for going Mad - poor Ld Dudley; & Mr Spencer Perceval & one of the Montagne's on Religious subjects. Mezzofanti, at Naples on learning Chinese - he uses, they say, in his Madness all the Languages, 35 in number, that he is acquainted with.[627] Mme Lefevre[628] is gone mad too of her usual May madness, the beginning of wh. showed itself by crumbling bread at dinner at Mr Cravens.

P'ce Borghese is to lie in state here on Monday.[629] They have found out 200£ more for Mrs Dodwell. Mr Seymour's is a happy menage - by all accounts.[630] Sir Wm Gell dined with us & he & Ch[i]averi[631] amused us in the E'g. Ld Northampton has written a Novel upon Bracciano.[632] The account of the late excursion there for Sir Walter is that they eat a large dinner, slept, breakfasted & came back!!

Yes'y I walked on the Pincio & called on Mrs Ashley & went to the Ara Coeli where Mass was chanting. I bought a Roman Pearl & three Rosaries - The short one is *Le Cinque piaghe di Christo*[633] - *Passionisti* - the other *Le sette dolore della Madonna.*[634] *Padre servili adolorati* & the Camaldolites. The *Saccone* with deads heads I am

---

[627] Cardinal Giuseppe Mezzofanti (1774-1849) was well-known in his day for his knowledge of 30-40 languages. In March 1832, he had visited the Chinese College in Naples, where following his exertions to learn Chinese, he had fallen into a fever during which he did not merely confuse his languages, but forgot them altogether. (See Charles Russell, *The Life of Cardinal Mezzofanti*, London, 1858, p.309).

[628] Anne, the wife of Charles Lefebvre (1775-1858), the prosperous owner of a large paper mill.

[629] Prince Camillo Borghese had died in Florence on 9 May. In 1803, he had married Napoleon's sister Pauline.

[630] George Hamilton Seymour, a career diplomat, had been sent on a special mission to the Holy See in Rome where he had taken up residence between March and September 1832.

[631] Luigi Chiaveri (1783-1837) was the stepson and associate of the banker Giovanni Torlonia. He acted as Danish consul in Rome over a number of years, and, in 1816, had helped the English find premises where Anglican services could be held in the city. He died in the cholera outbreak of 1837.

[632] A lake some 25 miles from Rome. *Murray's Handbook* (Central Italy) suggests that 'the baronial castles which still frown upon its banks carry us back into the feudal times more completely than any other objects within so short a distance of the capital.' (p.521). The novel does not appear to have been published.

[633] 'The Five Wounds of Christ.'

[634] 'The Seven Sorrows of the Virgin.'

sorry I did not buy, but it was too mornful with death's heads. We went to Caius Cestus.[635] Now the burial ground is beautiful, one mass of Cypress, aloes, roses & Rosemary blow about the tombs. Close to Shelley & Miss Bathurst's Tomb,[636] I gathered a Rose & put it into my book. On Ld Barringtons Tomb is an Inscription as to an excellent Father.[637] There is a very pretty Monument in White Marble to Miss Georgina Little.[638] Near it lies the infant child of Mr Wm Lambton,[639] & further on Ch's Dudley Ryder, the son of the Bishop of Litchfield, a Midshipman drowned in the Tiber 1825 along with five of the Crew of the *Naiad*. A Gothic Monu't to Mr Finch is at the end of the avenue of Rosemary & has violets all around it.[640] You see St Peters to gt advantage from the Walk, now trained with Roses planted by English hands. The Pyramid is going to decay, the wild plants have settled in its crevices - but as the gay pink Flowers hang in festoons about its dark grey walls discovered by time, it is an emblem of Life chequered & brightened alternately. From C. Cestus we we[nt] to S. Paolo fuori delle Mura - an example of folly in a poor fallen state like the Roman. The Church repairs are to cost a Million of Scudi: that is 200,000£. It is a small town in size. The bad air surrounds it & the Fathers have gone for the six Summer months to San Calista & in this spot the Pope is spending a sum that would clear & beautify Rome. Columns lie on the ground & all is far advanced. A gay young Priest did the honors to us & showed us the Convent newly cleaned up. Its magnificent Courts & gold Mosaique, its Antiquities, its Flower beds in Cloysters, the old Pictures of Nuns & Monks amongst whom are Sta Scolastica, its Corridors & his own room, a very nice little chamber. *A quoi bon*, renewing such an establishment.

---

[635] The tomb of Caius Cestius (died 12 B.C.) built in the form of a pyramid and near to which lies the Protestant cemetery.

[636] Rosa Bathurst, aged 16, had been drowned in the Tiber on 11 March 1824. Delécluze described her as 'gracieuse au delà de toute expression' and Stendhal maintained that 'plusieurs étrangers la trouvaient la plus belle personne de Rome.' See E.-J.Delécluze, *Impressions romaines*, Paris, 1942, p. 88. For a full account of the accident, see *Sketches from the diaries of Rose Lady Graves Sawle*, p.p., 1908, pp. 24-8.

[637] George, 5th Viscount Barrington had died on 5 March 1829, aged 67.

[638] Georgiana Little had died on 20 February 1829.

[639] Edward Lambton had died on 3 March 1830, aged 3.

[640] For details of Robert Finch (1783-1830), see Elizabeth Nitchie, *The Reverend Colonel Finch*, New York, 1940. Details of the tomb inscription are given on p.2 and there is a photograph of the Gothic monument on p.64.

18th May [1832]. To Frescati we went at 1/2 7. It is a melancholy way with its line of Aqueducts, its fountains, its old Towers, its wretched huts & still more miserable inhabitants. However, the birds & the wild flowers abound, & groups of stone pine surrounding the Old Towers relieve the eye from the monotony & black look of the Campagna wh. is produced by the colour of the ground. The climate is *not* clear, or italian like, it is quite certain. Heavy clouds hang about & yesterday there was a mist round Rome & its domes & palaces. Today is cold & sunshiney, nothing of the south wind here o'er a bed of violets. At the Nuova Trattoria we arrived, & went to the Duomo, where we looked at the Monument to the Pretender & the Car[dina]l di York who was Car[dina]l & Bishop of Frescati[641] - a noisy mass was dispatching with great vigour. How all brusquerie ruins dignity in everything & in the Catholic Religion where all is for effect.

With bad Donkies & savage Ciceronies we made our way up to Tusculum passing the Aldobrandini & the Rufinella.[642] The view from the top was spoiled for want of clearness & the entire & total desolation give one a feeling of awe along with the recollections of old stories, tho' according to Capt. Lushington & Mr L. Mason all is perfectly secure now. However a thousand fears of brigands came across me as we made our way for two miles thro' the woods down to the Camaldoli - & I did not like the savage looks of our Conductors. The Camaldoli lies near the bottom with its pompous gates & its walls & towers & fortified Approach, wh. with the woods of Stone Pine looks fine. Up to the Gates we walked & boldly asked admittance wh. was refused of course but we were gently admonished that there was an order at the Cross below that no woman should come up, but as we did not know that, they could only pity us. I never saw two such picturesque Figures as came to the Door to us. Black eyes & hair & a look of health & intelligence & if it had not been for the long white beard that bespoke age, they did not look more than thirty. The Pope Gregory 16 was a Camaldoli Monk here during 13 years & accordingly he visited a short time ago his brethren in a Coach & eight horses & the way was cut for him by wh. we returned to Frescati;

---

[641] The cathedral contained monuments to Prince Charles Edward Stuart, the Young Pretender, who had died at Frascati in 1788, and to his Cardinal brother Henry, whose father had made him Duke of York within the Jacobite peerage.

[642] The Villa Aldobrandini was well known for its magnificent views over the campagna. It was owned by the Prince Borghese. The Rufinella Villa had formerly belonged to the Jesuits, latterly to Lucien Bonaparte.

passing the Falconieri we again arrived at the Cappucines & to the Rufinella, where hearing loud vulgar english spoken by the Friars in the Garden sounded to me so odd. The whole beauty of Frescati is in its Trees. There are woods of Stone Pine & Ilex Avenues without end. As to the Villas, they are like Manufactories fallen to decay, & both Terraces, Statues & Jet d'Eaux, that have cost Millions, are in a ruined State. At 1/2 2 heartily tired we got some dinner at the Trattoria & went after to Grotto Ferrata. It is so long since I have seen beauty in the town classes of women that it struck me here: they wear red bodices, with falling shoulder straps & ribbons, red tight drawn hankerchiefs inside & white Veils.

Grotta Ferrata is miserable, eat[en] up with Malaria. Founded in the 10th Century by St Nilus, it has an old fortified Castle with Crenels & Towers. The attractions here are the 18 frescoes by Domenichino. The finest is thought to be the visit of the Emp'r Otho to St Nilus. The portraits in it are of the *amante* of Domenichino, of himself, of Guido & Guercino. I prefer that of the Demoniac boy, even to that of Raphael; in the transfiguration, the figure of the Saint pressing his finger on the mouth of the boy is very fine, while his hand reaches the sacred oil, & also the figures of the Father & Mother & children. We got back to Rome by 1/2 7, gloriously tired with our day.

19th May [1832]. After returning to Mr Cosvelt[643] & hearing of the feuds of Mme de Meuron & Ly. Wm Fitzgerald, we went to Sir Wm. [Gell], found him in his queer Room in his old Philosopher's dress, & after gathering all the Roses of his Garden, we went on to the Villa Spadana now Vigna Pallatina, more beautiful than any thing that ever was seen, & like the enchanted Gardens of Armida, with its roses of all hues, its beds of Larkspurs & the views of Rome thro' the tall Cypresses. The Master of it[644] is an evergreen & asked us to dine with him & Mr Craven & the Secretary & Sir William. Shall I ever see these old Men again? I hope so for I am very fond of Sir William. We after went to the ajoining Church of San Bonaventura & then to the Grand one of S. Giovani di Laterano. Then to the Pantheon. The Church was dark but the Chapels were partially lighted for E'g Service, & I looked at the Monument to C[ardina]l Consalvi & the Inscription in the Wall to Raphael by C[ardina]l Bembo. The *Ex Votos* are enormous to the celebrated image of the Madonna.

643 William Gordon Coesvelt (1766-1844), a collector of and dealer in paintings.

644 Charles Mills who had bought the property on the Palatine in 1816. He died in 1846.

20th [May 1832]. A fine bright Sunday. Went the Tour of the Pincio & Villa Borghese. The stone pine, Ilex avenues, & the Plane Trees are finer than any at Naples. Crossed the Town up to San Pietro in Montorio, where there are some fine Tomb[s] & a picture of gorgeous colouring in the style of Rubens. The outside of the Church, Sir Thomas Lawrence used to say, has the finest view in the World: distant Mountains covered with snow, the nearer Hills of Albano, Tivoli, Frascati & Palestrina, the Cypresses & Stone pines of the Villa Borghese, the Domes & Palaces of Rome, the most magnificent of wh. are at a distance, the long line of Aqueducts, the Gates of Rome, the Campagna & the windings of the Tiber, & near to the eye, orange gardens with fountains, & convents whose walls are ornamented with fresco paintings & whose well defended Courts you can look down into filled with shrubs & flowers!!! We came home but stopped to see Spilman[645] the celebrated Confectioner, enamoured of his art - his sweetmeats & cakes being thought the best in Europe. "Ah," he said, "comme on les aime ces Buns; et cette scotch Marmalade, comme on l'aime!"

Heard the majority against reform.

23d of May [1832]. Yesterday we left Rome at 7 to go to Tivoli. It is impossible to see any country more unhappy & solitary looking than that between Rome & Adrian's Villa, & yet herds of the brown eyed grey Cattle are continually met driven by Men on horseback with long poles, a cloak before fastened on their horses & a feather & a rose in an old black hat. Herds of Goats also & a few country people - but few tho'. We first came to a sulphureous Lake where the Risings petrify like stalectites - & the whole road smells most nauteously - next comes Adrian's Villa, a large mass of, to me, inexplicable building, with such beautiful Cypresses & stone Pine, & Fern & wild flowers as I never saw before in my life. The stone pines are so large & majestic, the cypresses so tall & thick, that there must be something in the soil that produces them thus. We then wound up Hills thro' Olive woods to Tivoli situated on a rich wooded bank opposite. The town is neither as dirty or ragged as a Neapolitan town would be, & the peasant women are beautiful with clear complexions like rouge, & rich brown eyes like gypsies, set out by ribbons & scarlet & white dress, but there is a melancholy in this spot & in all the environs of Rome not to be ex-

---

[645] Spillman in the Via della Croce was warmly praised by Mariana Starke - see *Travels on the Continent*, London, 1820, Appendix, pp.109-110.

pressed or explained; for the ground is a vivid green, & the sky is bright & the Sun shines - & birds are in abundance, Nightingales, & our old English friend the Cuckoo. I can only explain it by saying, We come from Naples where all is gay & brilliant. At the inn at Tivoli we got Donkies, & went the Tour of the Cascatelles.[646] The first view is spoilt by artificial banks built since the River burst its boundaries five years ago. The best view to my taste, & lovely it is, is just passing a little Chapel which I have a view of (by the by in England) under the house of Catullus. This house belong[ed] to the French of the order of St Francis, but it was suspended & sold by Napoleon to P'ce Massimo who now possesses it. After passing this spot, the views towards Rome are perfect Pictures, wh. one can see were studied by Claude & Poussin, & then we got to Horace's Villa occupied by the Hermites of St Antonio. Waterfalls I dont care for, & I own that neither the great fall of the Cascatelles enchanted me. The little white Chapel which pleased Pr. de Châteaubriand is formal & the views from the terraces over the Iron Manufactory are too great a display. Here is a Grotto of wh. I have a drawing. We went to the Villa d'Este where the plane trees are lovely & the avenues of Cypress & Ilex. The house is formal without grandeur, the frescoes within worn out, & all its magnificence gone to ruin. After dinner we set out again &, a thunderstorm coming on, we hurried back & got to Rome at 1/2 7.

24th [May 1832]. Went to the Villa Raphael where the Tree[s] & long grass almost prevent you getting into it. That we sd ever have thought of buying & settling in this place!! How things & people change & how times & wishes change. Now the *tristesse* of it kills me & I sd soon take fright as indeed I do often at my own voice & my own foot-steps. Mr Cosvelt, Mr Mills & Sir Wm Gell dined with us. They talked reform & Anti-reform - the 35 opposition made the hum in af-fairs. Went to C[amuccini]'s[647] pictures done by himself & very fine they are. San Francesco raising the young Man from the dead is for the new Church at Naples; a portrait of Thorwaldson excellent, & many historical pieces.

To Ignaccio's, who has Old Pictures, rings & cameos, cabinets, antiq-uities & trash of every sort & kind; a pretty ring is 10 Scudi. To the

[646] A series of cascades made by the river Anio.

[647] Vincenzo Camuccini (1771-1844), a leading Italian painter of the day, and also a col-lector. Some seventy pictures from his collection were acquired by the 4th Duke of Northumberland in the 1850s.

Library at the Vatican: a Dante copied by Boccacio, & a Dante illuminated, 1500, Beatrice painted in green in every page, always in green,
even in the skies; what a beautiful style of illuminating for fans this
would be. The Levee of the Duke d'Urbino 1500, then Portraits &
histories embellished with gold & arabesques in such taste! The Letters between Henry 8th & Anne Boleyn, very open, frank & affectionate without any affectation of propriety (see Prudery, Johnson's
Dict'y[648]). I sd like to have coppies of them & many other things I
saw. The Library is the most beautiful & gay looking of Rooms looking into the Gardens of the Vatican, all arches down the Room with
paintings of the Cinquecento, with views of St Peters as it then stood,
& arabesque[s] both on Ceiling & Pillars, all as fresh as if it had been
done yesterday. Chiaveri having addressed a memorial to the Pope for
permission for us to go down & see the Tomb of St Peters, we went to
the Church & the Custode came & lighted us into the Subteraneous
Chapel with one Torch. I own my feelings were disagreeable the
whole time, tho' here & there light & air came thro' the grating. There
is a finely ornamented Chapel to St Peter, & Tombs of persons whose
Monuments are in the Church, Christina Q. of Sweden, the three Stuarts, some heathen Emp'rs & *una Sybilla* amongst bas-reliefs & Mo-
saiques. I am glad to get up to open day & expressed to Georgina & to
Papa that I would rather be devoured by wild beasts than buried in a
Vault!! We [were] walking about St Peters long, & were struck with
the fading of the pictures & the way that the mosaique stands time.
Thorwaldson's is the worst M[onumen]t in St Peter's[649] & Canova's to
Pius 6, a Braschi I think, the best.[650] It is calm, glorious, & hopeful, &
as a Pope or praying Saint ought to be represented. Down here lamps
burn day & night.

Pictures of the Vatican. *The Vision of San Romualdo* by Andrea Sacchi
- the copy is in the Church, *a Doge* by Titian in a tight flowered dressing gown & Night Cap, *La Madonna di Foligno & St Bruno* - the finest pictures there. *Sta Michellina*, by Baracci: how much brighter is
the ancient coloring than the Modern Copies. Four heads copying well
from Raphael 7 guineas - Pinocchio an old Picture all gilding in the
style of Pietro Perugino. A Minerva wise indeed & lovely! in the new
building, & I sd like all the Trepieds, Vases & Tables in the old Stanze
- but Statues weary me & I am no lover of the Antique. I went to the

---

[648] Prudery defined as 'overmuch nicety in conduct'.

[649] Monument of Pius VII (d.1823).

[650] Pope Pius VI (1717-1799) was born Count Giovanni Angelo Braschi.

Capitol but liked the halls opposite to it with the Busts from the Pantheon better. What a pity it was to move them & place them in a place like a Shop!!

Galileo Wisdom itself.
Annibal Carraci by Carlo Maratti
Leonardo da Vinci by Canova
Perugino - a satirical Caricaturist.
Tasso interesting & melancholy-looking by Canova
Raphael by Carlo Maratti - not very good
Two very good of *Pius 7* & *Leo 12*.
Ariosto - spirited & clever, but not sensible, with a Beard & a wreath of Laurel - born 1474 died 1533, the bust by Canova.
It is a very interesting collection.

Mrs Ashley came & talked english news & reform. We went out at 5 to Sta Croce & then to the prettiest sight at Rome: the procession of the Penitents of the Via Cruxis in the Coliseum. The female penitents carry a black cross also. This seen for the 20th time is an impressive & beautiful sight when the lights & shadows fall towards Sun set.

Sunday 27 [May 1832]. It rained as it rains in Italy; however we got to Cammuccini's:
2 of Bellini, the only I ever saw,
a Claude, a *Duke d'Urbino*, & a Magnificent *Portrait of Sebastian del Piombo* (I forget by who).
San Stefano Martyr, by M.A. di Caravaggio - very fine.
There is a Portrait of a complete blue stocking or learned Lady: young, sensible, dirty & a slatern (of Vittoria Colonna I am sorry to say) by her admirer M. Angelo Buonarotti & finished by his scholar Venusti.

Today I am very unwell & Georgina very unhappy at the Albano excursion not being to be. We hear that Ld Grey[651] is in again to govern a country which he has made ungovernable. We went to say Adieu to our amusing gay friend of five entire years. I do not say long years. He felt it, & so did I much - so ends all friendship, remember Chateaubriand's passage in *Les Martyrs* "sur le port de la vie!" I am dismalled,

---

[651] Charles Grey, 2nd Earl Grey (1764-1845), Prime Minister during the passage of the Reform Act of 1832.

quite. We go tomorrow, the Cholera is at Geneva & we shall be shut into Italy if we do not make haste.

Hotel de York, Florence, June 2d [1832]. It rains & every thing looks as dismal as if it were Milan. There is a provincial & John Bull look here very striking. Four days journey have tired me to death, & if it has not been for the uncommon event of a glass of Monte Alcino wine & nine hours sleep, I sd be extinct, but here I am as usual deafened with the bells of the Duomo, & watching the green, bronze, & purple Umbrellas & the shop of Curiosities wh. is unluckily vis-a-vis of us. We are going to the Pitti & to the Gallery. The Pitti has some of the Rooms shut up but what are open are superb beyond any thing in Italy in paintings, ceilings, gilding & Mosaique Tables, which is the Furniture of an Italian Palace. The pictures are the first in Italy. *La bella di Tiziano* - a fair fat beauty, a blonde with golden hair & brown eyes, the handsomest thing in the world, but no shape at all or elegance, like our Van Dykes or Sir J. Reynolds's beauties. She has pearls in her hair, a petticoat of brocaded stuff, Marie Louise brown velours sleeves puffed in the Spanish taste which all the old painters used in costume. Another perfect Portrait of Titians is the picture of C[ardina]l Hypolito di Medici in his hungarian dress of brown velvet & green feathers in a Cap - this portrait wd rival the Cesar Borgia at Rome. For his romantic story, see Northcote's *Titian*, 1st Vol. page 118.[652] *The 4 Philosophers*, glorious, by Rubens. *Cardinal Bentivoglio* by Vandyke. *The Secretary of Leo 10*, by P. Veronese, perfection of a Portrait. The Georgione of 3 Persons, so very famous, supposed to be Calvin, Luther & his wife. *La Madonna della Seggiola*, Raphael, & another Raphael as fine called *La Madonna de Baldaretrini*. *Leo the 10 & the Cardinals* Raphael, much finer than that at Naples. *La Madonna con diversi Santi* by Fra Bartolomeo, a picture by Raphael of a beautiful Italian with a white Veil, & a white dress lined with folds. *Charles I* [&] *Henrietta Maria* in two panels & one picture by Vandyke. We had enough of Perfection. All these pictures are in such magnificent Gold Frames, with such Carving, & hung on green or crimson silks or velvets.

At the Gallery, I was disappointed in finding the Portraits of Painters shut up, but in the School of Barrocchio are some Caravaggios & Velasquez's *Philip 4 on horseback* that bear looking at after what we had seen. In the V[enetian] School, a Giorgione Knight, a Venetian Noble thought fine - an ancient composition in Bellini style, a superb *Por-*

---

[652] James Northcote, *The Life of Titian*, 2 vols., London, 1830.

trait of a Warrior by Seb. del Piombo, & such a magnificent Bassano, the three Bassano's & Titian being all introduced into the Picture. I saw Benvenuti Cellini's things again. In a Corridor are some Bas-reliefs relating to Valombrosa, very curious, Effigiato nel 1495, & some miracles of Saints 1515, very beautiful. There is a bust of Machiavelli very ugly with a craning[?] back chin I dislike so much.

It rains & Florence with its heavy massive walls & great Palaces looks dismal, but the shops are excellent & it seems the sort of place where people eat & drink & dress & are silly & frail according to the scotch phrase. Not so Rome & Naples. "Je me glorifie d'avoir ete a Rome, je me felicite d'avoir ete à Florence," & I forget the third, wh. M. de Fontenaye used to say. For a wonder yesterday being Sunday it did not rain & I dragged Papa up to Fiesole & walked up the stony pavement to the Church of the Franciscans, the outside of wh. is graceful & picturesque with its Saints canopied & uncanopied, its bits of Gothic & its Cloysters, the Stone Cross, & the Old Franciscan Friar scolding the beggar who has got food at the Convent door. The Language to my ears (who understand not Spanish) is Spanish - & then we looked at the view of the vale of Florence, criticized its want of picturesque beauty. It is the land of plenty to look at, but all is in strait Lines & no graceful curve even - strait houses, strait roads, strait trees, being Cypress, strait Vineyards, & strait walls of gardens. The plain is enormous & so is the Town seen from Fiesole. We went to a sad *triste* Villa Capponi to pay a Visit to Mrs Parker whose fat fair children are refreshing amongst the black & yellow Italians. Today went to Sta Croce, where they were pulling down the Draperies in an upholdstery [in] a very indecorous way while Mass was going on. Orsanmichele has fine painted windows. P'ce Poniatowski,[653] who is a bore of the first water, showed us his pictures himself. He cried up & puffed off all his things, China saucers & all, one after one. He has one fine Portrait in Vandyke's style - & his Gems & *Pietre dure* would take a week to see; there is a room full. He has china Cupboards without end - & he has a great treasure in a very fine Picture of Bianca Capella,[654] handsome but cross-looking, dressed & painted in Titian's manner.

653 Prince Stanislas Poniatowski (1754-1833), a collector principally known for his collection of Classical gems, most of which he himself had commissioned in the 'antique' style.

654 Bianca Cappello (1548-1587), a Venetian beauty who eloped to Florence where she became the mistress and subsequently the wife of the Grand Duke Francesco de Medici.

Lucca Baths 7th [June 1832]. I do pity my Aunt[655] from the bottom of my heart, how pity gets the better of all other feelings. Poor creature! In such a state of health & in such an unsettled, unhinged, uncomfortable state of mind, & wish & intention!! me, with all my bad Nerves, & bad spirits & fits of dejection, I feel calm & collected by the side of her, & what is more, reasonable. I begin, seeing her example, to think "we make the misery we find!!" She has made a home abroad, & adopted an Italian boy, & now rues both; not but that the home abroad is the one suited to her; but not this Home; & yet she can neither fix her mind to wander, or to a home. Oh we are silly, silly creatures, we women generally, without Chart or Compass on the wide world. She is a strong & dreadful Moral lesson, but indeed all is (except oneself) for by ones own experience, alas! one gains nothing I find, & that I am not in Miss Edgeworths first class, "of those who learn from their own errors."

The place is lovely, green & calm; a rushing stream, the noise of which is lulling beyond any sound, a house buried in flowers & trees beside its banks, rural & pastoral all around, the hill wooded & with here & there Cypresses near the Cottages - & there is a seclusion, a repose, a deep melancholy, an absence of all connected with the world & with civilized life astonishing & sublime. The country people are good, & look so, & are so as much as Italians know how to be. There is a perfect look of security - nothing savage or Salvator-like[656] in the woods & scenery. All calm &, except the rushing stream & my Aunt, not the sound of a leaf falling.

That this should be the home of a person of the world once! I think that Providence will spare her that great misfortune that will inevitably happen in Sandrino's turning out ill, which it is not probable she will live to witness. He is ill brought up as an idle gentleman; can waltz & ride, & instead of her having made him a good person in his calling, she has made him a silly person in a calling he can never have.[657] My Aunt is I think 62, she looks 72 & is a very decrepid Old Woman - her only pleasure is in having a listener, who or what she dont care. She has a Dog very well brought up. If she had educated the Boy like the

---

[655] Mary Brodrick, née Preston (c.1768-1834), the sister of M.T.'s mother.

[656] i.e. nothing like the wilder and more savage scenes of nature depicted by the painter Salvator Rosa (1615-73).

[657] In the 1840s, Alessandro Lena was serving as Deputy Harbour Master of Hong Kong. (See Mrs H. Stisted, *Letters from the Bye-Ways of Italy*, London, 1845, note p.5).

Dog, she would have done right. She has a   Portrait of the Duc de
Bordeaux wh. the D'esse de Berry has just sent her.

We left Lucca early Saturday & having changed our plan of going to
Modena by the Mountain road got to Florence by 6 - the way that the
people gather like savages about the carriages in these little Town[s]
of Lucca, Pescia, & Pistoia is quite extraordinary. At the dirty Hotel de
York we staid till 12 on Sunday [10 June 1832], wh. being Whit Sunday, we saw the Grand Duke & his black Cloth equipages, & suit[e]
go to the Duomo. For the first time the heat was great, but when we
got up to the Appenines delightful, & winding up those beautiful
Mountains in the still pure air of evening was charming - slept Sunday
Night at Covigliano - dined Monday at Bologna. All looks riches &
comfort & smart dress - kept in order by 5000 Austrian troops. The
black veils & the white veils & the high Combs of the women are so
pretty. Slept at Modena, where the women go to Mass in black silk
Mantillas over their heads in the Spanish style. Placentia - a dirty Inn -
they are ruined by the Steam boats from Genoa they say. Milan - news
of the D'esse de Berry in La Vendée.[658] She is no coward at least - in-
sinuations at Paris. I went out (for I had had a scene) very nervous to
some Shops to buy Combs for Ly Belhaven & myself, 3 at 9 Francs
each, 4 at 5 francs each, gold beads, one row, 38 Fr.

[15 June 1832]. Friday very hot day - got to Arona & enjoyed the
quiet of the Lake & the nice little Inn & the Moon at Night on the Water.

Saturday clambered up to the Statue not without trouble & unre-
warded for the Saint looks better from below.[659] Got to Domo d'Os-
sola to dinner, enjoyed the last walk that I shall ever take in Italy. The
E'g was mild & beautiful & the Mountains owing to the lateness of
the season were covered with snow. We walked up the Sacra Monte. It
is in a Chesnut wood & the Figures in the *Stazzioni* or Chapels are as
large as life & well grouped.

---

658 At the end of April 1832, Marie Caroline, Duchesse de Berry had landed near Mar-
seilles in the hope of gaining popular support to oust Louis Philippe in favour of her son
Henri, Duc de Bordeaux. Having failed in the south, she moved to the Vendée where, in
November, she was ultimately arrested and imprisoned.

659 The enormous statue of San Carlo Borromeo, 66 ft.high on a 40 ft. pedestal, which
had been erected in 1697.

At Sion, I saw a beautiful dog of the Grand St Bernard breed. At Martigny, disappointed always at never going to the Gd St Bernard. Lausanne - good Inn & beautiful Campagnes. At Coppet, nice fat amusing Children - so different from Italians & reasonable creatures.

[19 June 1832]. Geneva - got at 8 to the Hotel des Etrangers, very comfortable. Shops. Sunday in Switzerland - Swiss happiness, of people & children. My own low spirits. Dr Buttigni, & Georgina. His Anti-room & Study - curious. Mme de Noailles & her daughter: french *d'aujourd'hui*, emigration from Paris. Wash[ington] Irvine's *Alhambra* - amusing.[660] Lausanne - Mlle de Blonaye very pretty indeed - Chateaux, & disappointment about Mrs Cannings Monument.[661] Fribourg - an old Town like Berne & an old German Town of former greatness. Cathedral, & Mass & Music. D'esse de Blacas. Jesuits. Costume & [?] of Women. We went out of the road to a famous Hermitage[662] - like an old enchanter's habitation, where a[n] old Man & his wife live, the old woman without a grey hair in her head. A rich country to Berne. Uncomfortable Inn. Mr Wilmot. Mr Percy,[663] an unfortunate Man who dresses himself like a Monkey. Dress of Berneoise women. Switzerland filled with french emigrants.

La Croisee. 29th June [1832]. At a very clean tidy Inn on the way to Zurich where four roads meet.[664] We stopped to dine today at a great German Swiss Inn on a large scale, like something in Sir Walter Scott's Novels. I gave 12 Francs for the Bernoise Cap from the pretty Girl there. I never saw so much food or China or Cakes or Linen or such large bunches of Keys.

Zurich - Have passed two days in the dirty Inn of the *Epée*. I like this place the least of the Swiss Towns. It abounds in Children, Old Maids & ugly people, & in a sort of *tournure* which makes me know how much I care for *Ton* still, & for well-made Clothes. Not a Lady or

---

[660] Washington Irvine's *Tales of the Alhambra* had been published in May 1832.

[661] The monument by Bartolini that Sir Stratford Canning had erected to his first wife Harriet (1791-1817) in Lausanne Cathedral.

[662] The grotto of St Magdalene. *Murray's Handbook* (1838) considered it 'scarce worth a visit'. (p. 116).

[663] In 1830, Foley Wilmot had been promoted from Russia to become Secretary of Legation in Bern; Hon. Algernon Percy, British Minister in Switzerland 1826-32.

[664] Presumably the crossroads just south of Aarau, named Kreuzstrasse in *Murray's Handbook* of 1838, where there was an inn, the *Lion*.

Gentleman amongst them. Not so at Berne. Berne is so good. They are great gossips here at Zurich. I have lived much at the window & studied them, & know all the opposite neighbourhood, & the constant passengers over the wooden bridge. It is very amusing to do this & settle into a gossip when one has nothing to do. There is a Fair to wh. we went today - Toys, Glass, Linen, Shoes, Spectacles, Cakes, China, Flowers, Muslins, Prints (trash compared to English Prints now are the Swiss), & every sort of nonsense that can be thought of mixed up with every thing called necessaries of life, of which *Quincaillerie*[665] is the principal. Old Hist'y of Goethe's Print. Finished my 24 Hours, & having been to the Fair & the Market, finished the pleasures of the day.

On Tuesday the 3d [July 1832] we left the dirty noisy Inn at Zurich & went Voiturier[666] to Schaffhausen. Had an excellent specimen of a half German, half Swiss Inn at Eglisau, where we ba[i]ted, & a still better at the *Couronne* at Shaffhausen where there is a useful Landlord who speaks four languages, & set us off well on our German journey which, as we are for the first time travelling without that plague, a gold-laced Courier, was highly necessary, not speaking German. The Inns are exceedingly comfortable & the good living for those who care for it, prodigious in all sorts of drinking & wines, bread, butter, cheese &c. & every thing expressive of good Housewifery. Shaffhausen is lovely. The clear emerald Rhine rushes thro' a Valley of peace & plenty, with Swiss Farm houses all around & the prettiest Public walks in the German style surround the Ramparts. If any one could bear solitude & the german language, & likes health & pretty children, & cleanliness, & the sight of a well ordered Peasantry & *la bonne chere,*[667] neither to be found in France or Italy without money, let them come to Switzerland: but I don't suppose they cd find either society or litterature.

The 4th [July 1832] we passed thro' the Black Forest, literally black from its Fir Trees & charcoal Fires. La Vallée d'Enfer is like the de-

---

[665] i.e. hardware.

[666] i.e. hired a coachman and horses. This method of travel, in contrast to 'posting' involved regular stops so that the horses could be rested and fed (baited).

[667] 'good food'.

scent from the Spluegen into Germany.[668] Freybourg is an old Town; we had but just light enough left to see it & go to the Cathedral before we got Tea & went to Bed. The painted Glass there seemed to have many a legend of Knight & Lady of the olden time. We dined at Offenburg, an excellent Inn, crowded, as all the Inns are with Travellers going to & from Baden, Embs, & Wisbaden.[669] The Germans love travelling as much as they do eating & drinking. The posting is as good as elsewhere & the German Postillions no longer go at a footspace.

5th [July 1832]. We got in after dark to Radstat, where I heard a Band of a Regiment play a March & a Waltz so beautifully that I thought of nothing else for a day & night after. They were hardly Strains made for mortal Ears - it was so lovely - it must have been so to have struck me for now I am but little susceptible of the charms of music. It was calmer & softer & graver than Italian Music - & of a different nature from the music of Rossini that played in the gardens near us daily at Naples.

Georgina & I find much amusement in seeing a new people, new customs & new dress. Costumes like & yet not quite like those of England. Friday we stopped to see some Gardens of a Palace of the Grand D. of Baden, well worth the trouble. What most pleased me in them was a spot laid out with Terraces, Trees & Moss, & benches where the Court acted Schiller's Plays of wh. Georgina bought a Print. Got to the crowded Inn at Manheim on Friday E'g & Saturday to an excellent Inn at Mayence.

Sunday 8th July [1832]. Got up at four o'clock & walked down to the Steam boat that goes from Manheim to Cologne 110 miles in eleven hours. After seeing Italy & Switzerland, the scenery of the Rhine is nothing, but the whole is a comfortable & easy proceeding - a large commodious Cabin with Ottomans & windows below the deck, where people were reading, & writing, & talking, & some eating very substantial Luncheons indeed of mutton chops & White wine - or Caffey.

---

[668] *La Vallée d'Enfer* (*Höllental* in German), the Valley of Hell, which lies between Schaffhausen and Freiburg im Breisgau, is being compared to the *Via Mala*, the stupendous gorge above the village of Thusis on the Splügen road. The Splügen descends from Italy into the German-speaking, but Swiss, canton of the Grisons.

[669] Baden Baden, Ems and Wiesbaden, three of the most popular spas in Germany.

Les Eaux[670] I fancy furnished many a Conversation, but my *Voyage par Eau* rather amused me as well as making out & guessing the people. Madame Swagger, the wife of a Prussian Officer was the prettiest blonde I ever saw, of a good style enough, a coquette but not over done, but her ways amused me for the day. She had without exception the most graceful & beautiful figure I ever beheld - a blonde like Ly C. Poulett[671] or the Pulteney's, with dark & expressive eyes, wh. I sd. have been in love with if I had not been Miss Talbot. She was so perfectly dressed for the occasion like a Foreigner. They alone understand time & place wh. few english women do, & one cd not tell how & why she was dressed, wh. is or ought always to be the case with a pretty woman. I was sure she was someone of good birth & blood from a nameless sort of air & manner: but lo & behold when we got at 5 o'clock to Cologne, the shore was crowded with Idlers to see the Steam packet arrive. I said to Georgina, there is her Sister, & so it was, & there came on board the Mother & the Sister & the little brothers, & there was such kissing & rejoicing as made it evident they were all residents of the old Town of Cologne. We went on deck while the long ceremony of a German dinner took place. At one time we thought of going to Rotterdam & London but luckily we did not; as Mr Craven came back frightened, we heard, at the ceremony, in strong seas, of changing steam packets.

The Officers on board smoked after dinner & talked to their Ladies, but a word & a puff & a puff & a word succeeded each other alternately, while a long row of Passengers sat with a long row of Pipes immoveable as if they grew to them - & interupt[ed] not the labour of the hands. What an odd custom for a whole nation. The Steam boat stopped at Coblentz & at the large Towns to take up & set down passengers. A large bell rang & another answered, & all the people came running with pipes in their mouths. The shores crowded with persons in their Sunday dresses were pretty but as to the Romance of a *Voyage du Rhin* with *Childe Harold* in one's hand, as I had, it is now no longer to be had, & the celebrated Monastery on the Island is now a Pension where people may have Lodgings!![672] The *Cour Imperiale*, a

---

[670] 'the waters', i.e. experiences of watering places.

[671] Presumably Lady Catherine Poulett (1796-1816).

[672] The convent of Nonnenwerth formed part of territories ceded to Prussia in 1815. Sold to a private individual, and after the death of the remaining nuns, it became a hotel between the 1820s and 1830s.

horrid Inn at Cologne. The best Eau de Cologne 9 Francs a case of six bottles.

Landed in England Wed'y Aug. 1 1832. I am sorry that I have totally neglected my journal since we got out of the Steam boat on the Rhine at Cologne & had that tiresome long walk on Sunday over the bad pavement of Cologne to the horrid Inn we chose to go to instead of the good one we were recommended to. At Cologne ceased - the sunny South - the clear sky - a cheerful look, riches, comfort & happiness. At Cologne ceased Abroad & its joys. Then began - bad roads & *pavé*, wretched poverty, and untidy population, those horrid blue smock frocks which all the Men of the lower classes wear all thro' France & Belgium, & Coal Carts & coals & black smoke & cold, that made me wrap one's auld Cloak about one. Under these impressions we got to Aix La Chapelle, an ugly sort of French Town tho' Prussian, where we staid a Fortnight talking of the Cholera, reading the newspapers, & getting some decent clothing being in rags & tatters. There is without exception the very best mantua maker, or rather *Tailleuse*, in the world there whose taste & judgement are *sans peur et sans reproche*.[673] There we had cold weather for some days & then a heat or such a Heat succeeded as I have only felt at Naples in July, Ther 80. We went to Brussels where the Cholera was very bad - & had three days of Mantua Makers & Milliners. We got there on Sunday & were charmed with the good dress & air of decency & elegance of the children & of the women of all classes: little bonnets & squeezed-in waists, large sleeves & tournures are necessary appendages now to being a Gentlewoman. Heard of M[aria] C[opley's] marriage with Ld Howick & don't believe it.[674] The King is out of spirits they say, & Mr Taylor[675] says, would like his marriage, her fortune & a private situation, better than a precarious throne, & all the old big-wigs & bores he is forced to be civil to. Georgina lived in a nervous terror from Sunday to Thursday. Brussels is beautiful from its walks & Bellevue Gardens as far as

---

[673] The phrase is normally associated with the Frenchman Pierre Terrail, Chevalier de Bayard (1471-1524).

[674] Henry George Grey, Viscount Howick, married Maria, younger daughter of Sir Joseph Copley on 9 August 1832. James Stuart Wortley was also shocked at the announcement: 'he is so ugly & deformed, & has such an ugly temper, that I think poor girl she is taking a very questionable step. However, it is a great match.' See C. Grosvenor et al., *The First Lady Warncliffe*, London, 1927, Vol.2, p.151.

[675] Presumably Sir Herbert Taylor, private secretary of William IV, and brother of Sir Brook Taylor.

I cd see the only day I was out - & the Hotel de Bellevue was comfortable & the *Diner* perfect, & if it were not for the horrid cholera we sd stay some time. Mme de Marischal, Montagne du Park No 15 à Bruxelles has the prettiest bonnets in the world; we bought seven from her. Sismondi's *Republiques* 72 Fr.[676]

Just as our post horses came to take us to Engd., we got the newspapers wh. mentioned the death of Mr Scott & Mrs Robert Smith of the Cholera & of the violence with wh. it raged in London.[677] We sent away the post horses, & debated what was to be done, but resolved to return to Engd. Meanwhile an Invitation arrived for dinner from the King for us all wh. caused the Horses to be re-sent for & off we set thro' Lille to Cassel where we slept, & next day got to Desseins at Calais, where we shivered three days & 3 nights & then crossed to the white Cliffs!!! on 1st Aug't 1832. It really was a fine day & the fair wind made the passage a good one. The first thing that strikes one in ones own native Land after 5 years absence is the beauty of the horses, harness & what is called the Set-out of the Stage Coaches & carriages - & then the clean well dressed look of all the Men. Everyone looks thin to me, lankey & long, after the Swiss & the Germans & even the french & Italians: The french & Prussians both Men & women, if they are thin, are stuffed to have an in & out shape wh. is admired on the Cont.; here it is a long uniformity of back & shape that is quite peculiar now to Eng'd. The lower people look worn, mind & body, & the children impudent. For the women, what I feel is pity; the women look so very unhappy. Everyone is dressed the same, that is ill dressed with good Clothes. We came for some days to Seven Oaks, to be quite near London, wh. is infected, without sleeping there. The 64 miles from Dover here is a Park & so is all Eng'd wh. is the scenery England excels in. The gloom of the climate is terrible, but it is difficult to imagine revolution here or ruin. Every piece of ground & house beautified as much as it is capable of being. There is something wrong in Eng'd &, what is more, that can't be mended, but when one sees the flourish-

---

[676] The first edition of the *Histoire des républiques italiennes du Moyen Age* by Simonde de Sismondi had been published in 1809. See note 54.

[677] Elizabeth Smith (b.1803), daughter of Baron Forester and wife of Robert Smith (son of Lord Carington), had died on 23 July. 'She was at the opera on Saturday, and at twelve on Sunday night a corpse!' (See *Leaves from the Diary of Henry Greville*, London, 1883, p.3.) Harry Scott (b.c.1780), son of Rev. James Scott and brother to Jane, Lady Oxford, one of Byron's *amours*, had served as British consul in Bordeaux. He died on 24 July.

ing towns, roads, villages &c., it must last our time. We got to Tunbridge to the Sussex Hotel when the Pantilles were crowded with persons. In the Morn'g I came down to breakfast to a room with Carpets & Curtains & writing table & a balcony of flowers wh. consist of a row of stocks ....

[*Final 6 pages of volume cut out*].

****

Epilogue.
(written by Marianne Talbot after re-reading her journal in October 1842)

I have finished this huge thick volume & much pain has the reading of it given me. I brought these journals here intending to destroy half of them - now I cannot bring myself to do so - they are so full of interesting and amusing things to *anyone*, but to myself particularly so. I look on them as General confessions now of follies - but this vol. is less confidential & more sensible than the others are. What to do with them now My dearest Charlotte is no more, *I don't know*!!!

This volume closes the sixteen years of my residence abroad.

Sources and Select Bibliography

Manuscript sources.
In the hope of finding material about the Talbots in Naples from those who encountered them there, I examined the Acton Papers in Cambridge University Library, the Attingham papers (relating to William Noel Hill) in Shropshire County Archives, the Gell Papers in Derbyshire Archives, the Grafton Papers in the Suffolk Archives (Bury St Edmunds), the diary of Robert Grosvenor in the Bodleian Library, the Morier papers in Balliol College Library, the diary of Captain Henry Shiffner in East Sussex Archives, and the journal of Mary Anne Grant (subsequently Lady Meek) by courtesy of Michael Heath-Caldwell of Brisbane. While these sources helped to supplement information about their writers and their stays in Naples, they sadly provided little or no information about the Talbots. The Scott papers in the National Library of Scotland made less mention of the Talbots than might have been expected, but did provide additional information about activities which were jointly undertaken. Other material in the same library included one letter from Marianne to Sir Walter, as well as a letter, unrelated to the Scotts, written by Sir George Talbot to Lord Stuart de Rothesay in December 1829. The letters which Sir Walter Scott wrote to Marianne during his stay in Naples, copies of which I was sent by the Morgan Library, inasmuch as they were legible, confirmed events mentioned in her journal.

Printed sources.
Acton, Harold, *The Last Bourbons of Naples (1825-1861)*, London, 1961.

Alisio, Giancarlo et al., *Napoli com'era nelle gouaches del Sette e Ottocento*, 5th ed., Rome, 2004.

Apponyi, Rodolphe, *Vingt-cinq ans à Paris, 1826-1850 : journal du comte Rodolphe Apponyi, attaché de l'ambassade d'Autriche-Hongrie à Paris*, 3 vols, Paris,

Arbuthnot, Mrs Harriet, *The Journal of Mrs Arbuthnot 1820-1832*, ed. Francis Bamford and the Duke of Wellington, 2 vols, London, 1950.

Berry, M., *Extracts of the Journals and Correspondence of Miss Berry from the year 1783 to 1852*, ed. Lady Theresa Lewis, 3 vols, London, 1865.

Blessington, Countess of, *The Idler in Italy*, 2 vols, Philadelphia, 1839.

Buckingham, Duke of (Richard Grenville), *The Private Diary of Richard, Duke of Buckingham and Chandos*, 3 vols, London, 1862.

Burwick, Frederick, *The Journal of John Waldie Theatre Commentaries*, 1799-1830, accessible online.

Byron, Lord, *Byron's Letters and Journals*, ed. Leslie A. Marchand, 12 vols, London 1973-82.

Chateaubriand, *Lettres à Madame Récamier*, ed. Maurice Levaillant, Paris, 1951.

Christie's, *Mere Hall, Knutsford, Cheshire*, Catalogue of the Sale on Monday, 23 May 1994, on behalf of the Executors of the Late Mrs Helen Langford-Brooke.

Cole, Owen Blayney, 'A Last Memory of Sir Walter Scott', in *The Cornhill Magazine*, September 1923, pp. 257-267.

Crawley, C.W., *The Question of Greek Independence*, New York, 1973.

Dakin, Douglas, *The Greek Struggle for Independence 1821-1833*, London (Batsford), 1973.

Falk, Bernard, *"Old Q.'s" Daughter. The History of a Strange Family*, new ed., London, 1951.

Fox, Henry Edward, *The Journal of the Hon. Henry Edward Fox*, ed. Earl of Ilchester, London, 1923.

Gell, Sir William, *Reminiscences of Sir Walter Scott's Residence in Italy, 1832*, ed. James C. Corson, London, 1957.

Gell, Sir William, *Sir William Gell in Italy. Letters to the Society of Dilettanti, 1831-1835*, ed. Edith Clay, London, 1976.

Genoino, Andrea, *Le Sicilie al tempo di Francesco I*, Naples, 1934.

Greville, Charles, *The Greville Memoirs 1814-1860*, ed. Lytton Strachey & Roger Fulford, 8 Vols., London, 1938.

Gronow, R.H., *The Reminiscences and Recollections of Captain Gronow*, 2 vols, London, 1892.

Harris, Sir James, 3rd Earl of Malmesbury, *Memoirs of an ex-minister*, 2 vols, London 1884.

[Hogg, Edward], 'Walter Scott at Naples', in [Charles Macfarlane], *The Book of Table Talk*, London, 1836, Vol. I, pp.216-222.

Johnston, Henry McKenzie, *Ottoman and Persian Odysseys. James Morier, Creator of Hajji Baba of Ispahan, and his Brothers*, London, 1998.

Lane-Poole, Stanley, *The Life of the Right Honourable Stratford Canning*, 2 vols, London 1888.

Lévis-Mirepoix, Emmanuel de, *Mémoires et papiers de Lebzeltern*, Paris, 1949.

Lockhart, J.G., *The Life of Sir Walter Scott, Bart.*, New Popular Edition, London, 1893.

MacFarlane, Charles, *Popular Customs, Sports, and Recollections of the South of Italy*, London, 1846,

MacFarlane, Charles, *Reminiscences of a Literary Life*, London, 1917.

Madden, R.R., *The Literary Life and Correspondence of the Countess of Blessington*, 3 vols, London 1855.

Maillé, Duchesse de, *Souvenirs des deux restaurations*, ed. Xavier de La Fournière, Paris, 1984.

Malcolm, Alexander, *Letters of an invalid from Italy, Malta, and the South of France*, London, 1897.

Medlicott, C.L. and Camp, W.A., *St Marks Church, Talbot Village, A Victorian Dream*, St Mark's Church, 1996.

Murray's Handbooks:
Handbook for Travellers in Central Italy, London, 1843.
Handbook for Travellers in Southern Italy, (by Octavian Blewitt), London, 1853.
Handbook for Travellers in Switzerland, London, 1838.

Neumann, Philipp von, *The Diary of Philipp von Neumann 1819-1833*, ed. E.Beresford Chancellor, 2 vols, London, 1928.

Parry, John Orlando, *Victorian Swansdown. Extracts from the Early Travel Diaries of John Orlando Parry*, ed. C.B. Andrews & J.A. Orr-Ewing, London, 1933.

Ramage, Craufurd Tait, *The Nooks and by-Ways of Italy*, Liverpool, 1868. (Also the text edited by Edith Clay and published as *Ramage in South Italy*, London, 1965).

Severn, Joseph, *Letters and Memoirs*, ed. Grant F. Scott, Ashgate Publishing Limited, Aldershot, 2005.

Stendhal, *Promenades dans Rome*, ed. V. Del Litto, Grenoble, 1993.

Sultana, Donald, *The 'Siege of Malta' rediscovered. An Account of Sir Walter Scott's Mediterranean Journey and his Last Novel*, Scottish Academic Press, 1977.

[Talbot, Marianne], *The Sketch Book of the South*, London, 1835.

[Talbot, Marianne], *Past, Present, and Future*, 2 vols, London, 1850.

Trant, Clarissa, *The Journal of Clarissa Trant 1800-1832*, ed. C.G. Luard, London, 1925.

Uwins, Mrs [Sarah], *A Memoir of Thomas Uwins, R.A.*, 2 vols in 1, EF Publishing, 1978, (originally published London, 1858).

Index.

(Page numbers in *italics* indicate that there is a note related to the text reference; page numbers followed by 'n' indicate mention in a note but not in the text).

Fitzclarence, Col. George & Mrs *60*,61,64,128n,*132*
Fitzclarence, Mary *87-8*
Fitzgerald, Lady William 186
FitzGerald, Vesey 84,*115*,116,*158*
Fitzherbert, Mrs Maria Anne *21*,112
Fitzroy, Lady Isabella, see St John
Flahaut, Comte/Comtesse de & Mme *33*
Fleming, Admiral Charles *149*
Fodor, Josephine (singer) *21,65*
Fonig 3
Fordwich, Lord *45*,47
Forli, Mme de 127
Fornacello (near Vico) 98
Fox, Charles James 39,90
Fox, Charles Richard 87-8
Fox, Henry Edward (Blue Fox) 22n,24n, 25n,42n,44n,*82,86*,88,180n
Fox, Henry Stephen (Black Fox) *12*,20-1, 52,53,66,*79*,80,84-5,*86*,88
Fox, Mary *71*
Francavilla, Prince 56
Francesco 1 & Queen Maria Isabella (of Naples) 37,42,87,90,103-4,107,109-10, *142*
Frascati 172,182,185-7
Frederick III (of Germany) 10
Frere, John Hookham *152*
Galiati, Mlle *69*
Galzerani, Antonietta *79*
Garnier, Mr /Mrs 117,123,131,147,149, 155, 157,158,161,175,176,177n
Gell, Sir William 4,*5*,6,7,9,21,*24*,42,43, *44*, 46,47,50,51,53,54,56,57,58, 67,77,79, 83-88,90,92,94,*103*,104,108,113,118-9, 137-8,*140*, 142,*147*,151,153,154,155, 156,*157,158*, 161n,*162*,163,*168*,170,179, *180*,181,183, 186,188
George III 112
George IV 2n,5,*21*,52n,80,83,88,111, 119, *160*
Gerace, Prince/Princess 56,59
Gérard, François (painter) 3,66
Gertrude (novel) *26*
Giardinelli, Prince *171*
Gioja, Mme de *56*
Glenbervie, Lord/Lady 49n,*134*

Glenorchy, Lord & Lady (née Mary Turner Gavin) *45*,46,47,53,54n,56,57, 58,60,61,63, 68,69,75
Godiva, Queen 76
Goethe, Johann Wolgang v. 7n,14n,196
Golconda *149*
Gontaut, Duchesse de 5
Gordon, (Sir) Robert *11*,18,20,21n,23,51
Gordon, Duke & Duchess of *84*
Gore, Sir Charles Stephen *176*
Gow's band *161*
Graham Island 133n,141
Grandison, Sir Charles (novel) *6*,114
Grant, Mr *44*
Granville, 1st Earl *52*
Granville, 2nd Earl *45*
Graves, Lord & Lady *59*,74
Gray, Thomas *19*,70n,*106*
Greville, Charles 15n,58n,*66,69*,70,73n, 77,80,112n,131
Greville, Maj.Gen. Sir Charles J. *170-1*
Greville, Henry Richard 7n
Grey, Lord *190*
Gröditzberg, Mme Benecke v. *61*,62
Grosjean, Campagne, Geneva 25
Grosvenor, Robert *21*
Grotto Ferrata 186
Grotto of San Chrystoffe 100
Guccioli, Teresa *135*
Guiche, Duc de *33*
Guilford, Lord (Francis North) *25*,87
Guilleminot, Armand, comte de 3
Guilleminot, Mlle *65*
Gwynne, Miss 49
Haddington, Lady *64,67*,77,86
Hamilton, Lady Dalrymple *16*
Hamilton, Lady Susan 160
Hamilton, Terrick 23
Hammett, Alexander (US Consul) 161n.
Hanbury, Sir F. 42
Harrowby, Lord (Dudley Ryder) & Lady & family *111-2,114*,116,117,118,131
Heber, Bishop Reginald *8*
Helena Paulowna, Grand Duchess *5*,62
Henri, Mme (actress) 32
Herbault (Parisian milliner) *10*,34,67, 146

From the same publisher.

Two Victorian Ladies on the Continent 1844-5. An anonymous journal. Edited with notes by Michael Heafford, Postillion Books, Cambridge, 2008.
ISBN 978-0-9558712-0-7.

This is the journal of Miss W., an unmarried lady in her forties, travelling through France and Switzerland to Italy, accompanied by a teenage girl, Minnie, for whom she is acting as guardian and tutor. Like Marianne Talbot, Miss W. is well read and writes with fluency and humour. And yet, despite being separated only by some fifteen years, the two journals could hardly be more different. That written by Miss W. is based on letters she wrote to her family during her tour and composed in the knowledge that they would probably be read out loud for the entertainment of family and friends. As a result the journal has a sharply defined narrative structure into which people and events are explicitly introduced. Though of similar age, the two women differ markedly in personality, social status and attitude to life - differences which enable us to understand more fully the social scene of the period and the place of women, and men, within it.

The major task in editing Miss W.'s account lay in discovering the identity of the writer herself and of her companion Minnie. There being no information on the family provenance of the journal and the name of the writer appearing neither on the cover, nor indeed within the journal, it was only through clues within the text itself that identification for both women could be established. Following them to a successful conclusion helped to place the tour in a wider social context while opening up two very different and fascinating life stories. That of Miss W. revealed how she came to be making the journey in the company of a teenager to whom she was not related. The remarkable past of Minnie explained why it had been decided that she should make the tour with Miss W. It also showed how the tour changed the whole course of her future life. Following up the clues also led to the explanation of a more minor, but not less intriguing mystery: why the journal with entries for more or less every day of the tour which started in Boulogne on 9 April 1844 should end in Venice, over a year later on 3 June 1845 and in mid-sentence, with the words: 'The stillness..........'